COURTS AND POLITICAL INST

A Comparative View

The frontier between 'law' and 'politics' is not always clear-cut. A large area exists where courts operate, but governments and parliaments also make decisions. Tim Koopmans compares the way American, British, French and German law and politics deal with different issues: in many instances subjects which are highly 'political' in one country constitute legal issues in another. Is there, for example a 'sovereign Parliament' (as there is in Britain), or will courts control the compatibility of statutes with the Constitution (as in the United States and Germany)? How far can courts go in controlling the legality of administrative action? Are there general legal theories about the frontier between what courts and what politics can do? Koopmans considers case law on a range of issues, including human rights protection, federalism, separation of powers, equal protection and the impact of European and international law.

TIM KOOPMANS was formerly Professor of Constitutional Law at the University of Leiden as well as a judge of the Court of Justice of the European Communities. He was also Advocate General at the Dutch Supreme Court. He is a member of the Royal Netherlands Academy of Arts and Science and Honorary Bencher of Lincoln's Inn. His publications include many articles in Dutch, English and French on labour law, European law and constitutional law.

COURTS AND POLITICAL INSTITUTIONS

A Comparative View

TIM KOOPMANS

CAMBRIDGE
UNIVERSITY PRESS

PREFACE

Authors may not always be fully aware why they write their books. When composing this book, I felt that my reasons were simple and compelling. When I returned to teaching law at a somewhat advanced age, I happened to rediscover how much comparative methods help to develop students' ability to define legal problems and to collect materials for solving them. Moreover, there is something exciting for them in being exposed to ways of reasoning they are not familiar with. I wrote the book in the hope that any serious reader of it would have the same experience.

The reader I had in mind was the senior student of law, history or political science, not necessarily British or American, with a certain interest in general problems of law or politics, or with a cosmopolitan view of life in society. However, other readers, whatever their background or their vocation in life, may also benefit from the methods I have used for making foreign constitutional systems accessible by comparing them to others. Constitutional law, if well explained, is not all that difficult to understand.

The book could not have been written without the help of a number of persons and institutions. I am thinking, in particular, of the Cambridge law faculty, which provided me in 1999–2000, when I was Goodhart Professor of Law, with a tiny little office in the heart of the Squire Law Library, very close to the law reports. My Utrecht academic friend Tom Zwart helped me to collect materials; he also contributed to the evolution of my ideas by identifying new constitutional developments. Other friends and colleagues encouraged me to keep trying my hand at mastering some basic issues of comparative constitutional law. Finally, the Cambridge University Press assisted me in finding my style of writing.

The first two chapters of the book elaborate some ideas I had already developed in some of my earlier works, written in Dutch. Chapters 3 and 6 rely heavily, though not exclusively, on (respectively) the American and the French literature. Chapter 4 is mainly based on earlier publications of mine in English, French and Dutch, in particular on methods of human rights protection. Chapters 5, 9 and 10 are entirely original with regard to anything known to me in existing literature. The other chapters chiefly serve for giving cohesion to the book and transforming its text into a real *exposé*.

I owe the reader one final remark: it has been a great pleasure to compose this book.

T. K.

TABLE OF CASES

I. American cases

II. British and Commonwealth cases

III. French cases

IV. German and Dutch cases

V. European courts

ABBREVIATIONS

AC	Law Reports, Appeal Cases
Adm. Besl.	Rechtspraak Bestuursrecht (cases on administrative law, Netherlands)
AG	Attorney General
AJIL	*American Journal of International Law*
All E R	All England Reports
AmJCompL	*The American Journal of Comparative Law*
Art.	Article
Bell	John Bell, *French Constitutional Law*
BGB	Bürgerliches Gesetzbuch (German Civil Code)
BVerfGE	Entscheidungen des Bundesverfassunggerichts (decisions of the Federal Constitutional Court, Germany)
BVerwGE	Entscheidungen des Bundesverwaltungsgerichts (decisions of the Federal Administrative Court, Germany)
CC	Conseil Constitutionnel (Constitutional Council, France)
CE	Conseil d'Etat (Council of State, France)
ch.	chapter
Ch	Law Reports, Chancery Division
cl.	clause
CLJ	*Cambridge Law Journal*
CMLR	Common Market Law Reports
Cmnd.	Command Papers (studies submitted to the British Parliament)
C of E	Church of England
ColLRev	*Columbia Law Review*

Cranch	Cranch, ed., *Reports of Cases of the US Supreme Court 1804–1816*
DC	District of Columbia
DLR	Dominion Law Reports (Canada)
EC	European Community (or: Communities)
ECHR	European Court of Human Rights
ECR	European Court Reports
EHRR	European Human Rights Reports
ESC	European Social Charter
EU	European Union
FLR	Law Reports, Family Division
GLC	Greater London Council
HarvLRev	*Harvard Law Review*
ICC	Interstate Commerce Commission (USA)
ICLQ	*International and Comparative Law Quarterly*
IRA	Irish Republican Army
KB	Law Reports, King's Bench Division
Kommers	Donald P. Kommers, *The Constitutional Jurisprudence of the Federal Republic of Germany*
LQR	*Law Quarterly Review*
MR	Master of the Rolls
NedJur	*Nederlandse Jurisprudentie* (Dutch Law Reports)
NJW	*Neue Juristische Wochenschrift* (New Legal Weekly, Germany)
NO	Nationale Ombudsman (Netherlands)
PM	Prime Minister
QB	Law Reports, Queen's Bench Division
Rabelszeitschr.	*Zeitschrift für ausländisches und internationales Privatrecht*
RDP	*Revue du Droit Public* (Public Law Review, France)
Rec.	*Recueil des décisions du Conseil Constitutionnel* (or, as the case may be: *du* Conseil d'Etat)
RFDA	*Revue Française de Droit Administratif*
RFDC	*Revue Française de Droit Constitutionnel*
RIDC	*Revue Internationale de Droit Comparé*
s.	section

Series	European Court of Human Rights. Judgments and Decisions
TulLRev	*Tulane Law Review*
UCLA	University of California, Los Angeles
US	United States Supreme Court Reports
WLR	Weekly Law Reports

1

Introduction

1.1. Terminology

This book examines the legal relations between political institutions and the courts in some European countries and in the United States. The author happens to be interested in this theme and, particularly, in the boundaries between judicial and political activities.

At first sight, it is a somewhat unlikely subject. There seems to be little that judges and politics have in common. The dry atmosphere of the courtroom cannot be compared to the vividness of a debate in – say – the House of Commons or the American Senate. Judges are normally represented as somewhat elderly gentlemen, who try to look as wise as they are supposed to be; a gown and (in the case of English judges) a wig will strengthen that impression. Politicians, by contrast, radiate a cheerful kind of optimism, illustrated by a happy smile or a determined look on their faces; the image they evoke is one of willingness to tackle any problem humankind may find in its way. Two different worlds, one would be inclined to say. However, appearances are deceptive. I hope to show that it is far from easy to determine the borderline between the scope of judicial and political activities. To complicate things further, differences between legal systems also concern the exact location of this borderline. What is 'political' in some systems, for example in English law, may be the kind of problem to be solved by the courts in a different system, for example, under the Constitution of the United States. Capital punishment provides an example: its introduction, or reintroduction, is decided by political institutions in the United States, in fact by the state legislatures. And traditionally, the solutions adopted in the fifty states have not always been the same. The countries of Western Europe, on the contrary, have a hard and fast rule of law: the European Convention on Human Rights prohibits the application of the death penalty, except in time of war.[1] Subject to that exception, capital punishment is a legal and not a political issue in Europe.

It is true that the very existence of this borderline between political and judicial activities has been denied by some academics, who consider that any judicial opinion, on whatever subject, must be considered as a 'political' statement. That theory, though presented as 'modern' and 'critical' in the early 1980s, has since lost its appeal. Professional lawyers usually preserve the distinction between legal and political arguments nowadays, in Europe as well as in the United States. And they are right: nothing is gained by giving the concept of the 'political' such a wide scope that it includes court rulings on matters like divorce or bankruptcy.[2] There may be a problem in certain cases, when political rather than legal arguments are put forward in court decisions; but this problem is not solved by denying the distinction between the two kinds of arguments. As we shall see in the course of this study, the problem is particularly important when legal rules on relationships between public authorities, or between those authorities and the citizens, are concerned, i.e. in the area of constitutional and administrative law.

At this point, a first question of terminology emerges. The part of the law governing the relations between courts and political institutions, such as governments and parliaments, is known as 'public law' in many legal systems. The term is, however, slightly confusing when used in a study which is not confined to one legal system. The problem is, in particular, that the expression 'public law' is not part of traditional legal usage among English and American lawyers. It is the ordinary name for constitutional and administrative law in Dutch (*publiekrecht*) and in German (*öffentliches Recht*). It is in this sense that the expression will be used in this book.

This little terminological problem illustrates already one of the recurring difficulties of comparative legal research. In different legal systems, dissimilar concepts may exist; and if the same expressions occur, they often have a different meaning, or at least a different scope.[3] Among French

---

[1] Art. 1-2 Protocol no. 6 to the European Convention on the Protection of Human Rights and Fundamental Freedoms.

[2] See also Neil MacCormick, *Questioning Sovereignty: Law, State and Nation in the European Commonwealth* (Oxford, 1999), pp. 11–12.

[3] On problems of terminology in comparative legal research see David J. Gerber, 'Toward a language of comparative law', *AmJCompL* 46 (1998), 719; Geoffrey Samuel, 'Comparative law and jurisprudence', *ICLQ* 47 (1998), 817.

lawyers, for example, the expression 'public law' (*droit public*) has a more restricted meaning than among their Dutch and German colleagues, as it refers only to administrative law and not to constitutional law. That is not the only complication. In the United States, the concept of 'constitutional law' is used in a narrower sense than in Great Britain: it covers only the areas of law concerning the constitution which have given rise to judicial decisions. The relationship between President and Congress has not been the subject of any important body of case law, and the result is that it is chiefly examined in American books on 'government' or 'political science' rather than in those on constitutional law. I see no reason to adopt such a limited view of constitutional problems in this book. The comparatist has the advantage, however, that the case law of the United States Supreme Court on some constitutional matters, such as civil liberties and equal protection, is prolific. That circumstance, in itself, is a good reason to include American constitutional law in the analysis of problems concerning the relations between courts and political institutions.

According to this view, public law covers a large area of every national system of law. A respectable library could be devoted to American constitutional law, or French administrative law, alone. Consequently, it is an impossible task for one author to have a thorough command of this large area in more than one system of law; but he can nevertheless try to explore it.

As a lawyer, he is then faced with an additional difficulty. Frequently, it is hard to examine constitutional developments without taking a look at historical, social and political backgrounds. It is not possible to understand American case law on equal protection without some knowledge of the history of slavery and of racial inequality and oppression. Similarly, the peculiar characteristics of the French constitution of 1958 can only be fully grasped when they are considered as part of an evolution triggered by the political events of May 1958 and the ensuing birth of the Fifth Republic. It is an inadmissibly narrow conception of constitutional law, as Justice Frankfurter once put it in one of his individual opinions, 'to confine it to the words of the Constitution and to disregard the gloss which life has written upon them'.[4] The present author shares this broad conception of constitutional law, but he is aware that this does not facilitate his task. He

---

[4] Justice Frankfurter, concurring, in *Youngstown Sheet and Tube Co.* v. *Sawyer*, 343 US 579 (1952). Felix Frankfurter was judge in the United States Supreme Court from 1939 to 1962.

feels, however, that he has hardly any choice: a true understanding of the role of the judiciary in its relationship to the political institutions can only be gained after a careful examination of the constitutional background.

1.2. Comparative approaches

If it is already hard to gain a good understanding of public law in one legal system, what then is the use of comparisons between two or more systems? In answer to this question, different theories have been developed, some of them less convincing than others.

There is first a utilitarian answer: by learning from others, you can improve the quality of your own legal system.[5] It is quite possible that a well-considered use of comparative materials may help to solve legal questions of a more or less technical nature, such as liability of the employer for damage caused to the employee during working hours, or the position of the mortgagee in case of bankruptcy of the debtor. Thus, many provisions of the new Civil Code of the Netherlands have been inspired by solutions found elsewhere, for example, in the German or Swiss codes. However, it is difficult to see how this approach could possibly work in the area of constitutional law. American constitutional law, interesting though it may be, is very much a product of American history; it is part of American culture and attuned to American society. Constitutions are not very suitable commodities for export. It is true that, in the years following the Second World War, Americans sometimes attempted to impose their own constitutional standards on some of the defeated countries, but this operation was not a great success. During the American occupation of Japan, rumour had it that the new Japanese Constitution had been drafted by the legal advisers to the supreme military commander; but however that may be, the interpretation of the Japanese Constitution has always been completely at variance with constitutional practice in the United States. Identical words don't have necessarily the same meaning in different legal cultures.

A second aim of comparative law is the purely academic interest. We tend to be curious about things we don't understand, and we will try to find an explanation. Pascal said long ago, half mockingly, that it was 'an odd kind of justice' ('plaisante justice') which found its boundaries in the course of a

---

[5] See K. Zweigert and H. Kötz, *An Introduction to Comparative Law*, 3rd edn, trans. Tony Weir (Oxford 1998), no. 2–11.

river or a mountain range: 'true on this side of the Pyrenees, false on the other'.[6] In an intellectual climate affected by rationalism, academics will feel that there must be a justification for differences of this kind; their job is simply to find it. Montesquieu, also struck by differences among legal systems, made a fair attempt at discovering the reasons. He referred to elements like climate, religion, previous experience, morals and manners, and methods of government.[7] It is what we now would call a speculative generalization, more interesting to philosophers and sociologists than to lawyers. It is clear, for example, that democracy imposes its own requirements on legal evolution; but it is far from clear why some nations have a democratic tradition and others have not.

A third, and more idealist, vision of comparative law considers it as a modest means of fostering mutual understanding among nations and so, ultimately, of promoting peace. In the early nineteenth century, when comparative legal research began to develop as a special branch of legal science, there was much optimism that it would bring peoples together. A Dutch lawyer and politician expressed the opinion that it would bring about a new and international constitution, based on general principles of law growing into 'a world force'.[8] The evidence, sadly, does not support the idea that a better knowledge of the law and culture of other nations or groups will promote better relationships. The experience of the last quarter of a century can indeed be interpreted as showing the opposite: the mass killings in former Yugoslavia took place between ethnic and religious groups which knew each other only too well. At any rate, we are too sceptical nowadays to believe in easy methods of strengthening the forces of peace in the world.

The fourth view is based on educational considerations. One can only come to an understanding of a system of law by confronting it with a different system. The particularities of one system become apparent when other systems are found to be without them. This is, of course, part of a more general truth: having lived in the Amsterdam area during my childhood, I only discovered how flat the country was when I made my first

---

[6] Pascal, *Pensées*, no. 60 in the Krailsheimer translation (Harmondsworth, 1995); ed. Brunschvicq no. 294.

[7] *L'esprit des lois* xix, 4; in L'Intégrale edn (Paris 1964) p. 641. Also in: Montesquieu, *Oeuvres complètes*, Pléiade edn (Paris, 1951), vol. ii, pp. 396ff.

[8] Jan Rudolph Thorbecke, in 1841, in his 'notes' on the Dutch Constitution (*Aantekening op de Grondwet*).

trip to the Belgian Ardennes. This is the kind of experience which applies to the legal landscape as well as to the physical environment.[9] There is, however, a further perspective to the educational view of comparative law. The comparison shows us something about law and legal evolution generally. It allows us to develop ideas about the judicial interpretation of legal and constitutional provisions, about the use of broad and narrow notions and concepts, about the social and cultural factors influencing legal developments, about the relationship between law and politics, and half a dozen other fundamental problems. These problems can be analysed in the abstract – for example, on the basis of historical and sociological studies. They can also be concretized, by means of a study of constitutional practice, of case law on issues of constitutional and administrative law, and of the debates over those issues in various legal systems. This is, in the main, an empirical and inductive approach to important problems of public law and of the relationship between law, politics and administration.

It is this latter concept of comparative law which has provided the guideline for the composition of this book. Constitutional documents, statutes and legal principles are couched in words: for the lawyer, these words have their particular importance because of the possibility of human action they imply; they are, as one philosopher put it, 'guides to action'.[10] Often, this action follows its own course and develops its own dynamics; it may, therefore, give a meaning to the words the drafters of these words could not have imagined. The Constitution of the United States consists of words; but, as Justice Holmes once observed, these words 'have called into life a being the development of which could not have been foreseen by the most gifted of its begetters'.[11] We shall be trying to trace the processes which give rise to such developments in different legal systems.

1.3. Comparative methods

Much has been written about the 'methodology' of comparative law, and the debate is far from closed. Recently, a leading scholar wrote that this methodology is still at the experimental stage.[12]

---

[9] Zweigert and Kötz, *Introduction*, no. 2–IV.

[10] Karl Olivecrona, *Law as Fact*, 2nd edn (London, 1971), p. 252.

[11] *Missouri* v. *Holland*, 252 US 416 (1920). Oliver Wendell Holmes was judge in the US Supreme Court from 1902 to 1932.

[12] Zweigert and Kötz *Introduction*, p. 33. Further literature on page 32 of the work.

An additional difficulty is that contributors to the debate on comparative methods are usually interested in matters of private law. In that area, centuries of legal debate have helped to create a certain system of classification; the influence of Roman law and canon law is perceptible in many countries, particularly (but not exclusively) on the European continent and in Latin America.[13] That may provide a basis for comparative research. No such basis exists in the field of public law, where internationally accepted concepts and standards are much more difficult to find. There are only few common traditions, and public law often has a much more national character than private law. The notion of 'contract' in English law covers approximately – though not exactly – the same relations as those indicated by the concept of contract in French, Belgian or Dutch law. In contrast, the American expression 'separation of powers' and its French counterpart 'séparation des pouvoirs' concern entirely different matters. In the United States, the concept embodies not only the independence of the judiciary, but also the mutual autonomy of the legislative and executive branches of government, each of them having its separate tasks, powers and responsibilities. It is a general constitutional guideline, a fundamental principle underlying the American constitutional fabric. By contrast, the French expression refers only to the obligation of the courts to refrain from interfering in government and administration. From the French Revolution onwards, a rigid distinction has been drawn between the judicial and the administrative. Thus, similar expressions sometimes refer to different problems.

However, comparative study of public-law problems also has its brighter side: the number of fundamental problems is smaller than in private law. That is especially true if we limit our attention to States which are characterized as 'liberal democracies' in the literature on political science.[14] These States actually share some political and ideological traditions, which can briefly be summarized as democracy, rule of law, human rights protection and open government. Each of those traditions implies some of the basic assumptions which determine the working of the constitutional order: the role of representative bodies in legislation; the independence of the judiciary; protection of citizens against arbitrary government acts; participation of

[13] See Peter Stein, *Roman Law in European history* (Cambridge, 1999), ch. 5.

[14] Examples: S. E. Finer, *Comparative Government* (London, 1982), ch. II; Philippe Lauvaux, *Les grandes démocraties contemporaines* (Paris, 1990), ch. I-1; Arend Lijphart, *Patterns of Democracy* (New Haven, Ct., and London, 1999), chs. 1 and 14.

citizens in politics by free elections and public debate; autonomy in their own sphere of life. These States happen to have a similar economic order and an economic and social history with striking similarities: they were, until recently when these words went out of date, the 'Western', 'capitalist' and 'industrial' States, and most of them have been colonial powers. Within the scope of their basic assumptions, they encounter comparable problems. Questions arise, for example, as to the validity of legislation which violates human rights, or as to the rights of citizens to take action against irregular decisions by the administration. These questions do not arise in States under authoritarian rule: one-party States, States governed by a military junta, communist or fascist regimes. We shall restrict our inquiry to States of the liberal-democratic type.

Within this group of States I introduce a further restriction, by limiting my attention chiefly to the systems of public law of the United States, Great Britain, France and the Federal Republic of Germany. The reasons for this further restriction are mainly practical: materials are not always easily accessible, and my command of languages and appetite for reading have their own limits. The studies I actually did accomplish convinced me, however, that the comparison between American, British, French and German public law gives us the opportunity to discuss some basic problems concerning the relation between the courts and political institutions. I may, nevertheless, permit myself to make a few little excursions to places such as Italy, the Benelux countries and Canada.

If we take the basic assumptions of the liberal democracies for granted, further analysis will allow us to unearth a certain number of questions which are 'fundamental' in the true sense of the word: an answer to such questions *must* have been given before the system of public law could begin to operate. To give two simple examples: an Act of Parliament, a statute, is either unassailable or it can be struck down by the courts for violation of some higher law; Parliament and government either have their own independent powers or work together as interdependent bodies. The answers to such fundamental questions determine the way the system will be shaped. We can, therefore, try to invent two opposite answers to these questions, in order to create two extreme poles, linked by a continuum. For each question, some legal systems will be close to one of the two poles, but most systems find their place somewhere on the line between the two extremes. To study this, I shall use models: abstract solutions to general problems, sufficiently detached from reality to present the problem in a pure form, but close enough to reality to permit comparisons among actual systems of law.[15]

To put it another way, my method will consist in identifying some of the fundamental questions of public law in the four systems I propose to investigate; trying to find the opposing answers to each of these questions; and locating the four systems on the line between the two polar answers. The advantage of this method is that it can first give abstract answers, not encumbered by the compromises which characterize real life; but it then allows us to look into legal systems as they actually work and to measure the distance they keep from the abstract answers. The abstract model only serves as a yardstick for the comparison of the existing systems of public law; it does not express any value-oriented appreciation.

1.4. Legal approaches

The choice of method implies that certain subjects will not be discussed, although they might perhaps be considered as part of comparative public law and as having a link with our main theme, the relations between courts and political institutions.

First, I shall not seek to condemn or praise any legal system in particular, or any solution adopted in such a system. As far as possible, I shall refrain from assessing legal arrangements in terms of 'good' and 'bad'.[16] Assessments of that kind cannot be made without a profound knowledge of the relevant system of law and of the historical and social background. If 'native' lawyers have expressed their opinions, or even their moral judgments, it may be interesting to refer to these opinions and judgments, particularly when they are strongly held; but I shall not add my own appreciation. Some decisions of the US Supreme Court on the admissibility of abortion have given rise to a great political and moral debate in the United States; they also show something about the way the Court interprets the Constitution.[17] I intend to concentrate on the second aspect; the reader may benefit more from my reflections on the interpretation of constitutional provisions than from my

---

[15] See Claude Lévi-Strauss, 'Sens et usage de la notion de modèle', in *Anthropologie structurale deux* (Paris, 1973), ch. VI.

[16] See Philippa R. Foot, 'Approval and disapproval', in *Law, Morality and Society*, Essays in Honour of H. L. A. Hart (Oxford, 1977), ch. XIII.

[17] In particular: *Roe* v. *Wade*, 410 US 113 (1973); *Planned Parenthood of Southeastern Pennsylvania* v. *Casey*, 505 US 833 (1992).

opinions about abortion. More in general, I feel lawyers should be reticent about moral issues arising in legal systems other than the one they are used to. But, of course, Oscar Wilde was right in saying that 'one should not carry moderation to extremes'.

A second consequence of my choice of method is my view that constitutional provisions, rules of law, powers of institutions, should be examined in the framework of the legal systems in which they have developed. It is quite feasible to adopt a different perspective in studies of detail, by isolating a certain legal arrangement from its constitutional or legal environment. A study comparing the composition and the powers of the British Parliament with those of the American Congress might adopt such an approach.[18] It is, of course, interesting to know that a refusal of Royal assent to a bill passed by the British Parliament means that the bill will not become law, but that a veto of the American President can be overruled by Congress deciding by a qualified majority.[19] For the lawyer, this kind of information is not very helpful: he wants to know, rather, why the position of the President in the legislative process is so different from that of the British monarch. But he can arrive at this kind of understanding only by examining the position of the head of State in American and British constitutional law; and a true understanding of the presidential powers under the US Constitution cannot be gained without a thorough analysis of the American concept of separation of powers.

Most legal arrangements, however, cannot be isolated from their constitutional and legal background. A comparative study of such a famous institution as the French Conseil d'Etat would soon reveal that this body has no counterpart in countries like Britain or the United States. In these countries, the judicial tasks of the Conseil d'Etat are done by the ordinary courts, or by special 'boards' or 'tribunals', or not at all; the advisory functions of the Conseil d'Etat are scattered over a great number of persons and advisory bodies. These organizational differences reveal, however, a more profound problem: the tasks, powers and jurisdiction of a body like the Conseil d'Etat are not perceived in British and American legal thinking as necessarily belonging together. Therefore, the concepts used in the Anglo-American world lack the categories appropriate for defining the activities

---

[18] Example: Kenneth Bradshaw and David Pring, *Parliament and Congress* (London, 1972, paper 1973).

[19] Art. i section 7(2) US Constitution.

of the Conseil d'Etat.[20] As a result, these activities can be properly understood only when examined in their French setting. In this view, comparative legal research should first examine materials as they are considered in the framework of the relevant constitutional or legal system, by patiently and fair-mindedly analysing that system; the second task is then to determine the main characteristics of these materials by comparing them with the results achieved by the study of other legal systems.

For each of the legal systems to be included in the comparison, we should therefore try to scrutinize the concepts it uses. We cannot really understand the meaning of these concepts except by determining the framework within which the concepts have developed and play their role. The construction of the framework, in its turn, is based on certain principles which constitute the foundation stones of the system of public law. And that brings us back to our point of departure.

1.5. Outline of the study

For the purposes of this study, I shall assume that each of the four constitutional systems to be examined has a legislative, an executive and a judicial power. I shall take these three concepts for the moment in the sense they have according to the US Constitution, which is based on a distinction and a separation between these three powers.[21] I shall rely on this version of the famous doctrine of *trias politica* for heuristic purposes: it presents one of the few systematic starting points in the area of public law, and it can be easily understood, especially in its American form. Our problem is, therefore, not whether the *trias politica* idea, as it has been developed over the centuries, is still a correct political theory; it is rather whether this idea can be a useful tool for purposes of comparative research.[22]

My second assumption is that you learn more from studying the relationship between these three powers than from examining each of them individually. The position of the judiciary can only be understood by contrast with the activities of the legislative and executive bodies. The relationship

---

[20] See L. Neville Brown and John S. Bell, *French Administrative Law*, 5th edn (Oxford, 1998), ch. 1 and ch. 3 nos. 1–2.

[21] See Art. I s. 1, Art. II s. 1 and Art. III ss. 1 and 2, US Constitution.

[22] Compare Eric Barendt, *An Introduction to Constitutional Law* (Oxford, 1998), in particular ch. 1.

between the legislative and the judicial power presents a striking example. We can develop two basic models: in the first, laws passed by the legislative bodies can never be challenged before the courts, because these laws are the very foundation of the constitutional system in question; in the second, the constitutional system is founded on a written constitution which defines or limits the powers of the legislature and allows the courts to check whether legislation tallies with constitutional provisions. The first model is very close to the British doctrine of the 'sovereignty of Parliament'; the second embodies systems characterized by judicial review of legislation, such as the American and the German. When elaborating and developing this comparison, we shall discover the existence of systems which do not conform to either of the models but must more or less be considered as mixed. This is particularly the case with France since 1958.

Since legislation is normally considered as essentially a parliamentary task, the study of the two models will raise some general questions as to what parliaments and courts can be reasonably expected to do. That will ultimately result in some general considerations on the relationship between democracy and the rule of law. Hence it will compel us to face some arduous questions, which are frequently evaded in legal literature. They concern the division of labour between law and politics, lawyers and politicians, legal and political science. Together, they constitute a recurring theme, which is one of the main threads ('the red thread', we say in Dutch) of our study. The study will show that similar problems occur when we shift our attention to other relationships than those between courts and legislatures.

We can also use models when we study the relationship between legislative and executive power. The American constitutional system is based on a strict separation of these powers, and the courts sometimes have to act as umpires in case of conflict. However, parliamentary regimes such as those of Great Britain, Germany, Italy and the Benelux countries are based on collaboration and mutual trust between these powers. France, again, does not fit either of the two models, as its system is located in a somewhat uncertain position half way between them.

The relationship between executive and judicial power will allow us to examine how far the action of government and administrative bodies is subject to judicial control. In this respect, French administrative law is close to the model of total subjection. Systems which have been influenced by the French experience, such as Italian and Belgian, and to a certain extent also German administrative law, show some marked differences, but common law systems are still further removed from the model. The introduction of the general remedy for judicial review of administrative action in England and Wales in the late 1970s provoked, however, a new development which brought English law somewhat closer to the French model.

This use of a typological method for the relationship on each of the three sides of the triangle between the *trias* powers will, I trust, reveal something of the basic structure of the public law systems under consideration. It may, however, do more. If it works well, it may also constitute a useful tool for further comparative considerations. A simple example is the opposition between the completely centralized State and the State built on federal or confederal lines. Traditionally, France was considered as the prototype of the centralized State, the United States as the embodiment of federalism. Over the last fifty years, however, both systems lost something of their orginal clarity: France by regionalizing, and the United States by centralizing, tendencies. The typology may help to provide an appropriate analytical framework for a comparative study.

Likewise, and not surprisingly, the separation of Church and State lends itself to a typological approach. Such a separation has existed in the United States since Independence, and it is, as we shall see, strictly upheld by the US Supreme Court. There are interesting judgments on the implications of the separation, for example, for the admissibility of prayers in public schools. By contrast, England has an established Church ('the Anglican Church') headed by the British King or Queen. As a result, public life and ecclesiastical life are very much intertwined. France is again in an intermediate position: it considers itself as a 'lay republic' ('une république laïque'), but it used to be a Catholic nation under the monarchy, and it was only in 1905, more than thirty years after the founding of the Third Republic, that the last religious symbols disappeared from public buildings.

This method of using a typology and of founding it, in particular, on the old concept of separation of powers has not been taken from existing literature. The author developed this method when teaching comparative constitutional law, first to undergraduates, later to LLM students.[23] After his first experiences, he tried his hand at writing a comprehensive study based on this way of thinking. The book, written in Dutch in 1978, was well received – although the first review to be published thought it took the wrong subject – and it has facilitated the composition of the present

---

[23] At the universities of Leiden 1967–78, Utrecht 1998–99 and Cambridge 1999–2000.

study.[24] The book could not, however, simply be updated and translated into English. First, many important developments have since taken place in the area of public law: devolution in Britain; the introduction of judicial review of administrative action into English law; the changing role of the constitutional court in France; the 'cohabitation' which developed into one of the characteristics of French government; the 'conservative revolution' and its aftermath in the United States. One of the most conspicuous developments was the growth of the influence of judicial decisions on matters of public law, particularly in the European countries. In my view, that growth compels us to rethink the constitutional relationship between the courts and the legislative and executive bodies. The second reason for choosing a somewhat different focus is easier to explain: I am myself not the same person as twenty years ago, my ideas have evolved just as much as my subject matter. Moreover, my activities in the judiciary[25] may have had their effects on my opinions.

As a result, the present book is a completely new book, although readers of the earlier book in Dutch may occasionally recognise the tone of it.

---

[24] *Vergelijkend publiekrecht* (Deventer, 1978; 2nd edn 1986).
[25] 1978–1997: eleven years in the Court of Justice of the European Communities, eight years with the Dutch Supreme Court (Hoge Raad).

2

The sovereignty of Parliament

2.1. The parliamentary model

Relations between courts and political institutions cannot be properly assessed without a prior definition of the powers of the courts with regard to legislation. Do judges have to respect statutes validly approved by the competent political institutions in all circumstances, or are they, on the contrary, entitled to set aside or disregard statutes which, in their view, violate rules of higher law, for example, those of the constitution? This problem shows an interesting dissimilarity between the solutions adopted in British and in American constitutional law, which we shall consider first.

In nineteenth-century Britain, constitutional doctrine and constitutional practice came very close to what I shall call the 'parliamentary model'. In this model legislation adopted by Parliament is supreme: it cannot be challenged – not by the head of State, not by the government, not by the courts, not by the citizens.

The British doctrine of the sovereignty of Parliament embodied that rule: by issuing a statute, an Act of Parliament, the legislative bodies had the final say. No court was entitled to question the legal validity of a statute; and every law-making body in the country was subject to it.[1] For this doctrine, it is for the moment of no relevance that the term 'legislative bodies' includes not only both houses of Parliament – the House of Commons and the House of Lords – but also the Queen (or King), who must give the Royal Assent to a bill passed by both houses to sign it into law, under the responsibility of the Prime Minister. There is a debate among constitutional experts in Britain on the question whether the monarch is obliged to give assent after the bill has been passed in both houses; but we leave that question aside for the moment.[2] Dicey, who gave the British doctrine its classical

---

[1] See Finer, Bogdanor and Rudden, *Comparing Constitutions* (Oxford, 1995), ch. 3, nos. 10–12.
[2] See Geoffrey Marshall, *Constitutional Conventions* (Oxford, 1993), pp. 21–3.

formulation, explained the legislative procedure by defining the collaboration of Parliament and monarch as 'the Queen in Parliament' (this was in Queen Victoria's days), or just 'Parliament'. He went on to say that the sovereignty of Parliament 'means neither more nor less than this, namely, that Parliament thus defined has, under the English constitution, the right to make and unmake any law whatever; and further, that no person or body is recognised by the law of England as having a right to override or set aside the legislation of Parliament'.[3] Thus expressed, the doctrine has a disarming simplicity, although a Scottish lawyer might object that, since the Anglo-Scottish Union of 1707, constitutional matters are not part of English law but of the constitutional law of Great Britain.

Dicey's theory was a descriptive theory when it was written down: originally it had no normative purpose, it just endeavoured to describe how the constitution had in fact developed. However, theories are deceptive things: gradually, the doctrine of the sovereignty of Parliament was taken to mean that the British constitution *ought* to be arranged on that basis or, to put it differently, that the British constitution could only work well when it operated in accordance with the theory. Proposals to introduce a written constitution in Britain have sometimes been greeted with the argument that such a plan could not be realized because of its incompatibility with parliamentary sovereignty. An extreme case was a cabinet minister in the Wilson government who said of a plan to introduce an entrenched Bill of Rights that it would destroy the sovereignty of Parliament and thus constitute 'the most comprehensive scheme for the destruction of Parliament as the centrepiece of the constitution since the time of Charles I'.[4] Leaders of the Conservative Party, who have been bickering about continuing membership of the European Union since about 1985, used the unassailable character of the sovereignty of Parliament as one of their arguments.[5] Dicey's doctrine may thus have become a symbol of 'Englishness': it developed from a descriptive into a normative theory, and subsequently into a political guideline, even into an emotional catchword.

The elevation of the effective powers of Parliament into constitutional doctrine was the result of a slow development. Under the Tudor kings, it

---

[3] A. V. Dicey, *An Introduction to the Study of the Law of the Constitution* (London, 1885, 10th edn by E. C. S. Wade, 1959), ch. 1.

[4] Michael Foot, quoted in *The Guardian*, 18 October 1976.

[5] See Hugo Young, *This Blessed Plot: Britain and Europe from Churchill to Blair* (London, 1997), chs. 9 and 11.

was difficult to see how the evolution of the law, since 'time immemorial' (as English courts put it) in the hands of the Royal Courts of Justice, could be influenced by the way the King and his counsellors governed the country. The common law of England (and Wales) and the powers of the monarch belonged, in a way, to completely different categories of thinking. That situation changed in the course of the seventeenth century, when it became more and more apparent that kings were beginning to do a lot more than just quietly conducting wars and subduing rebellious barons. In the early part of that century, the courts began to hold that the King could not, on the basis of his powers and prerogatives as a monarch, make any change in the general law of the land without the support of Parliament. Elaborating this idea, the courts soon found that punishable offences could only be defined by Act of Parliament: the King could not, by his proclamations, 'make a thing unlawful which was permitted by the law before'. Sir Edward Coke, the famous judge who spoke these words, risked a conflict with the King. His Majesty found his judges obstinate, but his angry words, though unpleasant enough for Sir Edward and his colleagues, could not prevent the courts from further developing their case law in this way.[6] They thereby created a piece of what we now would call 'constitutionalism' in a nutshell; this was to become part and parcel of the common law of England.

The second step in the direction of the sovereignty of Parliament derived from the vicissitudes of the monarchy. In 1688, King James II fled the country after having dissolved Parliament. His son-in-law, William of Orange, landed in southern England with his Dutch troops and was able to negotiate a compromise with the English notables, rebellious members of Parliament included. The English Crown was offered to him and his wife Mary Stuart, a new Parliament was elected by a direct vote in the boroughs and counties, and the new King agreed to a strengthening in the position of Parliament as an institution. One of the first acts of the new Parliament was to adopt of a 'Bill of Rights' which reinforced the powers of Parliament. The courts accepted the new institutions.[7] They also hardened their attitude on the limits of royal powers. Taxes could only be levied, they decided, based on an Act of Parliament.

---

[6] See Roscoe Pound, *The Spirit of the Common Law* (Boston, Mass., 1921), ch. III.
[7] See Stanley de Smith and Rodney Brazier, *Constitutional and Administrative Law*, 8th edn (London, 1998), ch. 4.

A third element strengthened the force of these two developments. It was the gradual democratization of Parliament which gave the doctrine of parliamentary sovereignty a measure of democratic legitimacy. When, by the end of the eighteenth century, the accountability of ministers to Parliament was established inch by inch, and when in the early nineteenth century voting rights were extended to new groups of the population, the sovereignty of Parliament could be seen as part of an evolution towards more democracy. And that was more easily accepted when universal suffrage and cabinet government gave its present form to the relationship between the electorate, the House of Commons and the government.[8] Consequently, the doctrine of the sovereignty of Parliament began to assume a stronger position in the course of the twentieth century because it had democratic credentials.

Nevertheless, the scope of the powers of Parliament, its 'omnipotence' as it is sometimes called, owed much to the absolutist tradition which characterized English government before 1688. Tudor monarchs like Henry VIII and Elizabeth I ruled the country more or less single-handed. They might listen to some of their noblemen or clerical advisers, but they ultimately took the necessary decisions themselves. An adviser who was bold enough to oppose the King's wishes might pay for this error with his life. The monarchs also governed the entire country: there were no regional or local powers strong enough to resist royal commands. In modern terminology, we could say that the constitutional system was centralized and based on absolute rule rather than being characterized by competing powers or the existence of checks and balances. There have been interruptions in the evolution of this system, such as the English Civil War and the trial of King Charles I.[9] Moreover, after 1688, the centralism of the earlier kings gradually gave way to a more pluralist conception of the constitution. When Great Britain was created by the Union of 1707, the Scots were allowed to keep their own legal system and to remain outside the jurisdiction of the established Church of England. Further mitigations of centralization were to follow later.[10] It is, however, fair to say that the centralist and absolutist view of government persisted for a long time: for centuries, the system remained as it always had

---

[8] See A. W. Bradley, 'The sovereignty of Parliament', in Jeffrey Jowell and Dawn Oliver (eds.), *The Changing Constitution*, 4th edn (Oxford, 2000), ch. 2.

[9] F. W. Maitland, *The Constitutional History of England* (Cambridge, 1968), pp. 292–7.

[10] See A. W. Bradley and K. D. Ewing, *Constitutional and Administrative Law*, 12th edn (London and New York, 1997), ch. 3.

been, except for the growing influence of Parliament, later in particular of the elected chamber, the House of Commons. There is, therefore, a kind of artful deceit in the course of constitutional evolution in England: by slowly transforming the King-as-ruler into the King-in-Parliament, it put the absolute and central powers of the King into the hands of Parliament – first of the English, later of the British Parliament. Parliament inherited the King's position. Just as the King could do as he pleased in the sixteenth and early seventeenth century, so Parliament could, as a legislative body, do exactly as it thought fit under Dicey's theory.[11]

The success of the doctrine of the sovereignty of Parliament in England may have been encouraged by English conceptions of jurisprudence, legal theory and philosophy. The English intellectual climate has always been positivist. Theories of natural law have never been popular. Various elements may help to explain this situation. First, the influence of the Catholic Church and of the Roman law tradition was slight when compared to the situation on the European continent. Secondly, legal craftsmanship was very much practice-oriented: the training of practising lawyers was not in the hands of the universities but in those of the profession itself, in the so-called 'inns of court'. After the formative years of the common law, by the end of the thirteenth century, the common law courts were so faithful to the doctrine of precedent that solutions to legal problems could be found only by searching for earlier case law on the same or a similar point. The administration of justice developed into a technique, rather than representing the *ars boni et aequi* extolled by the Roman law tradition. A theory like the doctrine of parliamentary sovereignty could prosper because of its seemingly empirical and non-speculative character. And that was certainly the case when legal positivism in England found its philosophical foundation in the theories of the 'analytical school' at the beginning of the twentieth century. According to one of its leading philosophers, John Austin, the concept of 'law' is linked to the concept of 'sovereignty'. In this line of thought, all positive law is deduced from a clearly identifiable law-giver. 'Every positive law, or every law simply or strictly so called, is set by a sovereign or a sovereign body of persons.'[12] The doctrine of the sovereignty of Parliament fits well with such a theory. This may have had some importance because of

---

[11] See, generally, Jeffrey Goldsworthy, *The Sovereignty of Parliament: History and Philosophy* (Oxford, 1999), chs. 2-8.

[12] John Austin, *The Province of Jurisprudence Determined*, Rumble edn (Cambridge, 1995), lecture VI. See also Wolfgang Friedmann, *Legal Theory*, 5th edn (New York, 1967), ch. 22.

the popularity of Austin's view among English lawyers over a considerable period of time.

2.2. The impact of the British model

British constitutional law has often served as a model for other countries, in particular when Great Britain was at the height of its power during the nineteenth century. For countries in continental Europe, the British tradition embodied a combination of slowly evolving democracy on the one hand and a lack of revolutionary violence on the other.

Belgium provides an example. Its constitution was drafted in 1830, at the moment of secession from the Kingdom of the Netherlands, to which it had been (unhappily) united by the Congress of Vienna after the fall of Napoleon I. The framers of the constitution could not link up with Belgian traditions: at the time of the United Dutch Republics (1581–1795) the southern or Belgian provinces had been under Spanish and Austrian domination. The founders of the new nation admired the British constitution and attempted to write down the unwritten rules which determine the British constitutional framework. The outcome of their efforts influenced later endeavours of constitutional reform in other countries, especially in 1848 and subsequently, when the demand for popular government increased on the European continent. The Dutch Constitution was entirely recast in 1848, probably under the influence of revolutionary movements in Germany, France and Austria: and the liberalization of the constitutional system owed much to the – relatively – liberal provisions of the Belgian Constitution.[13]

There is one striking singularity in these attempts at laying down British constitutional rules in continental countries: the leading characteristic of those rules was disregarded. By formulating a Constitution that could be modified only by a special procedure, not by ordinary statute, the continental reformers adhered to a non-British conception: the Constitution established rules of 'higher law' which were binding on the legislature. Parliament could not, under the Belgian Constitution, make or unmake any law whatever, because it had to observe the provisions of the Constitution. If the Constitution prohibits censorship, a Belgian statute cannot compel the seeking of prior permission for press publications. The British

---

[13] On this development see W. van den Steene, *De Belgische Grondwetscommissie, Oktober–November 1830* (Brussels, 1963), 'Besluit'.

Parliament can legally do so; but learned opinion in Britain has it that Parliament will, in fact, never do so because it must be considered as the traditional defender of civil liberties. The Belgian Parliament is, however, under a legal obligation to refrain from legislation of this kind.

The supremacy of the Constitution does not necessarily imply that the compatibility of statutes with constitutional provisions will have to be assessed by the courts or by a judicial body. In Belgium and the Netherlands, the prevailing opinion insisted for a long time (and until fairly recently) that the legislative bodies are perfectly capable of respecting that obligation. Unconstitutional behaviour by representative bodies would, moreover, be punished by the electors.[14] It is only in the last twenty or thirty years that this optimistic view of politics has been slowly crumbling away, with the result that certain forms of judicial review of legislation have developed, particularly in Belgium.

A closer affinity with the British model existed in France under the Third Republic (1871–1940). It was, however, not the result of a conscious attempt to borrow from British constitutional law, but rather the product of happenstance; it came about more by fortune than by design. The Republic started indeed without a constitution, but with an elected Assembly. The defeat inflicted on the French by the Prussian army not only occasioned the collapse of the Second Empire, that of Napoleon III; it also gave rise to a 'convention of armistice' between the German and French generals. This convention stipulated that a national assembly was to be elected to decide whether or not to continue the war and, if not, how to negotiate a peace. The Assembly, once elected, had its own idea of its task: it appointed a head of the executive power 'under the authority of the Assembly', so that the country could again be governed. After a series of rebellions and other conflicts, and a period of uncertainty as to the future shape of institutions, the Assembly finally adopted three statutes on constitutional matters in 1875: one to create a Senate, one to organize the powers of the public authorities, and one to govern relations between the institutions. Together, these three statutes were considered as 'the constitution' of 1875. They have been modified by ordinary statute, though not very often. It happened, for example, when Versailles was replaced as the seat of the institutions by Paris.[15]

---

[14] On this argument see Allan Brewer Carìas, *La defensa de la Constitución* (Caracas, 1982), ch. 1.

[15] See Gabriel Lepointe, *Histoire des institutions du droit public français au XIXme siècle* (Paris, 1953), ch. x. See also Michel Winock, *La fièvre hexagonale: les grandes crises politiques 1871–1968* (Paris, 1986), chs. 1-3.

The circumstances surrounding the birth of the new Republic determined its character. The new constitutional system gave rise to what French authors call 'la république parlementaire', a form of government which would last in various guises until 1958 (with an interruption during the Second World War).[16] From a legal point of view, the system was very close to the model of parliamentary sovereignty: the Assembly was by far the most powerful institution; it could 'make and unmake' any law; its statutes could not be challenged; the validity of subordinate legislation and of administrative decisions depended on compatibility with the statute conferring the necessary powers. Politically, however, the situation in Paris could not be compared to that in Westminster: the political abysses were wider, the tone of the debate more violent, extremist groups and parties frequently tore the Assembly apart, and the instability of governments remained a difficulty until the dying days of the Fourth Republic in 1958. These important differences from the way in which government and politics were conducted in Britain should not obscure the fact that the constitutional systems of both countries were founded, during this period, on a similar legal basis.

A word should be added concerning Britain's influence on the constitutions of her former dominions and colonies. I shall take Canada as an example. For more than a century, the Canadian constitution was enshrined in a British Act of Parliament, the British North America Act 1867. It instituted, for reasons which do not concern us here, a federal system, dividing legislative powers between the central Canadian parliament (the 'dominion parliament' at the time) and the representative bodies of the 'provinces' (Quebec, Ontario etc.). This construction implies that the main characteristic of a sovereign parliament is missing: the legislative bodies are not free to regulate any subject they think fit; they have jurisdiction over some subjects but not over others. Nevertheless, many Canadian lawyers found it hard to renounce the British theory completely. They pointed out that the federal division of powers was the only obstacle to the sovereignty of parliament, since the British North America Act did not include a 'bill of rights' – unlike, for example, the US Constitution.[17] Some authors even developed the theory that the dominion parliament and the provincial parliaments

[16] See Dmitri Lavroff, *Le système politique français*, 5th edn (Paris, 1991), pp. 53–67; Jean Gicquel and André Hauriou, *Droit constitutionnel et institutions politiques*, 8th edn (Paris, 1985), pp. 629–50.

[17] See Peter Hogg, *Constitutional Law of Canada*, 4th edn (Toronto, 1997), s. 12.2.

were each 'sovereign within their powers', an expression which implies a somewhat peculiar concept of sovereignty. However that may have been, when the British Act was replaced by a real Canadian Constitution, in 1982, an entrenched bill of rights was added to it in the form of the Canadian Charter of Rights and Freedoms. As a result, legislative powers are limited not only by the federal division of powers but also by the rights and freedoms as constitutionally enshrined. The 1982 Constitution put a seal on this evolution by explicitly providing that the Constitution is the supreme law of the land and that any law inconsistent with it shall be of no force or effect.[18] The Canadian constitutional system has thus formally abandoned any association with the doctrine of the sovereignty of Parliament.

This little excursion illustrates that, outside Britain, the fortunes of this doctrine have had their ups and downs, but that, apparently, little is left of it.

2.3. British practice

The first characteristic of the parliamentary model is that it does not recognise any 'higher law' which could impinge on the validity of an Act of Parliament. Solemn declarations defining the rights of citizens, such as the 1688 Bill of Rights, are not considered by the English courts as overriding the provisions of a statute. They have the same rank in the hierarchy of rules. Even such a (seemingly) basic document as Magna Carta of 1215 could legally be abolished by ordinary statute. A 1920 judgment coolly observed that Magna Carta had not remained untouched: 'like every other law of England, it is not condemned to that immunity from development or improvement which was attributed to the laws of the Medes and the Persians'.[19] The same attitude is still prevalent. When Parliament decided to give effect to the substantive provisions of the European Convention on Human Rights in British domestic law, it made it perfectly clear that this statute, important though it might be, was just an ordinary statute like any other statute. Even if the courts find that provisions of a given statute are in clear violation of the Human Rights Act, that will not affect the validity or the enforcement of those provisions.[20] There is simply no higher law than the Act of Parliament, and even human rights protection cannot make

---

[18] Art. 52(1) Constitution of Canada. [19] *Chester* v. *Bateson* [1920] 1 KB 829.
[20] Section 4(6)(a) Human Rights Act 1998.

an exception to that rule. On the latter point, British constitutional law occupies a unique place in Europe.

A second characteristic of the system is that infringements of procedural requirements cannot be submitted to consideration by the courts. If a bill has passed both houses of Parliament, as shown by the parliamentary documents, and has subsequently received Royal Assent, it is to be considered as a statute; if rules of parliamentary procedure have been violated, that is of no concern to the judges. In answer to the argument that an Act of Parliament has been passed improperly, the court will merely say that it is for the legislature to correct it by repealing it: the court must apply the statute. Similarly, when one of the parties alleges that actual fraud has been committed, the court will react by holding that 'it is not open to the court to go behind what has been enacted by the legislature and to inquire how the enactment came to be made'.[21] Thus statutes cannot be challenged on formal grounds.

A third characteristic is that courts will not examine whether a statute is or is not compatible with rules of international law. An Act of Parliament cannot be *ultra vires*, i.e. beyond Parliament's jurisdiction. If a statute provides that it applies to the herring fishery in certain bays near the coast of Scotland, the judges will apply that statute even if they happen to be convinced that, according to rules of public international law, some of these waters are outside British authority. Conflicts of this kind have to be settled by the Foreign Office according to traditional case law, not by the courts. The accession of the United Kingdom to the European Communities, in 1973, did not immediately cause a change in judicial attitudes. It may have been clear that European Community law was to prevail over British statutes, and that British courts would have to apply a Community regulation rather than a British statute in case of conflict; but the political institutions had been aware of that problem, with the result that a statute was adopted with the very purpose of reconciling the primacy of Community law with the doctrine of the sovereignty of Parliament. The European Communities Act 1972 made Community law applicable in the United Kingdom; and for the purpose of the Act, Community law included not only existing but also future Community rules.[22] Quite obviously, the aim was to adjust the British

---

[21] *Hoani Te Heuheu Tukino* v. *Aotea District Maori Land Board* [1941] AC 388.

[22] See T. C. Hartley, *The Foundations of European Community law*, 4th edn (Oxford, 1998), pp. 250–7.

legal system to its integration into a European legal order without abandoning the doctrine of parliamentary sovereignty as the centrepiece of British constitutional law.

In the first years of British membership of the Community, however, English judges had difficulty in accepting the idea that Community rules could have priority over British statutes; they found it already a significant step to consider that these rules had the same effect as an Act of Parliament. This view was not in accordance with the case law of the Court of Justice of the European Communities and with opinions generally held in the other Member States. The House of Lords, acting in its capacity as supreme appeal court of the United Kingdom, finally accepted the primacy of Community law in unambiguous terms in the early 1990s.[23] The case concerned claims by Spanish fishermen to exercise rights of free establishment in EC countries under the EC Treaty, which were thwarted by a British statute instituting a licensing scheme for fishing in British territorial waters and in the contiguous zone. The House of Lords held that the statute was 'ineffective', thus recognizing that EC legislation was 'higher law' with regard to Acts of Parliament and that, to that extent, the doctrine of the sovereignty of Parliament did not apply.

If that is the result of British accession to the EC, one may wonder whether the British Parliament was legally entitled to approve it: could Parliament jettison its sovereignty without upsetting the entire constitutional system? The question was submitted to the Court of Appeal in 1971, before accession, but the Court left the question more or less unanswered.[24] Lord Denning, Master of the Rolls (president of the Court of Appeal), accepted the petitioner's argument that no Parliament can legally bind another, and that any Parliament can reverse what a previous Parliament has done. Nevertheless, he added, 'so far as this court is concerned, I think we wait till that day comes'.

Thus EC membership raises a more general question: can Parliament, under the doctrine of parliamentary sovereignty, tie its own hands and those of succeeding Parliaments? If, for example, Parliament itself adopts a statute imposing a particular procedure for a specific kind of legislation, or prohibiting the repeal of it, is it then a valid argument before a court

---

[23] *R v. Secretary of State for Transport* ex p *Factortame* (II) [1991] AC 603.
[24] *Blackburn v. AG* [1971] 1 WLR 1037. The expression 'Court of Appeal' refers to the Court of Appeal of England and Wales.

that Parliament has not respected these self-imposed requirements? The classic answer to this question was in the negative: the validity of a statute cannot be challenged, even if earlier statutes imposed requirements to be met by later statutes. The Privy Council, the British appeal court for cases from the dominions and colonies, developed a more subtle approach.[25] It accepted that dominion parliaments which had entrenched provisions on human rights, by prescribing that these provisions could be modified only by qualified majority, were not entitled to change or repeal these provisions by ordinary statute. In some cases such a statute, though having received Royal Assent, was considered as *ultra vires* and therefore invalid. Lord Pearce, speaking for the Court in a Sri-Lankese (then Ceylonese) case, used words to the effect that a sovereign Parliament could bind its successors by prescribing a certain 'form' for legislation in certain matters.[26] This un-Diceyan view is, however, usually considered as not applying to the mother country. It is not always clear why this should be the case.[27] The way in which the Human Rights Act 1998 was framed shows that, for Britain itself, the practice remains firmly embedded in the tradition of the parliamentary model, and that the Parliament in Westminster considers that it cannot bind its successors.

2.4. Subordinate and colonial legislation

Sovereignty of Parliament implies that the powers of all public authorities are subordinate to it. As a result, British Orders in Council – i.e. royal decrees made with the advice and under the responsibility of the government – ministerial regulations and local by-laws can be considered as validly made only if the authority to do so has been granted by Act of Parliament. If such authority is lacking, the piece of subordinate legislation in question is *ultra vires* and is therefore null and void.[28]

This strict view of the validity of subordinate legislation is scrupulously adhered to by the courts. Government efforts to make delegated legislation 'judge-proof' have generally failed. In a 1931 case, the Housing Act 1925 provided explicitly that certain schemes approved by the minister would

---

[25] The Judicial Committee of the Privy Council in fact consists of members of the Judicial Committee of the House of Lords. It still accepts appeals from certain Commonwealth countries, such as New Zealand and Trinidad and Tobago.

[26] *Bribery Commisioner* v. *Ranasingh* [1964] 2 All ER 785.

[27] But see H. W. R. Wade, *Constitutional Fundamentals*, 32nd Hamlyn lecture (London, 1980), ch. III.

[28] See H. W. R. Wade and C. F. Forsyth, *Administrative Law*, 8th edn (Oxford, 2000), chs. 1-2.

have the same effect 'as if enacted by this Act'; but the House of Lords held that the minister was not given the power to approve schemes which were not in accordance with the Act and that, therefore, the 'as if' clause could not apply to the approval of a scheme which was not compatible with the Act.[29] Parliament could perhaps avoid judicial scrutiny by giving a very broad definition of delegated powers in the Act, but such a device will not work very well either. In the first place, representative bodies generally dislike delegating wide and indeterminate powers, even to governments of their own political colour. And, secondly, it is by no means certain that judicial interference can be entirely ruled out in such a way. For more than a century, English courts have assumed that Parliament can only have intended that delegated powers will be reasonably exercised. If, for example, a government minister has issued a regulation which, though within the broad definition of his delegated powers, is considered by the court as arbitrary or unreasonable, the court will rule that Parliament cannot have intended to convey the power to issue unreasonable provisions; consequently, the regulation will be regarded as *ultra vires*.[30] In a very British way, the courts show a tendency nowadays to apply a less demanding test of reasonableness when the regulation has been issued by a representative body, such as a city council. But the test is very strict in cases of ministerial regulations or decisions by bodies like nationalized industries; the exercise of rule-making powers by these bodies is submitted to an exacting scrutiny.[31]

A similar test of reasonableness is applied to individual decisions issued by a minister or administrative body. Here, however, the result may be that reasons for the decision must be given, although the enabling statute is silent on that point. The Court of Appeal held, in a case concerning the British Nationality Act, that the statute did not require the Home Secretary to give reasons for refusing an application for British citizenship; where, however, the decision involved the exercise of discretion, he had to exercise that power reasonably, so that he was not relieved of the obligation to be fair in arriving at his decision. Therefore, reasons should be given.[32] Constitutional considerations can thus be conducive to the development of elementary rules of administrative law. The principle of 'legality' of administrative action, which is so important in many systems of law, particularly

---

[29] *Minister of Health* v. *R* ex p *Yaffé* [1931] AC 494.
[30] Example: *Kruse* v. *Johnson* [1898] 2 QB 91.
[31] See Peter Cane, *An Introduction to Administrative Law*, 3rd edn (Oxford, 1996), pp. 209–10.
[32] *R* v. *Secretary of State for the Home Office* ex p *Fayed and another* [1997] 1 All ER 228.

French and German administrative law, is in Great Britain founded on the sovereignty of Parliament.[33]

The view of the British courts on subordinate legislation was to have important effects outside the territory of the United Kingdom. In the eyes of British judges, colonial legislation was considered as, or assimilated to, subordinate legislation. When 'colonial charters' had been enacted for the different colonies by Act of Parliament, regulations issued by the colonial authorities were held to be *ultra vires* if they were not compatible with the charter. This compatibility was ultimately assessed by a British court, as appeals from colonial courts of appeal could always be brought to the Privy Council in London. Even in the early nineteenth century, the Privy Council held that colonial laws could not stand if they were opposed to the colonial charters or to other Acts of Parliament. That method of controlling colonial legislation remained in force once the colony concerned had its own representative body which, under the applicable colonial charter, was allowed to establish its own autonomous legislation in certain areas (normally not in matters of defence or foreign affairs). And this situation persisted when the 'white' colonies such as Canada and Australia were granted 'dominion status' and thereby became almost entirely independent. The Privy Council continued, however, to exercise its control over the compatibility of dominion legislation with the enabling Act of Parliament.[34]

For Canada, the implication was that Canadian legislation was considered *ultra vires* when it was contrary to the British North America Act 1867; that is to say that legislation was subject to judicial review, and that this was done by a British court, the Privy Council. The legal situation remained unchanged until Canada made an end to appeals to the London court after the Statute of Westminister, 1932, conferred full independence on the country. These developments revealed a strange constitutional paradox: in the name of the sovereignty of Parliament, the courts introduced judicial review of legislation by scrutinizing the compatibility of dominion legislation with the dominion constitution. The Canadian Supreme Court continued indeed to exercise this form of judicial review after the cessation of appeals to the Privy Council. Thus, constitutional evolution seems to show that, in the English-speaking world outside Great Britain, the heritage of the British doctrine of the sovereignty of Parliament may well have been exactly the

[33] See Jürgen Schwarze, *European Administrative Law* (London and Luxembourg, 1992), pp. 220–2.
[34] See Mauro Cappelletti, *The Judicial Process in Comparative Perspective* (Oxford, 1989), ch. 3-1.

opposite of what the doctrine intended: it established judicial review of legislation rather than the supremacy of the parliaments.[35]

There is a second aspect to the relationship between the 'sovereignty' of the Parliament in Westminster and the constitutional position of former British dominions and colonies. Autonomy in local and regional matters, and eventually full independence, were conferred upon these countries by Act of Parliament. The implication seems to be that the Westminster Parliament can also repeal statutes granting autonomy or independence. In the Diceyan view, it could 'unmake' any law it had made. Politically, such a repeal may have been most unlikely; but legally, it presented a real problem. Could the British Parliament repeal the British North America Act 1867 and thereby restore the *status quo ante* i.e. the semi colonial situation? The prevailing constitutional theory implied that it could. The question was submitted to the Privy Council when Canada abolished appeals to that august body after the Statute of Westminster, 1932, had granted the full powers of an independent State to Canada, matters of defence and foreign affairs included. The Court accepted that Canada, independent as it now was, was entitled to make an end to the appeals; but Viscount Sankey, speaking for the Court, added a caveat.[36] It was doubtless true, he said, 'that the powers of the Imperial Parliament to pass on its own initiative any legislation that it thought fit extending to Canada remains in theory unimpaired'. Indeed, he continued, the British Parliament could 'as a matter of abstract law' repeal or disregard the Statute of Westminster. But, as he added in a comforting tone, 'that is theory and has no relation to realities'; in truth, Canada must be considered as enjoying the full extent of self-government. It is perhaps disputable whether a theory which 'has no relation to realities' is, all things considered, a good theory; but the judgment constitutes a clear illustration of the hold which the theory exercises on the judges.[37] There are no perceptible signs that this hold is currently diminishing.[38]

The British North America Act 1867 retained its position as the constitution of Canada until 1982. Some amendments were made to it, for example in 1949, by British Act of Parliament, but only after the Canadian federal Parliament had expressed its assent. The delay in what was called the

---

[35] See also Edward McWhinney, *Judicial Review in the English-Speaking World*, 4th edn (Toronto, 1969), ch. 1.

[36] *British Coal Corp. v. the King* [1935] AC 500.

[37] See also Marshall, *Constitutional Conventions*, pp. 172–3.

[38] See *R v. Director of public prosecutions* ex p *Kebeline and others* [1999] 3 WLR 972.

'repatriation' of the Canadian constitution was not occasioned by Britain's unwillingness to relinquish one of its last legal links with the dominion, but by dissension in Canada itself, in particular between the federal government and some provincial governments, most notably that of the province of Quebec. Feelings ran high during this debate, since 'la belle province' insisted on a recognition of the right to secession. Ultimately, the debate led to an indistinct compromise satisfying nobody; later attempts to arrive at 'clarity' have so far been unsuccessful. The chief characteristic of the repatriated constitution are that it maintains the division of powers between the federal and the provincial authorities as established by the British North America Act 1867, and adds a Canadian Charter of Rights and Freedoms as part of the Constitution. In Westminster, however, the forms were respected until the last possible moment: the British Parliament adopted the Canada Act 1982 which repealed the relevant provisions of the Statute of Westminster 1932.[39]

2.5. Weaknesses of the theory

The doctrine of the sovereignty of Parliament has its strong as well as its weak points.

Its strength is twofold. As a theory, it is very simple: one doesn't need to be a lawyer in order to understand it. That is not true of constitutional theories generally. Besides, the doctrine has a kind of popular appeal because of its visible link with democracy. The assumption is, of course, that the representative bodies truly translate the feelings of the electorate; but then, of course, representative systems are in general founded on this assumption.

As a descriptive theory, the doctrine has some serious drawbacks. It cannot always explain what it sets out to explain. These disadvantages concern in particular the position of Britain in European and international developments, reliance on referenda for settling important constitutional issues, and the future of devolution in Britain.

The concept of parliamentary sovereignty is singularly inapt as a description of Britain's relationship with the European integration process. It is true that the European Communities Act 1972 had the very purpose of reconciling European rule-giving with the sovereignty of the British Parliament, but in many respects, it failed to do so. The Act presupposes that law-making

[39] See Hogg, *Constitutional Law of Canada*, s. 3.4; Marshall, *Constitutional Conventions*, ch. XI.

in the European Community is merely a matter of secondary legislation by means of regulations and directives established by the European institutions, in particular the Council.[40] Although that is one of the most important sources of EC law, it is not the only one. Other EC institutions help to shape the law: the Commission by its decisions on the way Treaty provisions are to be implemented, particularly if these decisions amount to a regular practice on certain points, for example in competition law; the Court of Justice of the EC elaborated certain principles of law, which it found either by disclosing basic ideas underlying Treaty provisions, or by relying on principles common to the legal systems of the Member States. The Commission's practice on competition matters and the Court's interpretation of general principles of law are part of European law to be observed by British institutions, courts included.[41] That conclusion is clear enough from the point of view of European Community law, but there is hardly a place for it in the constitutional theory prevailing in Britain.

Things are not much easier when we look at the influence of the European Convention on Human Rights. The rights and liberties enumerated by that Convention were finally made part of English and Scottish law by the Human Rights Act 1998, but the courts are powerless when faced with legislation which violates these rights and liberties. In a certain sense, it is worse: courts must interpret legislation in conformity with the provisions of the Human Rights Act, but they must still apply that legislation even if such an interpretation proves impossible. The implication is that minor sins are corrected and major sins forgiven.[42] The Human Rights Act does, however, allow for the role of judicial decision-making, in this case by the European Court of Human Rights. The Act assumes that the provisions of the European Convention must be interpreted in the way indicated by the European Court, and that British courts must follow that interpretation. That implies, it would appear, that the provisions of the Human Rights Act are to be interpreted and applied in the same way.[43]

---

[40] Regulations and directives are defined in Art. 249 EC Treaty (ex 189).

[41] See C. N. Kakouris, 'La Cour de Justice des Communautés européennes comme cour constitutionnelle: trois observations', in Ole Due, Marcus Lutter and Jürgen Schwarze (eds.), *Festschrift für Ulrich Everling* (Baden-Baden, 1995), vol. i, p. 629.

[42] See Rodney Brazier, *Constitutional Reform. Reshaping the British Constitutional System* (Oxford, 1998), chs. 1 and 8.

[43] See Art. 2(1) Human Rights Act. See also Conor A. Gearty, 'The Human Rights Act 1998 and the Strasbourg organs: some preliminary reflections', in Gavin W. Anderson (ed.), *Rights and Democracy: Essays in UK-Canadian Constitutionalism* (London, 1999), ch. 8.

European developments usually show their own dynamics, and their rhythm and course do not depend on British attitudes alone. That is probably one of the reasons why the attempt to pin down these developments to subjects defined by a British statute seems doomed to failure.

A second problem area concerns internal British matters. Recent history shows a number of occasions where decisions of great constitutional importance have in truth been taken by referendum rather than by Act of Parliament. The first occasion was when British membership of the EC was decided by referendum in the Wilson years. The political background was somewhat peculiar, as the Prime Minister was faced by internal disagreement in the Cabinet and refused to fight for his own point of view.[44] The referendum had only a consultative character, but it is not very likely that Parliament would have approved accession after a negative result. Parliament again resorted to a referendum when a second problem of constitutional reform arose, viz. devolution. The electorate of Scotland and Wales was asked to accept or reject legislation involving substantial decentralization of powers to regional authorities. Under the Wilson administration, a first plan was dropped because it failed to secure the required majority. In 1998, however, a second, revised plan was accepted, likewise by referendum. Somewhat later, the Blair Cabinet announced that it would submit British accession to the 'Euro-zone' (the single European currency) to a referendum.

A recurrent use of the referendum for solving important constitutional problems undermines one of the basic premises of the sovereignty of Parliament – the idea that the people decides by means of its elected representatives in the House of Commons. In 1999, however, the abolition of hereditary peers' membership of the House of Lords was achieved by statute.[45] It had been announced in the electoral manifesto which helped the Labour Party to win the general election. Apart from that, there is also reason to believe that it was not so much an important constitutional matter as a reform which was long overdue.

The third problem is devolution itself. Elected assemblies in Scotland and Wales have power to pass regional legislation. This legislation can be subjected to judicial scrutiny because these assemblies have only limited

---

[44] On this episode see Roy Jenkins, *A Life at the Centre* (London, 1991), ch. 22.

[45] This reform did not affect the position of the Judicial Committee of the House of Lords. The Committee consists of judges who are formally elevated to life peerages.

powers. The theory is that the Parliament in Westminster, as Parliament of the United Kingdom, retains its full legislative powers, and that British statutes will, therefore, continue to be as unassailable as before devolution.[46] The question is, of course, whether such an uneven system will remain unchanged in the future. Scottish and Welsh assemblies may wish to exclude British legislation on matters which have been 'devolved' to them. If such a wish were to be honoured, a first step would be made in the direction of a federal system. Federal developments elsewhere in Europe, particularly in Belgium, show that such a system does not work very well without judicial review of legislation. A white paper published on the earlier plan for devolution, in the 1970s, had already drawn attention to this possibility.[47] Judicial powers have already become more important because an Act of the Scottish Parliament is considered as 'law' only if its provisions are within the legislative powers of that Parliament. The Scotland Act provides, moreover, that a provision is outside these powers when it is incompatible with any right protected by the European Convention. That is a first step in the direction of judicial review of legislation for violation of human rights and fundamental freedoms.[48]

As a normative theory, the doctrine of the sovereignty of Parliament is losing some of its attractiveness. The most important reason is anxiety about human rights protection. Doubt is steadily growing as to whether the assessment of the need to restrict the exercise of these rights, for example in emergency situations, can be entirely left to the good sense of the parliamentary majority of the day.[49] The Human Rights Act 1998 seems conceived in such a way as to save, as a French expression has it, both the goat and the cabbage. Even the greatest democrat will have to admit that, nowadays, confidence in political leaders is not what it was. It was eroded earlier on the European continent, perhaps because of certain disillusioning experiences which, so far, are unknown to Britain. One might think, for example, of the political instability in France in the days of the Fourth Republic, or the street violence in Germany in the later years of the

---

[46] See Rodney Brazier, 'The Constitution of the United Kingdom', *CLJ* (1999), 96.

[47] Cmnd 6585 (Devolution to Scotland and Wales, supplementary statement), nos. 12–14. See also P. Craig and M. Walters, 'The courts, devolution and judicial review', *Public Law* (1999), 274.

[48] See, respectively, Art. 29(1) and Art. 29(2)(d) Scotland Act.

[49] See already Sir Leslie Scarman, *English Law: The New Dimension*, 26th Hamlyn lecture (London, 1974), chs. II and VI; Lord Hailsham, *Hamlyn Revisited: The British Legal System Today*, 35th Hamlyn lecture (London, 1983), chs. II–IV.

Weimar Republic. Although developments in Britain are not comparable, confidence in politicians is diminishing. There have been various scandals concerning Members of Parliament in recent years; one has even been accused of accepting bribes for putting certain questions to the government in the House of Commons at question time ('cash for questions'). More importantly, people feel that political leaders are not always interested in a good parliamentary debate on important political issues: they prefer to command their troops and have no greater worries than their image in the media. Under these circumstances, doubts begin to arise about the democratic character of the parliamentary debate itself. An extreme example is that of the conservative Prime Minister Mrs Thatcher in the last years of her time in office: she was able to abolish, with the help of her (devoted) parliamentary majority, local government in London and some other large cities for no other reason, it appears, than the left-wing orientation (and action) of the local authorities.[50] What happened to local government might just as well happen to the freedom of assembly or any other civil liberty.

Summarizing the normative argument against the doctrine of parliamentary sovereignty, one might say that Britain may be in need of some more checks and balances than those provided by the present constitutional system.

---

[50] See David Butler, Andrew Adonis and Tony Travers, *Failure in British Government: The Policy of the Poll Tax* (Oxford, 1994), ch. 12; Hugo Young, *One of Us – A Biography of Margaret Thatcher*, new edn (London, 1991), ch. 22.

Judicial review of legislation

3.1. The constitutional model

The opposite of the parliamentary model is the constitutional model: it is at the other end of the scale. In the constitutional model, a parliament cannot be 'sovereign' or 'supreme' in any sense of these words, because its legislation has to be compatible with higher law, in particular with the Constitution, and this compatibility will not be assessed by the parliament itself, but by a judicial body.

The American system of judicial review of legislation comes very close to this model. In the United States, any court to which a case or controversy has been brought will have to examine the arguments of the parties concerning the compatibility of statutes with the Constitution. If the court comes to the conclusion that a statute is unconstitutional, it will not apply that statute (it will 'strike down' the statute, in professional legal language). American reality shows, however, a somewhat different picture, because important cases on the interpretation of the Constitution will nearly always be referred to the US Supreme Court in Washington. It is true that this Court is only the highest appeal court in the hierarchy of federal courts, and that each of the fifty states has its own hierarchy of courts, with its own supreme court;[1] but an appeal to the Court from state supreme courts is always possible if the compatibility of a state statute with the federal Constitution is raised. Moreover, the US Supreme Court is largely master of its own agenda: practically all cases are brought before it by means of *certiorari*, a remedy which, in American law, allows the Court itself to decide whether or not to take the case, according to 'sound judicial discretion'. In fact, according to a well-established practice of the Court, an affirmative decision follows if four judges (out of nine) are in favour.[2] Normally, no reasons are given for *certiorari* decisions.

---

[1] See Alan Grant, *The American Political System*, 6th edn (Aldershot, 1997), ch. 4.

[2] For the history of *certiorari* see Peter Linzer, 'The meaning of certiorari denials', *ColLRev* 79 (1979), 1227.

According to the prevailing opinion, a denial of *certiorari* does not imply that the Court agrees with the judgment of the lower court. There may be entirely different reasons for not taking the case: the problem to be solved is not important enough, or the facts of the case do not constitute a basis for a sound decision. The Court itself refuses to consider a *certiorari* denial as anything else than an indication that fewer than four judges thought revision of the lower court's judgment desirable on grounds of judicial discretion.[3] In the Court's view, therefore, there is an important distinction between a decision on 'cert-worthiness' and one on the merits. In practice, however, this distinction is sometimes blurred. There have been subjects on which the Court was very much divided, for example, on the compatibility of capital punishment with the Constitution in the 1970s; in such cases, the lines of partition within the Court in *certiorari* denials and in judgments on the merits were usually identical. Moreover, the Court has sometimes published minority opinions on *certiorari* denials; this occurred, for example, during the debates on the constitutionality of the Vietnam War, when the Court consistently refused to take any case involving that point.[4] *Certiorari* denials don't imply approval of the lower court's decision, said a 1972 judgment, but 'pointed dissents' may nevertheless give an indication as to what the dissenting judges think about the merits.[5]

Since the Court controls its own docket, it has the opportunity to select the areas of law which it thinks most in need of judicial guidance. There is little doubt that the Court focuses on the area of constitutional law. There may, now and then, still be important judgments on other subjects, such as competition law ('anti-trust law', in the American terminology), but it is safe to state that, over the last century, the Court has gradually specialized in constitutional matters. Authors generally assume, without any further comment, that the US Supreme Court exists for the sake of its constitutional jurisdiction.[6]

As far back as 1803, the Supreme Court explicitly held that courts have power to examine 'whether an Act, repugnant to the Constitution, can become the law of the land'. In a celebrated opinion, delivered by Chief

---

[3] Justice Frankfurter in *Maryland* v. *Baltimore Radio Show Inc.*, 338 US 912 (1950).
[4] *Mora* v. *McNamara*, 389 US 934 (1967).   [5] *US* v. *Kras*, 409 US 434 (1972).
[6] See Archibald Cox, *The Role of the Supreme Court in American Government* (Oxford, 1976), ch. 1; Robert F. Nagel, *Constitutional Cultures. The Mentality and Consequences of Judicial Review* (Berkeley and Los Angeles, 1989), ch. 2.

Justice Marshall, the Court confirmed 'the principle, supposed to be essential to all written constitutions, that a law repugnant to the Constitution is void'.[7] Chief Justice Marshall said that this principle was supposed 'to have been long and well established', but he added some arguments intended to demonstrate its wisdom. These arguments can be summarized as follows.

A first group of arguments concerns the position of the legislative bodies under the US Constitution. The Constitution defines and limits the powers of the legislature. It does so, firstly, by attributing certain powers to the federal Congress and leaving others to the state legislatures and, secondly, by forbidding Congress to make certain laws, for example, laws conferring titles of nobility or restricting the freedom of the press.[8] The authority from which these rules proceed is supreme, continues the opinion, because they have been established by the people itself. The people has indeed 'an original right' to establish the rules applicable to its future government, and it exercised this right by assigning to different institutions their respective powers. It is interesting to note that in this opinion, as in American writing generally, 'the people' is identified with the Constitution, just as the same concept 'the people' is identified with the representative bodies in British constitutional thinking. However that may be, Chief Justice Marshall's opinion hits the nail on the head when it concludes:

> The Constitution is either a superior paramount law, unchangeable by any ordinary means, or it is on a level with ordinary legislative acts and, like any other act, is alterable when the legislature shall please to alter it. If the former part of the alternative be true, then a legislative act contrary to the Constitution is not law; if the latter part be true, then written constitutions are absurd attempts, on the part of the people, to limit a power in its own nature illimitable.

Nearly two centuries later, one has to admit that this is forcefully expressed.

The second group of arguments is based on the role of the courts. 'It is emphatically the province and duty of the judicial department to say

---

[7] *Marbury* v. *Madison*, 1 Cranch 137 (1803). The text can be found in any casebook on American constitutional law.

[8] See, respectively, Art. 1, s. 8, and Tenth Amendment to the US Constitution; Art. 1, s. 9(3), and First Amendment to the US Constitution.

what the law is.' If two or more statutes conflict with each other, the courts will have to decide 'on the operation of each'; in the same way, the courts must determine whether to apply a statute or the Constitution if there is opposition between them. It is 'the very essence of judicial duty' to fix the scope of each of these conflicting instruments. The opinion expressly refutes the idea that this general rule might admit an exception when one of the conflicting instruments is a constitution rather than an ordinary law: courts cannot 'close their eyes on the Constitution' by looking only at the statute.

The third group of arguments examines the aims of the Constitution itself. This part of the opinion is, to say the least, not very convincing. It starts by stating that a written constitution, 'the greatest improvement on political institutions' (it had only been in force for fifteen years), must not be reduced to ineffectiveness because of the failure of Congress to take it into account. It then discusses the intention of the framers of the Constitution and states baldly that a different concept would be 'too extravagant to be maintained'. Moreover, the opinion continues, the Constitution directs judges to take an oath to support it (a weak argument, as members of Congress take a similar oath). Finally, the opinion relies on a textual argument: in declaring what shall be 'the supreme law of the land' the Constitution mentions itself first, and only then the laws of the United States, and not these laws generally but only when 'made in pursuance of the Constitution'.[9]

Later cases and later literature take this power of the courts for granted: courts can strike down legislation (federal or state) which violates the Constitution. The 1803 judgment, *Marbury* v. *Madison* (affectionately known as '*Marbury*'), has been subjected to detailed and repeated analysis; its reasoning has been scrutinized, or attacked as not very strong, but its result has never been questioned.[10]

One element is conspicuously absent from the Court's reasoning: no single word is devoted to the background of judicial review in British colonial history. Reading the opinion of the Chief Justice gives the impression that the Court's attitude is exclusively inspired by the Constitution. It is true that this document was the pride of the new nation at the time; and the Constitution is still an important part of American political mythology. However, colonial courts of pre-Independence days had to examine whether

[9] Art. VI(2) US Constitution.
[10] Example: John E. Nowak and Ronald D. Rotunda, *Constitutional Law*, 5th edn (St. Paul, Minn., 1995), ch. 1.

the legislation of New York, Virginia or Massachusetts was, or was not, compatible with British colonial charters laid down in Acts of Parliament; and that situation may constitute one of the clues to understanding the present American system. On this particular point the American literature is scant.[11]

When reference is made to a possible British background, it will usually concern a judgment of Sir Edward Coke in 1610, *Dr Bonham's* case. There, the English court held that, if an Act of Parliament is against common right and reason, or impossible to be performed, the common law will adjudge it to be void.[12] Such an opinion may look like a prelude to later American developments, but according to British authors that can hardly be so. It is not entirely clear whether the learned judge was actually stating a general rule of law or blandly asserting judicial power. What *is* clear, however, is that Coke's opinion had no follow-up if it was really intended as a general rule on the compatibility of statutes with rules of higher law. In the seventeenth century, English lawyers became the allies of Parliament in its struggles with the King, and they usually admitted that the common law could be changed by Act of Parliament (though not by the King acting alone). A century later, the theory that Parliament had the final say in matters of validity of legislation was well established.[13] From that point of view, *Marbury* v. *Madison* introduced a line of constitutional case law which was new and original.

But whatever the background, it is clear enough that British and American constitutional law are not part of the same 'family'. It is important to make this clear, because many introductory and general books about comparative law take a different view: they start by constructing 'legal families', in which legal systems are grouped together by their family likenesses. In this literature, the 'common law family' includes English and American law and the 'civil law family' most continental European systems, in particular French and German law.[14] It is true, of course, that the legal systems of the United States are based on a common law concept (except for that

---

[11] But see Charles Grove Haines, *The American Doctrine of Judicial Supremacy* (New York, 1914), chs. I–II.

[12] See Th. F. Plucknett, 'Dr Bonham's case and judicial review', *HarvLRev* 40(1926), 30; R. C. van Caenegem, *Judges, Legislators and Professors* (Cambridge, 1993), pp. 26–31.

[13] See ch. 2.1.

[14] See Zweigert and Kötz, *Introduction to Comparative Law*, ch. 5; Peter Cruz, *A Modern Approach to Comparative Law* (Deventer, 1988), ch. 5. An older source is H. C. Gutteridge, *Comparative Law* (Cambridge, 1946), ch. 6.

of the state of Louisiana), and that this conception originated in England. After Independence, the original thirteen states continued to develop their legal systems on the basis of the English heritage: they had no codification but relied on a case-by-case evolution of private law, founded on precedent, some of it English. It is quite possible, therefore, that the classification of legal systems into 'common law' and 'civil law' families facilitates comparative research in the area of private law; I have no considered opinion on that point. For the study of public law, however, the idea of legal families does not work.[15]

The fact that the English and American systems share, more or less, a common law background may have influenced the evolution of administrative law (although there are only a few parallels), but it had no impact whatsoever on the relationship between the legislative and the judicial powers. On this point, the United States took their own American course.

3.2. The impact of the American model

During the nineteenth century, judicial review of legislation remained very much an American phenomenon. It did not lead to constitutional debates in Europe, perhaps because most Europeans took a dim view of anything connected with America (Charles Dickens is the most obvious example). Some European observers, however, became interested in the peculiarities of the political evolution of the United States.

In the early part of the century, Tocqueville was already wondering, in his well-known book *Democracy in America*, at the power and responsibilities of the American judiciary.[16] In his opinion, judicial review of legislation was part of a specifically American conception of democracy which was completely at odds with the dawning democratic developments in Europe. 'I am not aware that any nation of the globe has hitherto [this was in 1835] organised a judicial power on the principles now adopted by the Americans.' However close the American practice might bring the courts to political issues, it was undoubtedly most favourable to the liberty of the citizens. Tocqueville clearly saw that contemporary democratic movements

---

[15] See also John Bell, 'La comparaison en droit public', in *Mélanges en l'honneur de Denis Talon* (Paris, 1999), p. 33.

[16] Alexis de Tocqueville, *De la démocratie en Amérique* (reissue, Paris, 1981), vol. I, part I, ch. 6; abridged translation published by Oxford University Press, 1946 (I used the 1959 reprint, p. 77).

in European countries, such as France and Great Britain, were seeking to obtain protection of these liberties by other methods.

More than half a century later, the English author James Bryce echoed this assessment. After describing the relationship between the US Supreme Court and the Constitution, Bryce exclaims that 'there is no part of the American system which reflects more credit on its authors or has worked better in practice.'[17] He also emphasizes, however, how delicate the courts' task can be, in particular in times of grave discord. Bryce explains in all fairness the *Dred Scott* case, an 1857 judgment concerning the legal position of negro slaves who had been temporarily taken to a state where slavery was forbidden, but who had afterwards returned to a slave state. The decision itself, holding that such a person was not a citizen capable of suing in a federal court, was not the most controversial part of the judgment: the Court had thought fit to add a not very tactful *obiter* (consideration not strictly necessary for arriving at its decision) as to the position of negro slaves in general. Bryce thinks the Court's judgment did much to precipitate the Civil War[18] – hardly a compliment to the Court's wisdom.

Among European observers, admiration of the American system was frequently mixed with feelings of unconnectedness: the American experience seemed to have no relevance to developments in Europe. Many authors explained the American particularities by pointing to the federal system, with its limitations on legislative powers. The implication was that the American experience was of no use to Europe, except perhaps Switzerland. In the course of the twentieth century, the mood among European observers of the American scene began to change: judicial review was also considered as an expression of the idea that protection of civil liberties might not be in safe hands if wholly entrusted to political institutions.[19] As faith in the reliability of political institutions, even when democratically elected, began to shrink in the course of the twentieth century, particularly after the experience of dictatorships and world wars in Europe, the relevance of the debate on judicial review became more and more apparent.

The first European country to introduce judicial review of legislation was Austria. It did not adopt the American model, but established a

[17] James Bryce, *The American Commonwealth* (1893; new and revised edn New York, 1924), vol. I, p. 256.
[18] *Ibid.*, vol. I, pp. 263–4. This opinion is shared by many American authors.
[19] For the first view: Dicey, *Introduction*, ch. III; for the second: Finer, *Comparative Government*, ch. 6.II.

'constitutional court' (*Verfassungsgericht*) to safeguard the constitutionality of legislation. After the fall of the Empire (or rather of the 'double monarchy', since the Austrian Emperor had also been King of Hungary), the new republican constitution of 1920 (re-enacted in 1945) was intended to reinforce the protection of civil liberties by setting up a specialized court, to which issues of compatibility of legislation with provisions of the Constitution could be referred.[20] The institution of judicial review was the fruit of an evolution unique to Austria: it resulted from Austrian debates on the protection of freedoms rather than from a study of the American situation.

Ireland followed suit in 1922, after independence. Although the situation was somewhat uncertain in the early years of the Republic, the 1937 Constitution included an explicit provision on judicial review of legislation. More than Austria, Ireland seemed to be inspired by the American model, and it allowed any court of law to test the constitutionality of legislation. As in the United States, important constitutional issues in Ireland are normally settled by the Supreme Court.[21]

After the Second World War, developments seemed to accelerate. When the Federal Republic of Germany was established, in 1949, it adopted a constitution (*Grundgesetz* or Basic Law) characterized by an emphasis on human rights, rule of law and federalism. It instituted a federal constitutional court with exclusive jurisdiction over problems of compatibility of federal or state statutes with the Basic Law. The Basic Law itself provides a sophisticated system of remedies available to anyone whose constitutionally protected rights have been violated by statutes, administrative decisions or court judgments.[22] Italy instituted judicial review of legislation by a specialized constitutional court when the monarchy was abolished. That is interesting because Italy was, at the time, a unitary state (it probably still is, in spite of a high degree of regionalization). In both Germany and Italy, the safeguarding of constitutionality was entrusted to a special court, a 'constitutional court'. This was to set a trend for most countries in continental Europe. It may have been inspired by considerations derived from

---

[20] See Mauro Cappelletti and William Cohen, *Comparative Constitutional Law: Cases and Materials* (Indianapolis, Ind., 1979), ch. 1-B.

[21] See James Casey, *Constitutional Law in Ireland*, 2nd edn (London, 1992), chs. 1 and 11; Brian Walsh, 'The judicial power, justice and the Constitution of Ireland', in Deirdre Curtin and David O'Keeffe (eds.), *Constitutional Adjudication in European Community Law and National Law, Essays in Honour of Justice Thomas O'Higgins* (Dublin, 1992), ch. 12.

[22] Arts. 93 and 100 Basic Law. I use the official translation published by the Press and Information Office of the Federal Government (1998 edn).

the somewhat specific nature of constitutional problems; it may also simply be due to the desire of governments and parliaments to have a direct say in the appointment of constitutional judges.[23]

The French Constitution of 1958, which ushered in the Fifth Republic, introduced judicial scrutiny of the compatibility of statutes with the Constitution before the statute is officially promulgated and published in the Official Journal. Strictly speaking, the French Constitutional Council (*Conseil constitutionnel*) does not exercise powers of judicial 'review', as it can only look into questions of constitutionality between the passing of the bill and the promulgation of the statute: it 'previews' rather than reviews.[24] In this system, private citizens cannot have access to the Constitutional Council. Nevertheless, the main characteristic of the system is that the final say on compatibility of legislation with constitutional provisions is not left to Parliament, but to a judicial body. Initially, the powers of the Constitutional Council were probably intended for settling conflicts between Parliament and the executive, conflicts made possible by the limitation of the legislative powers of Parliament under the 1958 Constitution. The development of institutions cannot, however, always be steered by those who established those institutions: since 1971, the Council has also checked whether new legislation is compatible with human rights and fundamental freedoms. That opened a new chapter in the Council's case law, which ultimately appears to bring the activities of this body more in line with those of constitutional courts elsewhere in Europe.

Spain, Portugal and Greece embraced the German model after the fall of their dictatorships in the 1970s. The Spanish arrangements, in particular, are very similar to the German forms of judicial review. In the early 1990s, Poland, Hungary and the Czech Republic introduced judicial review when the one-party state crumbled; the same is true of the Baltic countries. Swedish courts began to accept judicial review from 1964 onwards. Cyprus and Turkey introduced constitutional courts in the 1960s.[25]

Belgian developments show some similarities to those in France. When the country was 'federalized', an arbitration court (*cour d'arbitrage*) was established for solving conflicts of jurisdiction, in particular between national and regional governments. However, since 1989 the court has also been

---

[23] Compare Art. 94 s. (1) Basic Law.

[24] Cappelletti and Cohen, *Comparative Constitutional Law*, p. 47.

[25] Further materials in A. R. Brewer Carìas, *Judicial Review in Comparative Law* (Cambridge, 1984).

empowered to look into the compatibility of legislation with the principle of equality and with the non-discrimination rule laid down in the Constitution, as well as with the freedom of education (*liberté d'enseignement*) which, in Belgium, also concerns relations between Church and State.[26]

Only a few countries in Western and Central Europe were unaffected by this general evolution, for example, Denmark and the Netherlands. The Dutch case is, however, somewhat exceptional, as the courts can strike down statutes for not being compatible with human rights as enshrined in the European Convention on Human Rights. This amounts to a system of semi-review; it reduces the powers of the representative bodies on an important point.

Britain may have set the tone of the constitutional debate in the nineteenth century; the end of the twentieth century found her somewhat isolated. Changes occurring elsewhere scarcely affected British constitutional law: it remained very much as it always had been – nearly as immutable as other British institutions like the monarchy, the Wimbledon tennis championships and the 'last night of the Proms'.

3.3. American practice

The practice of judicial review in the United States is closely connected to the construction of the American Constitution. In its initial form, the Constitution was a very simple document: in seven articles, it laid down the great principles governing the division of powers between federal and state institutions and the separation of powers between the legislature, the executive and the judiciary. Only four years after the entry into force of the initial text, the first modification took place: ten amendments were added, together known as the American 'Bill of Rights'.

It is somewhat odd that the Bill of Rights, which was to become so important in American practice, was introduced more or less as an afterthought. The framers of the Constitution had emphasized that citizens' rights were sufficiently protected by state constitutions and by the limitation of the powers attributed to the federal institutions. In this view, the very construction of the new Constitution made it unnecessary to add a specific

---

[26] See Constance Grewe and Hélène Ruiz Fabri, *Droits constitutionnels européens* (Paris, 1995), par. 61. See also Louis Paul Suetens, 'Judicial review in Belgium', in E.Smith (ed.), *Constitutional Justice under Old Constitutions* (Deventer, 1995), p. 319.

'list' of citizens' rights and liberties. Not everybody was convinced by that argument. Thomas Jefferson, the Virginia statesman who was later to become the third President of the United States, immediately protested against the omission of a bill of rights. A bill of rights was, he said, 'what the people are entitled to against every government on earth'.[27] Only some years later, the Bill of Rights was enacted and submitted to ratification by the states, pursuant to Article v of the Constitution.

The Bill of Rights remained true to the original concept of federalism, by securing the liberties of the citizens only against possible violations by federal authorities: 'Congress shall make no law...' are the opening words of the First Amendment. The limits to be observed by state authorities were to be found in state constitutions.[28] After the Civil War, this concept was abandoned. The abolition of slavery was laid down in an amendment to the federal Constitution, and another amendment provided that citizens' voting rights could not be denied or abridged 'by any state' on account of race, colour or previous condition of servitude. In a more general way, one of the post-Civil War amendments, the Fourteenth, stipulates that 'no state' shall abridge the privileges and immunities of citizens of the United States, nor deprive any person of life, liberty or property 'without due process of law', nor 'deny to any person within its jurisdiction the equal protection of the laws'.[29] As we shall presently see, the case law of the US Supreme Court rediscovered the importance of these general provisions of the Fourteenth Amendment, in particular the equal protection and due process clauses, in the second half of the twentieth century.

The abolition of slavery and the principles expressed in the post-Civil War amendments did not put an end to discrimination against blacks in American society. In the Southern states, rules of doubtful legality (for example, on 'literacy tests' for the exercise of voting rights) were used to intimidate the former slaves and to keep them 'in their place'. Transgression of the written and unwritten rules of social behaviour was punished by a combination of white arrogance, violence by private groups and private armies (such as the Ku Klux Klan) and silent complicity on the part of the police and the courts. When migration of blacks from the Southern states

---

[27] See his letter to James Madison of 20 December 1787, in Frederick C. Prescott (ed.), *Alexander Hamilton and Thomas Jefferson* (New York, 1934), pp. 278–9.

[28] See Leonard Levy, *Constitutional Opinions, Aspects of the Bill of Rights* (New York and Oxford, 1986), ch. 6.

[29] Respectively: Thirteenth Amendment; Fifteenth Amendment; Fourteenth Amendment s.1.

to the Northern cities like Chicago and New York began, the immigrants, though initially happy to escape Southern practices of oppression, soon found out how much they were isolated, as a group, from the rest of the population.[30]

Over a relatively long period of time, the federal authorities and the federal courts proved unwilling or unable to enforce the values expressed in the Constitution. The US Supreme Court accepted, for example, legislation by Southern states obliging 'Negro children' to attend separate schools. The leading case concerned Louisiana legislation requiring separate accommodation for white and black railway passengers. It was not true, said the Court, that 'the enforced separation of the two races stamps the coloured race with a badge of inferiority'.[31] Separate facilities were not necessarily unequal; this was an expression of the 'separate but equal' doctrine which was to haunt debates on the racial problem for many years. The dissenting judge, Justice Harlan, stressed that the majority decision would 'defeat the beneficent purposes which the people of the United Stated had in view when they adopted the recent amendments to the Constitution'. After having emphasized that the Constitution was 'colour-blind', Justice Harlan somewhat caustically concluded that the 'thin disguise' of 'equal' accommodation for passengers in railroad coaches 'will not mislead anyone'.[32]

It was not until 1954 that the Court overruled its earlier 'separate but equal' decisions, in a historic case called *Brown* v. *Board of Education.*[33] Even then, it was not easy for the Court to refute a line of thinking which had characterized its attitude to racial problems and which, moreover, was considered by many Americans – politicians as well as lawyers – as the ultimate constitutional wisdom. The Court took its time before the decision was handed down. The case was, for example, re-argued after the sudden death of the Chief Justice and the appointment of his successor. Finally, however, the Court came to a unanimous decision.[34] Separate educational

---

[30] On this period see Hugh Brogan, *The Penguin History of the United States of America* (Harmondsworth, 1990), ch. 16; Nicholas Lehman, *The Promised Land – The Black Migration and How it Changed America* (London, 1991), chs. 2 and 4.

[31] *Plessy* v. *Ferguson*, 163 US 537 (1896).

[32] John Marshall Harlan was a judge of the US Supreme Court from 1877 to 1911. A second Justice John Marshall Harlan occupied the same position from 1955 to 1971.

[33] *Brown* v. *Board of Education of Topeka*, 347 US 483 (1954). There was a companion case, *Bolling* v. *Sharpe*, 347 US 497 (1954), but *Brown* is considered as the landmark judgment.

[34] On the decision-making process in *Brown*, see Bernard Schwartz, *A History of the Supreme Court* (New York and Oxford, 1993), ch. 13; Roger K. Newman, *Hugo Black, A Biography* (New York, 1994), ch. 29.

facilities, it now held, were 'inherently unequal'. Because of its general approach, the judgment heralded the end of the institutionalized system of
racial segregation; but it was only the starting point of a long process of
social change. The first reaction of the Southern states was a refusal to recognise that federal courts were competent to change Southern ways of life. The
federal government decided to risk unpopularity in the South rather than
give up its support of the federal courts. In the autumn of 1957, President
Eisenhower sent federal troops to Little Rock, Arkansas, in order to secure
access of two black pupils to the central high school. Things started to move,
but slowly. The US Supreme Court rejected the argument that the *Brown*
decisions were binding only on the states which had been parties to the
proceedings: 'the federal judiciary is supreme in the exposition of the law
of the Constitution', said the Court, relying, in a somewhat questionable
way, on *Marbury* v. *Madison*.[35] Other escape routes were also barred by
the Court. It held, for example, that Virginia legislation purporting to close
public schools, and to grant subsidies for white children attending private
schools, was unconstitutional. Whatever the motives of the state legislature,
the result of the statute was to uphold segregation.[36] Gradually, the Court
developed the implications of the principle of equality.

If school segregation is 'inherently unequal', there seems to be little reason
to accept segregation in the use of other facilities. Discrimination against
blacks in public transport, in the public galleries of courts or representative bodies, in prisons, in parks, on tennis courts and golf courses, was
consistently repudiated by the Court as unconstitutional. Moreover, other
distinctions than that between black and white made in state or federal
legislation began to be challenged. When a state welfare scheme made a
distinction between residents, i.e. those who had lived in the state for more
than a year, and non residents, the Supreme Court struck it down as incompatible with equal protection. But whereas race (or colour) was considered
by the Court as a 'suspect classification' which could only be upheld in
exceptional circumstances, other classifications such as age or wealth were
subjected to a less exacting scrutiny. Only gender-based classifications were
considered as nearly as suspect as those based on race ('quasi-suspect'). In
the 1970s the Court struck down rules implying sex discrimination in education, jury selection, membership of clubs, alimony and other matters. In
a similar vein, state laws prohibiting illegitimate children from inheriting

---

[35] *Cooper* v. *Aaron*, 358 US 1 (1958).
[36] *Griffin* v. *Prince Edward County School Board*, 377 US 218 (1964).

from their father were ruled invalid under a strict scrutiny standard.[37] In a case concerning mentally retarded people, the Court said that its refusal 'to recognise the retarded as a quasi-suspect class does not leave them entirely unprotected from invidious discrimination'; and it added that, to withstand equal protection review, legislation making distinctions such as those beteen the mentally retarded and others 'must be rationally related to a legitimate government purpose'.[38]

In other words: some distinctions between people, or classifications of people into groups, such as those based on race, colour or gender, will not be accepted by the Court under the equal protection rule, except when the purpose to be achieved is legitimate and virtually imposes such a distinction or classification (for example, female guards for women's prisons). Other distinctions or classifications will be accepted so long as they bear a reasonable relationship to the object of the legislative measure in question. Distinctions between married and unmarried people may, for example, be acceptable for tax purposes, or in family law matters like adoption; but that does not mean that the same distinction could be applied with regard to access to public parks. The standards are, however, not always crystal clear. When a Massachusetts statute made a distinction between married and unmarried persons for the prescription of contraceptives, the Court could not find how the distinction could be justified by the government's interest in regulating the distribution of contraceptives; but the dissenting opinion of the Chief Justice criticized the decision for its weak link with the provisions of the Fourteenth Amendment. The Court might have passed, said the dissent, 'beyond the penumbra of specific guarantees into the uncircumscribed area of personal predilection'.[39]

The *Brown* decision was not only important because it opened a new chapter in the Supreme Court's case law; it also triggered off new political developments. Racial discrimination, tacitly condoned by many Americans for many years, became a political and social issue. There had been earlier attempts to attack racial segregation, particularly during the mid-1930s, in the progressive (or 'liberal') climate created by the Roosevelt administration; but the problem did not have political priority at that time. After *Brown*, serious efforts were undertaken to translate the values implied in the

---

[37] See Louis Lusky, *By What Right?*, 2nd edn (Charlottesville, Va., 1978), chs. XIII–XIV; Schwartz, *A History of the Supreme Court*, ch. 14.

[38] *City of Cleburne* v. *Cleburne Living Center*, 473 US 432 (1985).

[39] *Eisenstadt* v. *Baird*, 405 US 438 (1972).

post-Civil War amendments into statutory provisions. This led ultimately to civil rights legislation, in particular to the (federal) Civil Rights Act 1964. It can be considered as a somewhat belated adjustment of the law to the Constitution, but it helped the courts to uphold constitutional standards. In the South, civil rights associations and black movements began to press whites to stop discriminatory practices, by peaceful means such as mass demonstrations, sit-ins, civil disobedience and political participation. In the North, education became the critical issue, as living conditions in the great cities had *de facto* produced 'black' and 'white' neighbourhoods, and therefore black and white schools. In the 1970s measures were devised to put an end to this informal segregation, for example, by means of 'bussing' (i.e. conveying children compulsorily to schools outside the area where they lived); but these measures were very unpopular.[40]

For our purpose, it is perhaps more important to show the influence of these events on the Supreme Court's case law. In the early post-*Brown* years, the Court built on its earlier decisions on the Bill of Rights, especially on First Amendment liberties such as freedom of speech and of the press. As these liberties were now used as a weapon in the battle for equal protection, in which the Court was one of the prime movers, the Bill of Rights was more and more interpreted in such a way as to allow demonstrators to pursue their ends. Demonstrations were regarded as a form of speech protected by the First Amendment; freedom of speech meant freedom to express opinions, either verbally or non-verbally. Convictions of student leaders and church ministers for disturbing the peace, or obstructing public passages, when staging protest actions were overturned by the Supreme Court on this ground. Similarly, picketing stores or bars that maintained segregated counters was considered as a lawful exercise of constitutional rights.[41]

Civil rights case law began, in a way, to share the dynamism of the Court's equal protection decisions. When a police commissioner in Montgomery, Alabama, brought a libel action against a newspaper for implying that the Montgomery police force had harassed non-violent demonstrators, the Court held that the Constitution limits the state's power to award damages for libel in actions brought by public officials. Otherwise, critics of official conduct might be deterred from voicing their criticisms, a situation which might discourage 'the vigour' and 'the variety' of the public debate

---

[40] See Charles R. Morris, *A Time of Passion. America 1960–1980* (Harmondsworth, 1986), ch. VII.
[41] *Cox* v. *Louisiana* (*Cox I*), 379 US 536 (1965).

(it might have a 'chilling effect' as later case law would put it). Therefore, First Amendment liberties required a federal rule prohibiting public officials from recovering damages for a defamatory falsehood relating to their official conduct, unless the official could prove that the statement was made with 'actual malice' (i.e. in the knowledge that it was false or with reckless disregard of whether it was false or not).[42]

Decisions like this had an importance which went far beyond problems of racial equality: henceforth, 'public officials' were not in the same position as other people with regard to the law of libel. The consequence seems to be that, because public debate must be uninhibited, public officials have to suffer defamation more meekly than others. Later, the category of 'public officials' was extended to 'public figures', including even a university football coach. The Court had difficulty in defining the concept, however. Some judges relied on the idea that public figures had 'voluntarily exposed their entire lives to public inspection' (they probably didn't have the Queen of England in mind), whereas private individuals shrouded theirs from public view. Justice Brennan, then one of the leading judges of the 'liberal wing' of the Court, thought this at best a legal fiction. Free expression, he said, needed breathing space. Public discussion of public issues should not be hampered by self-censorship.[43]

The difficulty is, of course, that First Amendment standards developed in the battle for equal protection must also be applied to demonstrations or actions with less benign purposes. The problem arose very pointedly during the Vietnam War, when students publicly burned the American flag to illustrate their unwillingness to participate in the war effort; this happened when a large majority of Americans were still in favour of American armed intervention in Vietnam. The Court held that state legislation prohibiting such 'desecration' of the American flag violated the First Amendment, as flag burning should be considered as 'symbolic speech'. Many honest American patriots (and many conservatives) were shocked by these decisions.[44]

In order to understand the full scope of the Court's case law on civil liberties, it is important to realize that the Court has gradually relinquished the rule that the Bill of Rights is not binding on the states. It did not accept the opposite view, according to which the Fourteenth Amendment,

[42] *New York Times Co.* v. *Sullivan*, 376 US 254 (1964).
[43] *Gertz* v. *Robert Welch Inc.*, 418 US 323 (1974).
[44] See Robert H. Bork, *The Tempting of America. The Political Seduction of the Law* (New York and London, 1990), ch. 4.

by inserting the due process clause into the Constitution, had had the effect of incorporating the entire Bill of Rights in the guarantees to be respected by the states. The Court adopted a selective approach, by including in due process only rights it considered as 'fundamental'. In the long run, however, almost every right protected by the Bill of Rights was held to be fundamental and therefore incorporated in the due process clause of the Fourteenth Amendment. The effect of incorporation was to bring the states up to federal standards as developed by the US Supreme Court. This line of case law has been particularly important in criminal law, where the Court steered legal evolution in the 1960s and the 1970s by a bold interpretation of the Bill of Rights, particularly of the Fourth, Fifth and Sixth Amendments.[45] There is litttle doubt that the Court's libertarianism had the effect of slowly strengthening centralizing tendencies in the evolution of the United States and of thus changing, almost imperceptibly, the division of powers between federal and state institutions.

3.4. Judicial restraint and activism

One of the charms of American constitutional law is the availability of terminological resources. The system of judicial review of legislation is operated by the courts, with the result that problems are much more conceptualized than, for example, in English or Dutch law. New concepts are coined as new problems arise. We saw some examples in the preceding section ('suspect classification', 'chilling effect', 'public figure', 'symbolic speech', 'incorporation').

The description of judicial attitudes in terms of 'activism' versus 'restraint' is also an American invention.[46] The concept of restraint was well explained in a dissenting opinion by Justice Frankfurter, in a case concerning the compatibility of new legislation with the requirements of the Constitution. He said:

> This legislation is the result of an exercise by Congress of the legislative power vested in it by the Constitution, and of the exercise by the President of his constitutional power in approving a bill and thereby making it 'a law'. To sustain

---

[45] Examples: *Mapp* v. *Ohio*, 367 US 643(1961); *Argersinger* v. *Hamlin*, 407 US 25 (1972).

[46] I have not been able to trace the origin of the terms. For an unlikely theory, see Arthur M. Schlesinger Jr., *A Life in the 20th century*, vol. i, *Innocent Beginnings 1917–1950* (Boston and New York, 2000), pp. 421–5.

it is to respect the actions of the two branches of our government directly responsible to the will of the people and empowered under the Constitution to determine the wisdom of legislation. The awesome power of this Court to invalidate such legislation, because in practice it is bounded only by our own prudence in discerning the limits of the Court's constitutional function, must be exercised with the utmost restraint.[47]

The difference in attitude is well illustrated in the early reapportionment cases, in which the Court took an activist stand in spite of Frankfurter's admonitions. In these cases, state laws were attacked for violating equal protection, on the ground that electoral districts were unequal in population. The background was legislative inaction after a period of massive migration from the country to urban areas, and this problem had a very American twist since the immigrants into the cities were mainly blacks. In 1946, the Court stated that it must remain aloof from the determination of such issues.[48] Justice Frankfurter, speaking for the Court, explained that involving the judiciary in the politics of the people was 'hostile to a democratic system'. He added: 'Courts ought not to enter this political thicket.'

In a 1962 case, which concerned a Southern state (Tennessee), the Court overturned its earlier decision.[49] Justice Brennan, speaking for the Court, held that the rights asserted by the applicants were within the reach of judicial protection under the Fourteenth Amendment. His opinion does not go into the relationship between courts and politics in general; instead, it examines the scope of the doctrine of 'political question' as it had been developed by the Court itself. In a number of cases, the Court had dismissed actions for non-justiciability on the ground that they presented a political question. Justice Brennan found, however, that the earlier cases were not relevant to the present situation. Moreover, he said, there was no reason to extend the concept of political question to reapportionment cases. The argument was that these cases concern only the compatibility of state action with the federal Constitution, not questions to be decided 'by a political branch of government coequal with this Court' (presumably Congress or the President). Justice Frankfurter, along with Justice Harlan,[50] dissented. With his usual eloquence, he emphasized that the federal Constitution does not offer 'a judicial remedy for every political mischief, for every undesirable exercise of legislative power'. Ultimately, he argued, reliance must be

---

[47] *Trop* v. *Dulles*, 356 US 86 (1958).   [48] *Colegrove* v. *Green*, 328 US 549 (1946).
[49] *Baker* v. *Carr*, 369 US 186 (1962).   [50] The second Justice Harlan.

placed on an informed, critically minded electorate. However correct this last remark may be, it also shows the weakness of the argument: the political process was, in a way, distorted by the inequality of electoral districts, and the bodies elected on this basis were probably not very keen on changing the boundaries. In such a situation legislative inaction is likely, and that might ultimately result in a permanent under-representation of minorities.

The alternative presented its own difficulties, however. Two years after the Tennessee decision, the Court had to specify the standards to be applied.[51] The majority decision repeated the reasons for judicial interference. 'Legislators represent people', it said, 'not trees or acres'; they are elected 'by voters, not farms or cities or economic interests'. Equal representation of citizens was 'a bedrock of our political system'. Every vote should therefore have an equal weight. In an armed dissent, Justice Harlan (Frankfurter had retired) listed ten considerations which had been rejected by the Court, for example, geographical criteria such as the course of waterways or mountain ridges. He questioned the wisdom of the Court's attitude. Later case law was to confirm his doubts. The standard of 'one person, one vote' did not really help in reapportionment. A mathematical equality of every vote cast cannot be achieved in a majority system of voting in electoral districts. The Court had rather to examine what degree of inequality was still acceptable – hardly a judicial task. So the Court got entangled in the 'political thicket', exactly as Justice Frankfurter had predicted, and it gradually had to loosen its supervision over such matters. Although the Court's case law had the important effect of encouraging state legislators to revise existing boundaries, its jurisprudential merits were less impressive, as it proved impossible to formulate workable standards. Thus the reapportionment cases illustrate the risks of judicial activism. Cases in which federal courts struck down reapportionment plans devised by state legislatures, and appointed 'experts' to draw a new plan, tended to irritate politicians as well as voters. Ultimately, the Court limited its supervision to reapportionment schemes which were so irrational 'on their face' that they could only be understood 'as an effort to segregate voters into separate voting districts because of their race'.[52]

One of the rare occasions on which the Court itself examined the respective roles of legislature and judiciary in general occurred in 1938. In a fairly innocuous case concerning a federal statute prohibiting interstate shipment

---

[51] *Reynolds v. Sims*, 377 US 533 (1964).   [52] See *Shaw v. Reno*, 509 US 630 (1993).

of milk, the Court added a footnote clarifying its review standards; but it did so in a somewhat oblique way.[53] In this case, it said, there was no need to consider 'whether legislation which restricts those political processes which can ordinarily be expected to bring about repeal of undesirable legislation, is to be subjected to a more exacting judicial scrutiny under the general prohibitions of the Fourteenth Amendment than are most other types of legislation'. Similar considerations might apply, the footnote added, with regard to statutes directed at particular religions or racial minorities, as prejudice might curtail 'the operation of those political processes ordinarily to be relied upon to protect minorities'. It would seem that this explanation gives a valid justfication of the reapportionment cases, as well as of *Brown* and its aftermath.[54] However, the post-*Brown* years also showed examples of judicial activism which are not covered by the rationale expressed in this '*Carolene Products* footnote'.

In a 1972 judgment, the Court held that capital punishment was a 'cruel and unusual punishment' forbidden under the Eighth Amendment and that state statutes carrying death penalty clauses could not be applied. The judgment led to an outcry: popular opinion in the United States was (and is) very much in favour of the death penalty for serious crime; academic lawyers were wondering how the Court could read something in the Bill of Rights its framers could, at the time, not have been aware of; moreover, the reasoning of the Court appeared weak, as part of the majority found capital punishment in itself 'cruel and unusual', whereas other justices founded their view on the practice of it, which involved a disproportionate number of blacks. For whatever reason, the Court changed its mind a short time later.[55] Many states reintroduced or introduced the death penalty in the 1980s, and the Court put no obstacles in their path. Ultimately, it seemed to abandon any attempt to bring constitutional elements into the debate on capital punishment: for a long time, it refused to consider specific issues, such as the case of convicted minors or the cruelty of particular methods of execution.[56]

---

[53] *United States* v. *Carolene Products Co.*, 304 US 144 (1938).

[54] See John Hart Ely, *Democracy and Distrust: A Theory of Judicial Review*, 11th edn (Cambridge, Mass., 1995), ch. 4.

[55] Respectively: *Furman* v. *Georgia*, 408 US 238 (1972); *Locket* v. *Ohio*, 438 US 586 (1978).

[56] See Russell Baker, 'Cruel and usual', *New York Review of Books* 47/1 (20 January 2000). However, in June 2002 the US Supreme Court decided that the death penalty was a cruel and unusual punishment when applied to mentally retarded people. It is possible that this has opened a new chapter in its case law on capital punishment.

There are occasions, however, where the Court ventures into new areas, provokes resistance in society, but sticks to its guns. This is what happened in the abortion cases. In 1973, the Court ruled that state statutes prohibiting abortion were unconstitutional, at least as far as abortion during the first three months of pregnancy was concerned (the Court allowed regulation during the second period of three months and prohibition during the final period).[57] The decision was based on the due process clause of the Fourteenth Amendment; according to earlier case law, due process included protection of 'privacy'. The abortion decision held that the concept of privacy was 'broad enough to encompass the woman's right to terminate her pregnancy'. The decision was severely criticized. Religious groups were outraged; they were even able to gather momentum by pointing to the consequences of excessive liberalism as practised, they argued, by the Court. Conservative politicians tended to agree with the latter point of view; that was particularly important when the United States was under conservative leadership during the Reagan years (1980–8). Moreover, many lawyers attacked the Court for imposing its own moral views on society without a clear basis in the Constitution; they argued that nothing in the Constitution even remotely addressed the problem of abortion. It was tempting to conclude, according to one author, that the Court had set itself above the Constitution.[58]

The 1973 abortion judgment, *Roe* v. *Wade*, was considered very much the work of the 'liberal wing' of the Court. After the appointment of conservative judges during the Reagan years, attempts were made to overturn it. In a 1989 case, which concerned state legislation on medical procedures to be followed in case of abortion, one of the justices, Justice Scalia, stated that *Roe* should be expressly overturned, but the majority upheld the statute without bringing *Roe* into question.[59] Some years later, the point at issue was explicitly whether *Roe* should be overturned; but the Court refused to do so, Justice Scalia dissenting (*Roe* was 'plainly wrong', he said). For the majority ('conservatives' included) *Roe* was the precedent to be followed, whatever one's personal opinions.[60] It would indeed have been difficult, after twenty years of relative freedom of abortion, to restore the earlier situation. In other words: society had adapted to *Roe*, and overturning it might have given rise to more vehement opposition than the *Roe* judgment itself had done.

---

[57] *Roe* v. *Wade*, 410 US 113 (1973).   [58] Lusky, *By What Right?*, p. 20.
[59] *Webster* v. *Reproductive Health Services*, 492 US 490 (1989).
[60] *Planned Parenthood of Southeastern Pennsylvania* v. *Casey*, 505 US 833 (1992).

My last example of the problems concerned with judicial activism is affirmative action. The term – another one coined in the American debates – denotes forms of reverse discrimination in favour of racial or other minorities, which are intended to counterbalance the adverse effects of the lack of esteem they enjoy in society. When racial desegregation did not lead to a significant increase in the admission of black students to the universities, programmes were framed to rectify this situation; after all, the Court had proclaimed that what the Constitution required was a system not of white schools and black schools, but of just schools. One of the remedies was a quota system: a certain percentage of the available places was reserved for blacks. Students could therefore be refused admission although they were better qualified than members of the favoured minority who had been admitted – and, in a certain sense, they were refused because of their race. What happened in education served as a beacon in other areas: quota systems were introduced for engaging employees, for rules on promotion, for government contracts etc. After some time, these programmes concerned not only blacks, but also Hispanics, Asians and other minority groups, and finally women.[61]

The Court proceeded very carefully. In an early case, on quotas for black students, Justice Brennan voiced the feelings of the Court by recognising that the Constitution was colour-blind, but by adding that colour-blindness should not 'become myopia which masks the reality that many "created equal" have been treated within our lifetimes as inferior both by law and by their fellow-citizens'.[62] In later cases, the Court began to submit affirmative action programmes to strict scrutiny. In a 1989 case, it struck down a city programme requiring construction contracts to guarantee at least 30% participation by of businesses owned by certain minorities (blacks, Hispanics, Indians and others). The Court found that this was a violation of the equal protection clause, as no evidence existed of earlier discriminatory practices.[63] Justice Brennan was one of the dissenters. In a concurring opinion, Justice Scalia accepted the majority view that strict scrutiny must be applied to any classification by race, whether or not its asserted purpose was 'remedial' or 'benign'. He went one step further, however, by insisting on the colour-blindness of the Constitution and by expressing the view that

---

[61] See the indignant comment of Bork, *The Tempting of America*, ch. 4.
[62] *Regents of the University of California* v. *Bakke*, 438 US 265 (1978).
[63] *Richmond* v. *J. A. Croson Co.*, 488 US 265 (1989).

unequal treatment in law is an inappropriate remedy for unequal treatment in society.

The attitude of the Court shows a degree of hesitation which is not entirely in keeping with the importance of the problem in society. Nearly half a century after *Brown*, it is still difficult, if not impossible, to trace the boundary between acceptable and unacceptable programmes of affirmative action.[64] In a way, the present judges are paying the price for the courage of their predecessors in trying to banish any form of discrimination from American society. Judges may sometimes overplay their hand. In the debate in the United States, the Court has occasionally been accused of a desire to impose its own moral standards, or play a role in American politics, under the cover of its interpretation of the Constitution. When reviewing the Court's case law since *Brown*, one rather feels that it has been carried away by the impetus created by its own decisions. Taking equal protection seriously, it could hardly help getting entangled in social problems nobody has been able to solve so far.

3.5. Collisions with politics

The activist attitude of the Supreme Court in the 1960s and 1970s, and the problems connected with the affirmative action programmes in the 1980s, had the effect of bringing the Court into the heart of political debates in the United States. That had occurred before, however: there have been earlier periods in which the Court held the political spotlight because of decisions not everybody was pleased with. It happened in the years immediately preceding the outbreak of the Civil War, when abolitionists (opponents of slavery) rebuked the Court for closing its eyes to the rights of the black population.[65] It happened again in the beginning of the twentieth century, when the Court consistently invalidated state legislation aimed at protecting employees on the ground that it violated the freedom of contract, which was then considered as a 'liberty' covered by the due process clause of the Fourteenth Amendment. There has always been an area of tension between the voluntarism of American politics and the restraint on political action the Court reads in the Constitution.

---

[64] See also *Metro Broadcasting Inc.* v. *FCC*, 497 US 547 (1990), defining 'benign race-conscious programmes'.

[65] See ch. 3. 2.

The dilemma was well expressed by Justice Holmes, dissenting in a case which involved the validity of a New York statute on maximum hours for workers employed in bakeries. The majority opinion considered that this restraint of the freedom of contract amounted to a violation of the liberty of the citizen under the Fourteenth Amendment.[66] Justice Holmes strongly criticized the result:

> This case is decided upon an economic theory which a large part of the country does not entertain. If it were a question whether I agreed with that theory, I should desire to study it further and long before making up my mind. But I do not conceive that to be my duty, because I strongly believe that my agreement or disagreement has nothing to do with the right of the majority to embody their opinions in law.... I think that the word liberty in the xivth Amendment is perverted when it is held to prevent the natural outcome of a dominant opinion, unless it can be said that a rational and fair man necessarily would admit that the statute . . . would infringe fundamental principles as they have been understood by the traditions of our people and of our law.

The Court, however, continued to erect barriers to the progress of social legislation for at least another thirty years. Politicians began to show their uneasiness. President Theodore Roosevelt occasionally attacked the Court for having lost contact with the realities of life in society. In his 1912 presidential campaign, he even developed a plan for 'recall' of judicial decisions by democratic process; but he lost the election.[67] For a long period of time, the fate of social legislation rested ultimately with the judges.

Things came to a head-on collision in the thirties. President Franklin D. Roosevelt (Teddy's nephew) had been elected on a programme which announced a 'New Deal', a coherent set of measures intended to defeat the economic depression and combat massive unemployment. This New Deal, slightly social-democratic in European eyes, was vehemently attacked by opposition groups in the United States as introducing communism into the Western hemisphere ('The red New Deal with a Soviet seal...'). The Roosevelt administration had some difficulty in pushing its legislation through Congress, and it was greatly dismayed when, subsequently, various new statutes were declared unconstitutional by the Supreme Court. The

---

[66] *Lochner* v. *New York*, 198 US 45 (1905).

[67] See William H. Harbaugh, *The Life and Times of Theodore Roosevelt*, new edn (London and Oxford, 1975), ch. xxv.

grounds advanced by the Court were not always the same. Some statutes, particularly on labour law, were struck down for violating the freedom of contract; in other cases, the Court gave a narrow interpretation to the scope of federal powers, for example, to the concept of 'interstate commerce'; in a third group of cases, it did not accept the constitutionality of the delegation of regulatory powers to the President, at least not to the extent that the New Deal legislation had practised this.[68] When the Court struck down three statutes in a single day, the President was furious. In public speeches he made scathing remarks about the 'nine old men' who tried to obstruct the will of the people; and he announced measures to deal with the problem. 'We have reached the point as a nation,' the President solemnly declared, 'where we must take action to save the Constitution from the Court.'[69]

Roosevelt announced his measures at the beginning of his second term of office in 1937, after a landslide victory in the presidential elections (only two of the then 48 states went to the Republican candidate). He presented a plan to improve the working methods of the Court. Under this plan, assistant judges could be appointed for every member of the Court who was over seventy (there were six justices in that category); these assistant judges would have full voting rights in the deliberations of the Court. Public opinion took this for what it probably was, a 'court packing plan'. It met with serious opposition, even among the President's allies, and among Democrats who had helped to give the proper form to the New Deal. Many Americans were shocked by the careless way in which the President intended to treat the Court. The legal committee of the Senate pulled the plan to pieces in a devastating report. Before the full Senate could start its debate, the Court created a sensation: in a 5–4 decision, it sustained a state statute on minimum wages, explicitly overruling its earlier case law which had held that every violation of the freedom of contract was incompatible with the due process clause. That had been 'a departure from the true application of the principles governing the regulation by the State of the relation of employer and employed', the Court now said.[70] The minority judges emphasized that the meaning of the Constitution could not change 'with the ebb and flow of economic events'.

---

[68] A famous case was *Schechter Poultry Corp.* v. *United States*, 295 US 495 (1935).

[69] See Schwartz, *A History of the Supreme Court*, p. 233. See also Roosevelt's 'fireside chat' of 9 March 1937 in J. G. Hunt (ed.), *The Essential Franklin Delano Roosevelt* (Avenel, N.J. 1995), pp. 133 ff.

[70] *West Coast Hotel* v. *Parrish*, 300 US 379 (1937).

When the Senate finally rejected the President's plan, the Court had also overruled its recent judgments on the concept of 'interstate commerce'. It abandoned the narrow interpretation it had given to this expression, thereby widening the scope for federal powers of legislation. This was a very important judgment, as it opened a new chapter in the Court's thinking on the extent of federal powers.[71] Shortly afterwards, some vacancies occurred in the Supreme Court; they allowed Roosevelt to appoint new justices, more in tune with his own view of the Constitution. It should be added that this time the President used his authority well, by appointing some of the most distinguished judges the Court ever had (in particular Justices Black, Frankfurter and Jackson). And so the clash between the Supreme Court and the President ended in a way nobody could have foreseen.[72]

Politically speaking, the next collision episode showed exactly the opposite picture: the activism of the Court caused irritation and anger among Republican politicians in the 1970s and 1980s. Rephrasing this idea in a somewhat malicious way, one could say that the Republicans tried to catch votes by channelling irritation over the Court's decisions into distaste for the Democrats, both being accused of 'liberalism', one of the major sins in the American political climate of the 1980s. In the 1968 presidential election campaign, the Republican candidate, Nixon, had already promised that he would, when elected, abolish the system of 'bussing', which was extremely unpopular among the middle classes.[73] He could, of course, do no such thing after his election; but he had set the tone for subsequent Republican campaigns. Some observers are inclined to think that dissatisfaction with the Court's case law had the effect of improving the electoral performance of the Republican party and strengthening the position of conservative candidates within that party.[74]

During the Reagan years, the President deliberately used his power to appoint justices to the Supreme Court so as to get a 'conservative majority' in the Court. Sometimes, however, things went wrong. The President needs

---

[71] *National Labor Relations Board* v. *Jones & Laughlin Steel Corp.*, 301 US 1 (1937). For later case law on this point, see *Heart of Atlanta Motel* v. *United States*, 379 US 241 (1964).

[72] See on this episode: Robert Jackson, *The Struggle for Judicial Supremacy* (New York, 1941), chs. 4-7; James McGregor Burns, *Roosevelt, The Lion and the Fox* (London 1956), ch. 15; Howard Gillman, *The Constitution Besieged: The Rise and Demise of Lochner Era Police Powers Jurisprudence* (Durham, N.C., and London, 1995), ch. 4.

[73] 'Bussing' was compulsory ferrying of white schoolchildren to black neighbourhoods and vice versa; see ch. 3.3.

[74] See Morris, *A Time of Passion*, ch. VII.

the agreement of the Senate for these appointments ('advice and consent'), and American Senators are experienced politicians who are suspicious of any guidance from the White House. When the president nominated Robert Bork, known for his sarcastic comments on the Court's case law concerning equal protection and civil liberties, the Senate committee organized public hearings which resulted in three days of aggressive interrogation. The nominee had to explain how he felt about freedom of expression, why he thought sex discrimination was not a proper subject for judicial interpretation, what his political convictions were, and even why he had a beard.[75] Bork took the honourable way out by withdrawing. On other occasions, appointments ran smoothly through the Senate. President Reagan accomplished his aim of securing a conservative majority in the Court; some of his appointees, such as Justice Scalia, were very capable professionals.

Judges do not always behave in accordance with the expectations of those who appoint them. Judging a case is not only a matter of having opinions, but also of looking into the evidence, listening to the arguments and respecting the precedents. In spite of its conservative majority, the Court refused to overturn *Roe* v. *Wade*, although the liberalization of abortion was a thorn in the flesh of most American conservatives.[76] Nevertheless, there is little doubt that the post-Reagan Court toned down the activist character of earlier case law. It was not willing to be guided by the dynamics of judicial law-making and, occasionally, it put the brakes on developments which had been triggered in the 1960s and the 1970s, for example in the area of criminal procedure.

Like any other court of law, the US Supreme Court is not much given to considerations on its own role: it just decides cases. When comparing judgments of the present day Court with those of twenty or thirty years ago, however, one cannot fail to be impressed by the differences in emphasis. Nowadays the Court prefers to limit the scope of the problems submitted to it; it is less inclined to generalize. The circumstances of the case in hand are more important; formal elements such as admissibility (standing, mootness) play a greater role. As Justice Ginsburg said, speaking for the Court in a case where a federal court of appeal had struck down a statute after having given it a very broad interpretation: 'a more cautious approach was

---

[75] Report in the *New York Times*, 13, 17 and 20 September 1987. Bork was also considered by some senators as an accomplice of President Nixon in the Watergate scandal.
[76] See ch. 3.4.

in order'.[77] A cautious attitude may be less exciting for authors and commentators, but that does not necessarily mean it is less satisfactory for the evolution of the Court's case law. Nor does it mean that conflicts between the Court and political leaders can be ruled out in the future. American society is deeply divided on many of the issues which come before the Court; choices made by the Court, or adhered to in its case law, may once more run into political resistance in the future. The volatile character of American politics does not agree very well with the consistency the Court tries to achieve in its interpretation of the Constitution.[78]

[77] *Arizonans for Official English* v. *Arizona*, 520 US 43 (1997).
[78] See R. Hodder-Williams, 'Constitutional legitimacy and the Supreme Court', in Gillian Peele, Christopher J. Bailey and Bruce Cain (eds.), *Developments in American Politics* (London, 1992), p. 139.

The growth of judicial power

4.1. Constitutional courts: Germany

At first sight, the main difference between the systems of judicial review
of legislation in the United States and in Germany is that the latter country has specialized constitutional courts, exclusively competent to assess
the compatibility of legislation with constitutional provisions. The Federal Constitutional Court (Bundesverfassungsgericht) performs this task
with regard to compatibility with the federal constitution, the 'Basic Law'.
The difference from the American situation is not as great as it appears,
however, since the *certiorari* system in the United States allowed the US
Supreme Court to develop informally into a specialized court for constitutional matters.[1] However, as the Bundesverfassungsgericht (or BVerfG, in
the strange German abbreviation) is not an appeal court, special remedies
have been created to provide access to it.

The Basic Law itself establishes seven of these remedies.[2] Details are
governed by federal statute; there is a Federal Constitutional Court Act or
Bundesverfassungsgerichtsgesetz (BVerfGG). Two of these remedies are of
particular importance for our subject. First, other courts faced with the
argument that a federal or state statute is incompatible with the Basic Law
will refer that problem to the Federal Constitutional Court, which will then
decide the issue by way of a preliminary ruling. Secondly, anyone who alleges that one of his or her basic rights, as enumerated in the Basic Law, has
been violated by any public authority can bring a 'constitutional complaint'
before the Federal Constitutional Court.[3] This second remedy allows private citizens and corporations to submit constitutional problems directly
to the constitutional court, but only once the ordinary remedies have been
exhausted. That condition had the effect of elevating the constitutional
complaint into a kind of super-appeal: the petitioner must first work his

---

[1] See ch. 3.1.   [2] Art. 93 s.(1) under 1-4b, and Art. 21 s.(2) Basic Law.
[3] Respectively: 'konkrete Normenkontrolle' and 'Verfassungsbeschwerde'.

way through the ordinary court system before he can apply to the constitutional court with the argument that the courts which have heard the case
have disregarded one or more of his constitutional rights. German lawyers
have been extremely clever in transforming the rights maintained before
the ordinary courts into basic rights justifying a constitutional complaint.
I should add that the Basic Law helped them to do so as some provisions
on basic rights are very broadly worded (for example, the inviolability of
the 'dignity' of every human being and the right to 'free development of his
personality' in Articles 1 and 2). However that may be, the constitutional
complaint developed into the main avenue for bringing a matter before the
federal constitutional court. The Court itself encouraged this development
by putting emphasis on the basic character of procedural guarantees; and
as these guarantees are relevant to any kind of litigation, the Court was
able to broaden its jurisdiction. Important elements of German procedural
law, in civil and criminal as well as administrative matters, have been adjusted to constitutional requirements as understood by the constitutional
court.

Germany has been a federal republic since 1949, but the division of
powers between the federation (*Bund*) and the states (*Länder*) is less complex and less rigid than under American constitutional law. The Basic Law
recognises the existence of 'concurrent' legislative powers for a long list of
matters.[4] There is no double hierarchy of courts as in the United States.
However, specialized courts (with specialized supreme courts on top) have
been created for particular areas such as administration, tax, social security
and employment. Moreover, there is no strict separation of powers between
the legislature and the executive: Germany has a parliamentary system of
government where the distinction between the respective tasks is not particularly important so long as the government enjoys the confidence of the
parliamentary majority. As a result, there is less litigation on the scope of
powers and responsibilities than in the United States. Individual rights give
rise to a seemingly endless stream of cases, however.

In the view of the constitutional court, the Basic Law does not simply lay down individual rights. The position of these rights in the constitutional system as a whole, and the mutual relationship of these rights,
establish what the Court calls an objective order of values ('objektive
Wertordnung'). The Basic Law supports this view by referring, for example,

[4] Art. 74 Basic Law.

to 'the constitutional order' and the 'free democratic basic order' of the Federal Republic; moreover, it obliges the *Länder* to act in conformity with 'the principles of the republican, democratic and social state governed by the rule of law'.[5] Obviously, specific provisions of the Basic Law should be interpreted against this background. That is presumably why, in the eyes of the constitutional court, the meaning of individual rights can never be determined by merely looking at the constitutional provision on which the right in question is founded. In a 1973 case concerning a wholly invented interview with an Iranian princess who had been a person of some fame, the Court considered the relationship between the freedom of the press, the protection of privacy and the law of tort.[6] It then attempted to strike a balance between the rights and interests which were at issue: the constitutional protection of the freedom of the press alone was not a sufficient argument for deciding the case in favour of the newspaper. This kind of balancing test is rarely used by the US Supreme Court when interpreting the First Amendment. If a conflict with other constitutionally protected rights is likely to arise, the American court will probably consider that freedom of expression is so basic to the working of a democratic system of government that it has a 'preferred position' among human rights. Such a view would be inconceivable in the case law of the German constitutional court; as a result, it lacks something of the rugged individualism of its American counterpart.[7]

One of the consequences of the German court's attitude is its method of explicitly defining and analysing the requirements of law and order in case of conflict with individual rights and liberties. When, during the 'leaden years' of the late 1960s, terrorist attacks and urban guerilla activities resulted in emergency measures and the exclusion of 'radicals' from public service, the constitutional court went out of its way to identify the reasons for these measures and determine the seriousness of the infringements of human rights they might cause.[8] It is a safe way of treading on dangerous ground, but it does not necessarily make for easy reading.

---

[5] Arts. 9(2), 20(3)-(4), 21(2) and 28 Basic Law.

[6] BVerfGE (*Entscheidungen des Bundesverfassungsgerichts*) 34 no. 25, *Princess Soraya*, 1973. Partial translation into English in Donald P. Kommers, *The Constitutional Jurisprudence of the Federal Republic of Germany*, 2nd edn (Durham, N.C., and London, 1997), p.124.

[7] See ch. 3.3. See also David P. Currie, *The Constitution of the Federal Republic of Germany* (London and Chicago, 1994), ch. 4.

[8] Example: BVerfGE 39 no. 16, *Radikalenerlass Schleswig-Holstein*, 1975. Also in Kommers, p. 229.

The values embodied in the Basic Law are not always explicitly mentioned in its provisions. Occasionally this is the case: for example, the principle of equality before the law.[9] More often than not, however, the Basic Law seems to enunciate general concepts which do not have a clear and well-defined meaning. Choices often have to be made by the courts, particularly the Federal Constitutional Court. The framers of the Basic Law were aware of this consequence, but they preferred to accept it, possibly because of a certain distrust of the political process, which may well have been inspired by the sad experience of the dissolution of the Weimar Republic in the early 1930s.[10] One of the key concepts is the notion of *Rechtsstaat* (approximately 'the State governed by the rule of law'). According to the Bundesverfassungsgericht, this constitutional concept embodies certain values, in particular the protection of legal certainty (*Rechtssicherheit*), which is a general principle of law. That principle, in its turn, implies protection of legitimate expectations (*Vertrauensschutz*). Citizens should know what their legal position is; they should know what they can reasonably expect from statements or activities by public authorities. If the authorities have, for example, created the impression that they will follow a certain policy, they cannot unexpectedly take a different line to the detriment of an individual citizen who had every reason to believe that his case would be considered in the same way as previous cases. That is true even when the new decision is entirely compatible with the legal provisions on which it is based; even when it is more in conformity with these provisions than the earlier decisions had been. On similar grounds, legislation with retroactive effect is prohibited, unless it imposes no burdens on the citizens.[11]

These examples show that the constitutional court has an abstract and highly deductive style of reasoning. The facts of the case do not seem to matter very much; the tone of the judgment is professorial rather than judicial. Dissenting opinions, permitted since 1971 (but only in the Federal Constitutional Court) do not lead to biting remarks or to a genuine debate; they retain the quiet character of academic exposition.

The search for a balance between different rights and interests also characterizes the attitude of the Court with regard to the respective roles of the

---

[9] Art. 3(1) Basic Law. See also Arts. 3(2)–(3).
[10] See Currie, *The Constitution*, ch. 1-II; Peter Badura, *Staatsrecht* (Munich, 1986), ch. A-3.
[11] Example: BVerfGE 13 no. 19, *Grunderwerbsteuergesetz Hamburg*, 1962.

legislature and the judiciary. On the one hand, the Court recognises that a certain freedom of choice is inherent in the very act of legislation; on the other hand, it tries to reconcile this freedom with the enforcement of the values it has to protect. The interpretation of the principle of equality illustrates this approach. Sometimes the Court is very strict. Even in its early years, it held that the special provisions of the German Civil Code concerning illegitimate children's right to inherit could not stand the test of the equality principle. Very soon, however, it also recognised that the legislative bodies have a certain freedom to 'mould' equal protection in such a way as they consider justified: within that margin, they are free to shape the equality as they think fit (*Gestaltungsraum*). This concept was initially used – as it still is – in cases where equality arguments were directed against territorial reshuffles, such as combinations of *Länder* or of cities.[12] Later it acquired a wider significance. In 1957, the Court found that an electoral threshold of 5% (Germany has a nation-wide system of proportional representation) was not incompatible with the requirements of equal protection. After having considered the arguments for and against the threshold, the Court held that the decision to establish it remained within the *Gestaltungsraum* of the legislature.[13] Similarly, the Court allowed a federal statute to make a distinction between political parties that were and that were not represented in the *Bundestag* (the directly elected house of the federal parliament) with regard to matters such as the granting of broadcasting time and of subsidies for electoral campaigns.

For some matters, however, the Court allows no freedom at all to the legislative bodies. In examining the constitutionality of distinctions between men and women, for example, the Court applies a strict scrutiny test. One of the reasons may be that Article 3 of the Basic Law has a 'specific' rule on equal rights for men and women, over and above its 'general' clause on equal protection; the Court may also have thought that the distinction between men and women is based on a 'suspect classification', but it did not use that expression. Rules of private international law referring to the nationality of the husband when considering (for example) the law to be applied to matrimonial property, were struck down as violating the equality of men and women. Regulations concerning night work by female employees could not be upheld, although social considerations might tell in favour of certain

---

[12] See BVerfGE 1 no. 10, *Südweststaat*, 1951; BVerfGE 84 no. 10, *Stadt Aschendorf*, 1992.

[13] BVerfGE 6 no. 10, *Sperrklausel*, 1957. See also Currie, *The Constitution*, ch. 6–v.

prohibitions.[14] In these cases, it is the Court itself which defines the exact standards implied by the Basic Law.

The debate on judicial activism did not leave Germany untouched. The expression 'judicial restraint' can even be found, in English, in a judgment of the constitutional court. The case concerned the treaty-making power of the federal government; the Court rejected a constitutional complaint from the Bavarian state government against the approval of a treaty with the German Democratic Republic (the eastern part of Germany, then still under Soviet domination). The principle of 'judicial self-restraint', said the Court, is intended to leave space for free moulding of policy which the Basic Law leaves to other constitutional institutions. Justice Frankfurter might have said the same – albeit, probably, in more accessible language. In other cases involving treaties the Court was also inclined to leave considerable latitude to the federal government.[15]

Occasionally, the criticism (or accusation) of judicial activism has been levelled at the Bundesverfassungsgericht. It happened, in particular, when the Court struck down a recently adopted federal statute liberalizing abortion legislation.[16] The public debate had been turbulent, and when the Court examined, in its judgment, exactly the same arguments and views that had already been discussed in the Bundestag, the Court seemed to take sides in the political debate but came to a different assessment. It was extremely difficult to make a clear distinction between the constitutional, moral, political and religious points of view; the Court, the critics said, had missed the opportunity to clarify matters by a rigorous legal analysis.

A comparable debate ensued on the constitutional court's 'crucifix judgment'.[17] The Court held that a Bavarian statute requiring a crucifix to be hung on the wall of every class-room in state schools (*Volksschulen*) was incompatible with the freedom of religion as established by the Basic Law. The reaction in the region was one of pained disbelief. Roman Catholicism had been part of Bavarian life just as much as beer-drinking at the annual

---

[14] Respectively: BVerfGE 63 no. 12, *Irakischer Ehemann*, 1983; BVerfGE 85 no. 18, *Nachtarbeiterinnen*, 1992.

[15] BVerfGE 36 no. 1, *Grundlagenvertrag*, 1973. See also BVerfGE 66 no. 3, *Mittelstreckenraketen*, 1983; also in Kommers, p. 155.

[16] BVerfGE 39 no. 1, *Schwangerschaftsabbruch*, 1975 (Kommers, p. 336). The minority of two included the only female judge. See also BVerfGE 88 no. 21, *Schwangerschaftsabbruch II*, 1993 (Kommers, p. 349). Further explanations in Alec Stone Sweet, *Governing with Judges: Constitutional Politics in Europe* (Oxford, 2000), p. 109–13.

[17] BVerfGE 93 no. 1, *Kruzifix*, 1995 (Kommers, p. 472). See also the comment by C. Grewe and A. Weber in *Revue Française de Droit Constitutionnel* 25 (1995), 183.

Oktober Fest. The Bavarian Prime Minister thought the gentlemen in Karlsruhe (in Baden-Würtemberg, where the Court is located) had not the faintest understanding of life in Bavaria; in a first emotional comment, he even said the government of the *Land* would have to reconsider its relationship to the federal authorities. The *Land*, however, subdued its passions after a time; its parliament adopted a new statute on state schools which was only slightly different from the old one.

In spite of the ups and downs in the Court's popularity, judicial review of legislation seems firmly established in Germany. The Bundesverfassungsgericht is one of the constitutional courts which have a great authority: its judgments have a profound influence on legal and political developments in the country.[18] The role of the Court, and the authority it enjoys, can be explained by legal reasons such as its constitutional position and the scope of its jurisdiction. There is perhaps also a historical dimension: the emphasis on the rule of law (*Rechtsstaatlichkeit*), and the self-evident acceptance of judicial guardianship of it, show some distrust of the political process and a corresponding faith in the work of courts. The recent past of Germany may make that attitude understandable. The Nazi regime made a semblance of respecting the legal rules when it assumed power in early 1933, only to use these rules for purposes which were completely at odds with their original aims. A German author has defined this phenomenon as the 'perversion' of a legal order.[19] That historical element may explain why the emphasis of the constitutional court's case law is not primarily on guarantees of the proper working of the political process, as it often seems to be in the United States; the German court rather defines the constraints which constitutional requirements impose on that process. This does not mean, however, that the German court has remained safely outside 'the political thicket': decisions like the abortion and crucifix judgments brought it right into the heart of the political debate. That is, perhaps, the price to be paid for a sophisticated system of legal protection.

4.2. Semi-review: France

Judicial review in France is more difficult to fathom than in Germany. French constitutional law seems to be in a continuous state of flux, sometimes briefly interrupted by periods of real commotion or of relative quiet.

---

[18] See also Grewe and Ruiz Fabri, *Droits constitutionnels européens*, no. 67.
[19] Fritz von Hippel, *Die Perversion von Rechtsordnungen* (Tübingen, 1955).

Moreover, the French version of judicial review is far removed from the constitutional model in its pure form. We have already seen that the Third Republic (1871–1940) had a constitutional system which was closely akin to the parliamentary model as embodied by the British tradition; and the Fourth Republic (1946–58) remained very close to it, by combining a written constitution in the true sense of the word with the supremacy of parliament but without judicial review of legislation. It was only under the Fifth Republic (from 1958) that a judicial body was set up to supervise the constitutionality of legislation; and this happened more or less by accident, as the initial aim of judicial control was limited to the settling of disputes between the executive and the parliament.[20]

We take up the story in early 1958, when the rulers of the Fourth Republic, overcome by their inability to solve the Algerian crisis and by their fear of an invasion by rebellious troops, appealed to Charles de Gaulle, of Second World War fame, to sort things out. He was appointed Prime Minister under the existing rules; informally, he became the political leader of the country, as he had been at the Liberation in 1944. De Gaulle, however, had made no secret of his desire to reconstruct the entire political system. The outline of the reform had already been described in an address he had delivered in Bayeux, Normandy, in 1946, when he had left politics in a discontented mood.[21] France, he explained, needed a complete renovation: in order to gain self-confidence, to recapture her glory and to take her legitimate position among the nations (I use some Gaullian language here), she should be brought under strong leadership. In the crisis situation of 1958, de Gaulle believed (or said he believed) that the country, deep in its heart ('le pays dans ses profondeurs'), really wanted the same. A new constitution should be prepared, centred around a strong executive, a president of the Republic with more than nominal powers, and a parliament with restricted tasks and responsibilities. The same year, the new Constitution was completed, and adopted by referendum. De Gaulle became the first President of the new Republic.[22]

One of the typical features of the 1958 Constitution is the limitation of legislative power. The Constitution enumerates the subjects to be regulated

---

[20] See ch. 2. 2 and ch. 3. 2; Lavroff, *Le système politique français*, ch. 11.

[21] See Charles de Gaulle, *Mémoires de guerre*, vol. III, *Le salut* (Paris, 1959), *Documents*, 'discours de Bayeux'.

[22] See also Charles de Gaulle, *Mémoires d'espoir*, vol. I, *Le renouveau* (Paris, 1970), ch. 1; Pierre Viansson-Ponté, *Histoire de la République gaullienne*, vol. I (Paris, 1970), ch. 1.

by statute (*loi*). Matters which are not part of this legislative field (*domaine législatif*) are removed from the jurisdiction of the legislative bodies; the government can issue regulations (*règlements*) for such matters. Thus the government has autonomous regulatory powers for all matters that are not covered by the *domaine législatif*. The Constitution states explicitly that matters other than those within the province of the *loi* have a regulatory character.[23] Under its rules, regulatory powers are usually exercised by the government (sometimes the Prime Minister, sometimes the Cabinet), but occasionally by the President of the Republic.

The demarcation between the *domaine législatif* and the *domaine réglementaire* is not a perfect example of clarity. In legislative practice, it is often difficult to determine what the 'subject' of a statute is: the Constitution couches its categories in abstract terms, without taking heed of the policy considerations which may have guided the drafters of the bill. The text of the Constitution makes things worse, by using two different concepts to indicate the subjects of the *domaine législatif*: statutes 'fix the rules' for some subjects (such as nationality), but 'determine the fundamental principles' for others (such as education). It is not always easy to make distinctions between rules and principles, or between fundamental and other principles, particularly as rules or principles which once had little importance may later become fundamental owing to new developments.[24] Differences of interpretation are, therefore, perfectly possible. In the new constitutional framework, the solution of these problems could not be left to parliament: it was considered to be one of the parties to the conflict, and the unhappy experience of the Fourth Republic had shown how ineffective it could be. A mechanism of arbitration was therefore necessary.

That mechanism was provided by the creation of the Constitutional Council (*Conseil constitutionnel*). The Constitution describes its task in broad terms, however: the Council is to rule on 'compatibility with the Constitution'.[25] Organic laws (statutes required by the Constitution for certain specific matters, for example the electoral system) must be submitted

---

[23] Art. 37(1) Constitution 1958. An English translation of (most of) the Constitution can be found in John Bell, *French Constitutional Law* (Oxford, 1998), pp. 245ff.

[24] See also Louis Favoreu (ed.), *Le domaine de la loi et du règlement*, 2nd edn (Paris and Aix-en-Provence, 1981); the booklet summarizes an oral debate.

[25] Art. 61 Constitution 1958. The Council has other tasks, in particular with regard to litigation resulting from elections, which do not concern us here. Further explanations in Didier Mauss, 'The birth of judicial review of legislation in France', in Eivind Smith (ed.), *Constitutional Justice under Old Constitutions* (The Hague and London, 1995), p. 113.

to the Constitutional Council before being promulgated. Ordinary statutes *can* be submitted to the Council before their promulgation, by the President of the Republic, the Prime Minister, the president of the Senate or the president of the National Assembly. Since 1974, sixty deputies (members of the National Assembly) or sixty senators have been entitled to do the same. Bills referred to the Council can be promulgated only after the Council has issued a declaration of compatibility with the Constitution.

It is doubtful whether, initially, the Council was considered as a genuine court. Its decisions are binding, but it examines the texts submitted to it *in camera* and the parties to the conflict have no opportunity to make their views known. In fact, there is hardly any procedure as such.[26] The composition of the Council is non-judicial: three out of nine members are appointed by the President of the Republic, three by the president of the National Assembly and three by the president of the Senate; no professional qualifications are required. In the early years, the Council consisted of elder statesmen rather than specialists in law.[27] The manner in which cases can be brought before the Council seems to indicate that the decision to be taken is considered as a political expert opinion, not as a judgment. Private citizens or corporations cannot bring an action before the Council. Once the statute (or organic law) in question has entered into force, it cannot be challenged by private parties on constitutional grounds. In the early 1980s, there were plans to modify the Constitution in order to permit private individuals to challenge the validity of statutes before an ordinary or administrative court (*exception d'inconstitutionnalité*); that court was then to refer the matter to the Constitutional Council for a preliminary ruling on the constitutionality of the statute. These plans did not materialize, however, and in the hustle of French politics they were quickly forgotten.

The Constitutional Council developed into a true constitutional court because of its decisions. It soon opened up new avenues. In the early years of the Fifth Republic, the Council duly gave its decisions on the respective areas of jurisdiction of parliament and government; and similar problems have occasionally reappeared since.[28] From the 1970s onward, however, the Council has mainly examined whether the bills submitted to it are

---

[26] See Thierry Bréhier, *Le Monde*, 31 October 1998.

[27] See Dominique Turpin, *Contentieux constitutionnel* (Paris, 1986), nos. 186–97.

[28] Examples: CC 11-8-1960, *Redevance radio-télévision*, Rec. 25; CC 30-7-1982, *Blocage des prix et des revenus*, Rec. 57, also in Bell, *French Constitutional Law*, p. 284. See also Louis Favoreu and Loïc Philip, *Les grandes décisions du Conseil constitutionnel*, 6th edn (Paris, 1991), nos. 7 and 35.

compatible with the constitutional protection of civil liberties. In French legal terminology, civil liberties and fundamental freedoms are incorporated in 'le bloc de constitutionnalité'. This was quite a step, since the 1958 Constitution does not enumerate rights and freedoms in the way the German Basic Law does, or the American Bill of Rights. The preamble to the Constitution affirms, however, that the French people 'solemnly proclaims its attachment to the rights of man ... such as are defined by the Declaration of 1789' (that is the famous 'Déclaration des droits de l'homme et du citoyen'), 'confirmed and completed by the preamble to the 1946 Constitution'. The latter preamble also referred to the 1789 Declaration; besides, it reaffirmed 'the fundamental principles recognised by the laws of the Republic'. In a 1971 case which concerned freedom of association, the Constitutional Council held that this freedom was part of the fundamental principles recognised by the laws of the Republic and solemnly reaffirmed by the preamble to the Constitution. Therefore, the Council said, the creation of associations cannot be subjected to any kind of control or authorization by the administrative authorities. In a later case, the Council found that provisions of a finance bill submitted to it violated the principle of equality as proclaimed in the 1789 Declaration and solemnly reaffirmed by the preamble to the Constitution.[29] In this roundabout way, the Council made itself the protector of civil liberties against possible infringements by the legislative power.[30]

The next step followed in 1981. That year, the Gaullists and their allies, in power since 1958, lost the presidential elections to the socialist Mitterrand who, once in office, dissolved the National Assembly in order to get a left-wing majority in parliament (the President of the Republic has some powers which can be exercised without ministerial countersignature; the power of dissolution is one of these). This gamble having been successful, the left-wing coalition started to carry out its electoral programme, which involved nationalization in industry, banking and insurance. The Gaullists had the feeling that 'their' republic was being brought into disrepute and danger by these actions, and that every effort should be made to stop the perversion, as they saw it, of the institutions established by the 1958 Constitution. One of the methods they used was systematic submission of bills to the

---

[29] Respectively: CC 16-7-1971, *Liberté d'association, Rec.* 29 (Bell, p. 272; *Les grandes décisions* no. 19); CC 27-12-1973, *Taxation d'office* (Bell, p. 346; *Les grandes décisions* no. 21).

[30] See J. C. Beardsley, 'The Constitutional Council and constitutional liberties in France', *AmJCompL* 20 (1972), 431.

Constitutional Council. They could limit their action to submitting the bill; it was not necessary (although it was permitted) to explain why or on what point the text was incompatible with constitutional provisions. This strategy had a double impact on the position of the Constitutional Council. First, the systematic submission of bills to the Council tended to transform it into a court of appeal against political decisions. After the end of the political debate and the final vote of the Assembly and the Senate, the Council had the last word by scrutinizing the bill before it could be made law. Secondly, the undirected way in which the appeal was often made had the effect of compelling the Constitutional Council itself to exercise its imagination to discover what constitutional problems the text might give rise to. There is little doubt that the Council's case law on civil liberties owes a good deal to this peculiar situation.[31]

This evolution increased the political importance of the Constitutional Council, all the more so because the left-wing parties, once again in opposition, followed the Gaullist strategy by applying systematically to the Council. The Council's case law, in its turn, tended to extend the *bloc de constitutionnalité*, with a resulting growth in the importance of constitutional law. The 1789 Declaration and the 1946 and 1958 preambles turned out to constitute real sources of constitutional norms. The 1946 preamble opens, for example, by referring to 'the victory won by free peoples over regimes that tried to enslave and degrade the human person'; according to the Constitutional Council, this means that the dignity of the human person is a value protected by the Constitution. The same status was attributed to the freedom of education and the freedom of conscience.[32] Gradually, the width of the Council's powers of assessment has become comparable to that of the Bundesverfassungsgericht in Germany. It is much more a true court than in its early days, and its composition as well as its way of proceeding are beginning to show judicial characteristics.[33]

When compared to its American and German counterparts, the Constitutional Council seems more inclined to respect the assessments of the representative bodies. In its judgment on the nationalizations of

---

[31] See C.Vroom, 'Constitutional protection of civil liberties in France: the *Conseil constitutionnel* since 1971', *Tulane Law Review* 63 (1988), 266.

[32] Example: CC 23-11-1977, *Liberté d'enseignement*, Rec. 42 (Bell, p. 319; *Les grandes décisions* no. 27).

[33] 'Le Conseil se juridictionnalise', according to Jacques Robert, former member of the Council, in an interview by Dominique Rousseau, *RDP* (1998), 1748 ('Neuf années au Conseil constitutionnel').

ne representative bodies rather than by the government. Forceful argu-
ts can be advanced in favour of that view, but it is doubtful whether the
ers of the 1958 Constitution were really of the same opinion. On that
t also, French constitutional law may be in the process of losing some
s originality.[38] A new institutional balance is slowly developing and the
culties it encounters have an uncanny resemblance to the problems met
where.

4.3. Human rights protection: the Netherlands

Kingdom of the Netherlands was established in 1815, after the fall of
oleon I. Initially, the Belgian provinces were part of it (they had been
er Spanish and Austrian domination when the northern provinces were
pendent republics); but Belgium seceded in 1830. The Constitution of
new Kingdom clearly reflected British influence.[39] It gave a prominent
e to the legislative power. The parliament (or 'States-General', in the old
gnation current in republican times) was not 'sovereign' in the Diceyan
e of the term, as it had to observe the provisions of the Constitution. The
stitutional system seemed, however, to be based on the assumption that
legislative power was limited only by its own assessment as to what kind
tatutes might possibly be contrary to the Constitution. The prevailing
ression in the Netherlands was, at the time, that a decent government
a decent parliament would never act in violation of the Constitution.
he Constitution was modernized in 1848, when revolutions had broken
in the main capitals of continental Europe. In accordance with the spirit
he times, provisions were introduced to reduce royal prerogatives and
phasize ministerial accountability. More or less accidentally, a sentence
added declaring that 'statutes are inviolable'. The idea expressed by that
tence was to remain the basis of much constitutional thinking for about
ntury, although one of the leading politicians of the day expressed his
givings at an early stage: he thought the new provision was a 'slogan'
ich would 'act as a shield against the Constitution', making everybody
l 'outside a closed door'.[40] Knocking at that door started only after the

ee Dominique Rousseau, *Droit du contentieux constitutionnel*, 2nd edn (Paris, 1992), 1st part;
ernard Chantebout, '1958–1998: est-ce encore la même Constitution?', *Recueil Dalloz* (1999),
hr.12.
ee ch. 2. 2.
He was Jan Rudolf Thorbecke, a former law professor who was then a leading liberal politician.

1981,[34] it referred to the right of property included
although the conditions for the exercise of this rig
stantial change, it retained, said the Council, its
However, as the 1958 Constitution put 'the nation
within the *domaine législatif*, the importance of th
to be weighed against the urgency of the nationa
statute submitted to the Council justified these m
them as appropriate methods for promoting econ
bating unemployment. The Council then explains t
its own judgment on this point to that of the legisl
misuse of powers or manifest error of assessment –
as the nationalizations do not restrict the area of p
a degree that no significant room is left for it. As
for dispossessed owners, the Council held that the
not been sufficiently respected and that the statute
the compensation in a way more favourable to th
approach of protecting individual rights, and reco
with the political decisions that have been taken,
Council's attitude. As soon as equal protection of
concerned, however, the Council is merciless. Dist
and women, or between citizens and aliens, are nor
exacting scrutiny.[35] The Council refused, however, t
tionment of electoral districts; it indicated that it mig
in case of manifest error in evaluating the relevant d

One other development of the Council's case law is
years, its strictness in tracing the exact boundaries t
the parliament and of the executive appears to have
of parliamentary procedure, it leaves matters very i
the Assembly or the Senate itself.[37] And when determ
domaine législatif, it follows a method of reasoning
that new rules which direcly affect the rights of citizens

by t
men
fran
poi
of it
diff
else

The
Nap
und
ind
the
pla
des
sen
con
the
of
im
and

out
of
em
wa
sen
a
mi
wh
fee

38

39
40

---

[34] CC 16-1-1982, *Loi de nationalisation*, Rec. 18 (Bell, pp. 273 and
no. 33).
[35] CC 18-11-1982, *Quotas par sexe*, Rec. 66 (Bell, p. 349); CC 22-1-1990
33 (Bell, p. 347). See also Alec Stone, *The Birth of Judicial Politics i
Council in Comparative Perspective* (New York and Oxford, 1992),
[36] Further: Bell, ch. 6.
[37] Example: CC 23-1-1987, *Amendement-Séguin*, Rec. 13 (Bell, p. 305
du Sénat, Rec. 79 (Bell, p. 126; *Les grandes décisions*, no. 45).

Second World War. In the first part of the twentieth century, the rule of inviolability became one of the main assumptions underlying the case law of the courts, and it also became accepted wisdom among constitutional lawyers.

The rule was thought to mean that judicial review of legislation, in whatever form, was excluded. The thinking behind this was that the legislative bodies would be sufficiently aware of the constitutional implications of bills they were examining. As they could not be supposed to have any inclination to violate the Constitution, because of the very position they occupied in the constitutional system, judicial supervision of the constitutionality of legislation was superfluous; and as it was superfluous it was dangerous, because the search for violations of the Constitution might entice the courts into the area of politics. Some spice was added to this opinion by the generally accepted view that constitutional questions had a predominantly political character. The example commonly quoted concerned the electoral system: the Constitution provided that it should be 'based on' proportional representation, and, so the argument ran, it was for the legislative bodies and not for the courts to decide whether or not a certain threshold (minimum number of votes required for a share of the seats) was compatible with the notion of proportionality. In other words: in the view then prevailing, the matter was to be settled by political debate.[41]

As a result, the case law of the Hoge Raad (supreme court in private and criminal law, as well as in tax matters) showed some degree of similarity with British cases, where courts refuse to discuss the validity of statutes duly adopted by Parliament. In matters of constitutionality, the legislative bodies had the final say. Courts did not examine whether an act of the legislature was *ultra vires* or whether the statute had been adopted under the influence of fraudulent deceit. It was a system of beguiling simplicity, but it came to an end in 1953.

During a revision of constitutional provisions provoked by the end of constitutional links with Indonesia, Parliament adopted an amendment intended to adjust the Constitution to coming changes in international law, in particular to the requirements of European integration as they were then in the air. Technically, the amendment was so clumsily drafted that it had to be redone in 1956. It was only then that constitutional lawyers began to discover the full scope of the modification. In the 1956 version,

---

[41] On the Dutch electoral system see Hans Daalder, in S. E. Finer (ed.), *Adversary Politics and Electoral Reform* (London, 1975), p. 223.

the Constitution paves the way for far-reaching forms of international integration. It provides that legislative, administrative and judicial powers can be transferred to institutions of international organizations, and that provisions of international treaties 'which, according to their nature, are capable of binding the citizens' shall have this binding force after publication; they will then prevail over earlier or later provisions of national law in case of incompatibility.[42]

The purpose of the constitutional amendments was to 'open' the Constitution to the European integration process: 1953 was, after all, the year in which the first European Community, the European Coal and Steel Community, started its activities, and the year 1956 was characterized by vehement debates on the question whether a European Defence Community should be established. There is little doubt that, from this point of view, the amendments have had the intended effect.[43] It had also an effect, however, which went far beyond the object the drafters had in mind. The new constitutional provisions did not have a limited scope, in the sense that they merely recognised the priority of European Community law over national statutes; they concerned rules of international law in general. International rules of whatever origin take precedence, under the 1953–6 constitutional amendments, as soon as these rules can be considered as 'capable of binding the citizens'.

The meaning of the latter expression was gradually developed by the Hoge Raad in a number of cases starting in the early 1960s. In one of the first judgments, in 1960, a lower court had made a distinction between 'provisions which, by their nature, can be directly applied by the courts' and 'provisions which have no other purpose than to give instructions to legislative or administrative bodies'. The Hoge Raad affirmed the decision on this point; it held that international treaty provisions which oblige contracting States to modify their legislation do not create any right a citizen can rely on before a national court.[44] Later case law gradually elaborated this idea. First of all, the Hoge Raad made it perfectly clear that the question whether a rule of international law has direct effect or not must be determined by the courts, regardless of opinions which may have been expressed

---

[42] See on the 1953 and 1956 revisions H. F. van Panhuys, 'The Netherlands Constitution and international law', *AJIL* 47 (1953), 537, and *AJIL* 58 (1964), 88.

[43] See T. Koopmans, 'Receptivity and its limits, the Dutch case', in St. John Bates *et al.* (eds.), *In Memoriam J. D. B. Mitchell* (London, 1983), p. 91.

[44] HR 13-4-1960, *AOW-I*, *Ned.Jur.* (1960), 436.

by the government or by members of the representative bodies. When deciding, the courts will have to analyse the provision in question and check whether its wording expressly assigns rights to individuals. This test has, for example, been applied to provisions of the European Convention on Human Rights formulating rights of individual citizens, like those on freedom of the press and of religion (Articles 9 s.1 and 10 s.1). A second test is whether the provision in question can affect the legal position of individuals without any implementing measure being taken by the national legislature. If that is not so, the provision cannot be considered as being 'capable of binding the citizens'. The mirror image of this test occurs when the wording of the international provision is aimed at a public body but that provision can be effective without any implementing measure by such a public body. The implication is that a rule of international law imposing a clear and unconditional prohibition on a public body can be construed as having direct effect, because such a prohibition creates a corresponding right which individuals can exercise and invoke before the courts. This conception of direct effect was not entirely original: it had already been developed by the Court of Justice of the European Communities since 1963.[45]

It was, however, the implementation of the European Convention on Human Rights which gave the most important blow to the traditional maxim of the 'inviolability' of statutes. Initially, this looked unlikely. The first cases on the impact of the Convention on Dutch legislation did not look very promising for human rights activists: Dutch courts followed a restrictive line when interpreting the rights conferred by the Convention, but they gave a broad scope to the exceptions, like those in Article 9 s.(2) and Article 10 s.(2) of the Convention (limitations... prescribed by law and... necessary in a democratic society in the interest of public safety, for the protection of public order, health or morals...). In a famous judgment of 1962, the Hoge Raad held that legislation limiting the right to organize religious processions to places where such processions were customary before 1848 (i.e. to the then Catholic regions of the country) was not contrary to the freedom of religion as protected by Article 9 of the Convention. The court examined the reasons the legislative bodies had adduced when the 1848 rule was framed, and found that the main reason had been the protection of public order, one of the grounds justifying an exception under Article 9 s.(2) of the Convention. Considering whether such a reason could

---

[45] Case 26/62, *Van Gend en Loos* [1963] ECR 5.

still be considered as valid in 1962, the court stated that the question was whether a 'reasonable legislator' could still think that the rule was necessary for the protection of public order, and it simply said that it was 'not inconceivable' that a reasonable legislator would think so.[46] This judgment has been much criticized, as showing somewhat excessive deference to the legislature. There were also commentators, however, who considered the judgment as typical of the Dutch courts' view on judicial attitudes to the European Convention.

These same judicial attitudes began to change after 1962. The first signs occurred in the late 1960s and early 1970s, when Article 10 of the Convention, on freedom of expression, began to be quoted more frequently than the corresponding Article 7 of the Dutch Constitution. Difficulties arose on the relationship between public order and freedom to express opinions in new and different forms. It was the time of the great Vietnam demonstrations and, more generally, of student and youth rebellions; protesters manifested their opinions by wearing sandwich-boards, waving flags or shouting slogans, and even by distributing blackcurrants on the highway during rush-hours. The constitutional provision covered only the freedom of the press, with the result that the new problems were more and more frequently examined by the courts on the basis of the Convention.

This development was helped by the case law of the European Court of Human Rights. Judgments condemning the Netherlands for not complying with the Convention were initially greeted with dismay. After some time, Dutch lawyers began to ask how Dutch legislation on such matters as disciplinary measures for conscripts and rights of appeal for psychiatric patients could possibly violate human rights provisions.[47] Such studies led inevitably to the conclusion that the Dutch courts themselves had power to strike down national rules which were not in conformity with the Convention, and that it was really not necessary to wait for decisions of the European Court. As a result, Dutch courts began to develop a line of investigative case law.

A new chapter was added to the debate by the appearance upon the scene of a new generation of lawyers. They tended to see the law as more value-oriented than previous generations had done. Protection of human

---

[46] HR 19-1-1962, *Geertruidenberg II*, *Ned.Jur.* (1962), 107. The case concerned a small town in the Catholic south of the country where it appeared impossible to establish that processions had taken place before 1848.

[47] See, for example, ECHR 8-6-1976, *Engel*, Series A no. 22.

rights acquired a new emphasis: it is also a kind of ideology, sometimes even a creed. The lawyers of the post-1960s generation established thriving associations and successful journals on human rights, penal reform, the protection of minorities and the emancipation of women. They advocated full application of the European Court's case law; they studied American constitutional law and were impressed by the contribution the US Supreme Court had made to the evolution of society. And, most importantly, they pinned their faith on the activities of judges, not on politics.

All these circumstances helped to create a psychological climate in the legal profession which tended to promote a more activist stand on human rights protection. A first outcome was the view that the European Convention's provisions defining human rights could be directly applied and were thus capable of overruling national legislation, statutes included, under the Dutch Constitution. A second step followed when the Hoge Raad tacitly accepted that these provisions could have only the meaning ascribed to them by the European Court's interpretation. The Hoge Raad held, for example, that a journalist who had obtained confidential information could not be compelled to disclose his source of information, since this would violate Article 10 of the Convention. In this judgment, the court overturned its earlier case law on matters of criminal procedure on the sole ground that, meanwhile, the European Court had decided otherwise.[48] A third development may have an even stronger and more lasting influence: the Hoge Raad started to scrutinize provisions of the Civil Code on the basis of its own, autonomous, view of the meaning to be attributed to the human rights provisions of the Convention. This line of case law concerned, in particular, Article 8 of the Convention, on the protection of 'family life', a provision which had not given rise to an important body of case law of the European Court but which turned out to provide important standards for reviewing rules of family law in the light of present-day conceptions of individual rights.

The first decision based on Article 8 of the European Convention concerned the position of aliens. Rules on expulsion of non-nationals, even when laid down in a statute, could not be applied, said the Hoge Raad, when they had the effect of splitting a family, by for example, expelling only one member of a family. His or her right to the protection of family life,

---

[48] HR 10-5-1996, *Van den Biggelaar v. Dohmen, Ned.Jur.* (1996), 578; ECHR 27-3-1996, *Goodwin,* 22 EHRR 123.

guaranteed by the Convention, should be upheld. Similarly, the Hoge Raad decided that divorced couples could continue to exercise parental authority over their children, although the Civil Code provided that parental authority ends upon divorce and that a guardian is then to be appointed for the children. In a later decision, the court recognised that unmarried couples can also exercise parental authority over their children. In both cases, the protection of family life as embodied in Article 8 of the Convention prevailed over Code provisions on guardianship of minors.[49] The court was not impressed by the argument that these Code provisions had been thoroughly revised in recent years. Similarly, the court held that the mother of an illegitimate child could not block recognition of the child by the biological father – the Code provided that recognition was not possible without her consent – if the man in question could prove he had lived with mother and child, his 'family life' then being protected by the Convention.

The upshot of these developments is that statutes became a good deal less 'inviolable' than formerly. Consequently, it seemed somewhat odd that Dutch courts could not rely on the Dutch Constitution when the compatibility of statutes with human rights standards was challenged. There appeared to be a lack of harmony in the Dutch constitutional system, as it allowed courts to refashion family law on the basis of human rights standards defined by an international treaty, but not on the basis of the Constitution. As a result of these misgivings, the debate on judicial review of legislation was reopened. However, during a comprehensive revision of the Constitution, in 1983, the States-General decided by a convincing majority to retain the principle of inviolability of statutes, albeit in more understandable language. The constitutional provision now states that courts 'shall not enter into examination of the constitutionality of statutes'.[50]

The courts, meanwhile, moved on. A new line of case law was introduced when Article 26 of the International Covenant on Civil and Political Rights (the United Nations Covenant), which embodies the principle of equality in very general terms, was considered as having direct effect. On that basis, administrative courts decided to strike down social security legislation, concerning pensions, on the ground that it made a distinction between male and female beneficiaries. Tax decisions began to challenge distinctions between residents and non-residents, and between owners and

---

[49] Judgments of 1984 and 1986: *Ned.Jur.* (1985), 510; (1986), 585.
[50] Art. 120 *Grondwet* (Dutch Constitution).

tenants of housing accommodation. Civil courts refused to accept a salary distinction between married and unmarried teachers; the Hoge Raad held that the distinction was discriminatory, because it was impossible to find a reasonable and objective justification for it.[51]

It is no exaggeration to say that human rights protection in the Netherlands is mainly enforced by the courts on the basis of European and international law. The European Convention on Human Rights and Article 26 of the International Covenant on Civil and Political Rights are regularly applied; in the process, the general wording of these provisions is translated by the courts into workable standards. A further source of human rights protection is European Community law. Problems such as equal treatment of men and women in employment, access to justice and discrimination against foreigners may be solved on the basis of the enforcement of EC rules and the interpretation given to these rules by the Court of Justice of the EC. The concept of 'indirect' discrimination – i.e. a distinction which is formally not based on a suspect criterion but which leads to the same result – was developed by the Court of Justice at an early stage. The first case concerned lower hourly wages for part-time workers in the textile industry, where the part-time work force usually consists of women.[52] Together with Article 26 of the Covenant, this concept became a formidable weapon in the hands of the Dutch courts.

One of the consequences of these developments is a more assertive tone in judicial decisions. Confidence in the wisdom of the representative bodies, which had characterized Dutch political culture for a considerable period of time, has begun to erode. One of the first examples was a 1989 case. A statute limiting students' rights under a 'study financing scheme' had been adopted in great haste by the two houses of Parliament in order to meet a financial deadline. Subsequently it emerged that university students already enrolled for certain courses, in the expectation that the scheme would apply to them, were retroactively deprived of benefit. The argument that such legislation violates legal certainty was accepted by the Hoge Raad; the court held, however, that it could not strike down a statute for other reasons than those covered by the 1953–6 constitutional amendments.[53] What was new in the judgment was the absence of the deferential tone towards the legislative

---

[51] HR 7-5-1993, *Antillean teachers*, Ned.Jur. (1995), 159.
[52] Case 96/80, *Jenkins v. Kingsgate Clothing Productions* [1981] ECR 911.
[53] HR 14-4-1989, *Harmonisatiewet*, Ned.Jur. (1989), 469.

bodies which had characterized earlier case law. Moreover, the court went out of its way to show the illegality of the measure, before deciding that it had no power to counter an illegality of this kind.

The constitutional law of the Netherlands presents, therefore, some particular characteristics when considered in a comparative perspective. It continues to repulse judicial review of legislation, unlike most other constitutional systems in continental Europe; but its conception of the direct effect of international law means that the techniques operated by the Dutch courts for protecting human rights are exactly the same as those developed by constitutional courts in reviewing the constitutionality of statutes. German and French experience show the importance of human rights protection for judicial review, so that the situation of the Netherlands is in truth not very far removed from that of its continental neighbours.[54]

4.4. The influence of the European courts

The way the Dutch courts rely on the European Convention on Human Rights exemplifies a more general characteristic of the evolution of public law in Europe in recent years: the growing influence of the case law of the European courts. By using the latter expression, I refer to the European Court of Human Rights (the Strasbourg court) as well as the Court of Justice of the European Communities and the court of first instance which is attached to it (the Luxembourg courts).

The influence of the European courts concerns only the European countries, and it does so in varying degrees. At this point a first distinction must be made. The provisions defining human rights and fundamental freedoms, laid down in the European Convention, are directly applicable in some legal systems, for example in French, Belgian and Dutch law, but not in other systems. English and Scottish courts were previously never tempted to apply the provisions of the Convention: they considered these provisions as standards the British legislature had to respect, not as rules of law to be applied by the courts. That point of view was consistently adhered to in English and Scottish law, until the provisions of the Convention were translated into rules of national law by the Human Rights Act 1998. The rights established by the Convention are, therefore, applied by the English courts because they

---

[54] See also T. Koopmans, 'La Convention européenne des droits de l'homme et le juge néerlandais', *RIDC* (1999-1), 21.

have been laid down in a British statute, but by the Dutch courts because the rules of the Convention themselves have the force of law.

This distinction has no importance for European Community law, which has in itself the force of direct application. From the very beginning of its case law, the Court of Justice of the EC has held that the provisions of the EC Treaty, and of regulations and directives based on that treaty, must be directly applied if their tenor allows it.[55] The courts of the Member States have accepted this view, albeit, sometimes, after a period of hesitation. They have also adopted the rule, developed by the Court of Justice, that provisions having such direct effect prevail over national legislation, even if that legislation is laid down in a later statute, a *lex posterior*. The Court of Justice considers this rule as one of the basic features of the Community legal order.[56]

A second important difference between the system of the European Convention on Human Rights and European Community law concerns interpretation. In EC law, the Treaty itself emphasizes that EC provisions are to be applied as they are interpreted by the Court of Justice. In order to ensure a uniform application of these provisions, the Treaty establishes a system of preliminary rulings: national courts faced with the problem of how to interpret the Treaty, or regulations or directives, can ask the Court of Justice to give an answer, by way of a preliminary ruling, to any questions of interpretation; supreme courts are obliged to put such questions to the Court of Justice.[57] It is generally accepted that the notion of a common market, on which the EC Treaty was initially based, implies the necessity of a uniform interpretation of EC provisions; otherwise an artificial deflection of trade might occur (for example, if rules on custom duties or value added tax had a different meaning in different Member States). National courts are therefore obliged to follow the interpretation of the Court of Justice. If a national court does not agree with the interpretation given by the Court of Justice, it is free to put further preliminary questions to the Court; but the answer of the Court to these further questions will be final and decisive.[58]

The European Convention on Human Rights does not provide for a system of preliminary rulings. National courts are not in a position to initiate

---

[55] Case 26/62, *Van Gend en Loos* [1963] ECR 5; case 106/77, *Simmenthal* [1978] ECR 629.

[56] Case 6/64, *Costa* v. *ENEL* [1964] ECR 585; case 148/78, *Ratti* [1979] ECR 629.

[57] Art. 234 EC Treaty (ex 177). The articles of the EC Treaty have been renumbered by virtue of the Treaty of Amsterdam, 1997.

[58] See case 66/80, *International Chemical Corp.* [1981] ECR 1191.

proceedings before the European Court of Human Rights. Individual petitioners can do so only after all domestic remedies have been exhausted, in accordance with the rules generally recognised in international law;[59] their complaint is addressed against the State in whose territory, or under whose jurisdiction, the alleged violation of human rights took place. The Convention does not say, either explicitly or implicitly, that national courts must follow the interpretation of the Convention developed by the European Court. Consequently, that is a matter of national law or of national practice. The British Human Rights Act requires the courts to take into account any judgment or decision rendered by the European Court. Such a rule does not exist in the Netherlands, but the Hoge Raad tends to follow Strasbourg decisions faithfully.[60]

The interpretations adopted by the European Court of Human Rights are not only relevant under a national constitution like the Dutch Constitution, which does not recognise judicial review of legislation; they also matter in constitutional systems, where it falls to constitutional courts to supervise the respect of human rights as embodied in the national constitution. The federal constitutional court in Germany considered that the case law of the European Court of Human Rights had a double role to play in German constitutional law. On the one hand, that case law fixes the limits of the obligations imposed on the Federal Republic by public international law; for that reason, German statutes will be interpreted and applied in conformity with it. On the other hand, the European Court's case law also helps to determine the substance and scope of human rights as defined in the Basic Law (*Auslegungshilfe*).[61] The German court thus attempts to bring a certain harmony into the application of the two systems of human rights protection, national and European.

It is, therefore, undeniable that national courts are influenced by the Court of Justice of the EC as well as by the European Court of Human Rights. That influence is easily perceptible with regard to the interpretation of individual provisions of EC law, or of the European Convention on Human Rights. The influence exercised by the European courts may, however, be of a much more general nature. I shall suggest some reasons

---

[59] Art. 35 s.(1) European Convention since the entry into force of the Eleventh Protocol to the Convention on 1 November 1998. See also ECHR 19-3-1991, *Cardot*, Series A no. 200.

[60] See, respectively, Art. 2(1)(a) Human Rights Act, 1998; HR 10-5-1996, *Van den Biggelaar* v. *Dohmen*, Ned.Jur. (1996), 578.

[61] BVerfGE 74 no. 23, *Unschuldvermutung*, 1987.

why this influence extends to the attitudes adopted by national courts with regard to the relationship between the judiciary and the political institutions in general. It may have prompted a change of attitude on three points: a decrease in the importance of codes and statutes as the primary source of law; a frequent reliance on general principles of law; and an increasing confidence in the creative talents of the courts themselves. I shall briefly elucidate each of these three developments.

On the first point, decreasing importance of statutes, it is fair to say that judges in national courts are getting used to the idea that the application of statutes will have to make way for higher law. The Court of Justice of the EC has the task of ensuring that 'the law' is observed; it exercises a general power of judicial review, under which it can annul regulations and directives infringing rules of law.[62] Such a general power of review is not available to national courts; when such power exists it will normally be exercised by separate constitutional courts. Besides, the Court of Justice assumes that rules of national law, statutes included, will always give way to Community law in case of conflict, and that all national courts have a duty, under the Treaty, to enforce this priority of Community law.[63] Thus, all national courts in the Member States of the European Union are brought into a position which enables them to strike down national statutes, and that possibility will be enhanced as the number of EC rules increases.

In a more indirect way, implementation of the European Convention on Human Rights has a similar effect. When following the interpretation of the Convention adopted by the European Court, national courts will tend to accept the priority of human rights protection as consistently sustained by the European Court. If they lack the power to set aside the application of a national statute on such a ground, they will try to interpret it in conformity with the standards developed by the European Court. The importance of the European dimension leads to a corresponding decline in the consideration given to the will of the State legislature.

On the second point, general principles of law, the European courts share a common attitude. These principles are of paramount importance for the evolution of European Community law and the definition of standards of human rights protection. For the European Convention, this development followed as a matter of course. The Convention utilizes vague and indefinite

---

[62] See Art. 220 (ex 164) and Art. 230 (ex 173) EC Treaty.
[63] See *Simmenthal* (quoted in note 55).

notions which need further explanation and interpretation; more often than not, the European Court is compelled to resort to general principles of law. It is, for example, impossible to find out what a 'fair' trial is, as required by Article 6 of the Convention, when no standards of fairness have been established. In matters of procedural law, certain forms of practice have been generally accepted in the European States, and the European Court has been able to extract certain fundamental principles of procedural law from that practice. On this ground the European Court held, for example, that the concept of fair trial implies that the suspect in criminal proceedings cannot be forced to collaborate in gathering evidence which may be used against him. This right of the suspect, usually referred to with the American expression 'privilege against self-incrimination', serves in its turn as a basis for a number of procedural rules developed by the European Court.[64]

The situation in European Community law is more or less comparable. It is true that the EC Treaty has some detailed rules on matters of economic law, such as free movement of goods and competition law. However, it is completely silent on general legal problems. It provides that the Court of Justice is to ensure that 'the law' is observed in the interpretation and application of the Treaty, but it fails to indicate how this 'law' is to be derived. There are no rules on sources of law, or on the relationship between Community law and national legal systems, or between Community law and traditional international law. There is only one provision which seems to give an indication: on a somewhat technical point, the liability of the Community for torts of the institutions and their agents, the Treaty refers to 'the general principles common to the laws of the Member States'.[65] This source of law has, in a way, been generalized by the Court of Justice. General principles of law such as legal certainty, protection of legitimate expectations and the principle of proportionality have been drawn from national systems of law and further developed by the Court of Justice. This has been particularly important in filling the gaps left by the text of the Treaty, or by applicable regulations or directives. An interesting example is the Court's ruling that the EC Commission must respect, in its investigations into anti-competitive behaviour by business corporations, the confidentiality of correspondence between the company and its legal advisers. The applicable regulation was

---

[64] See ECHR 25-2-1993, *Funke* v. *France*, Series A no. 256-A.
[65] Art. 288 EC Treaty (ex 215).

silent on the matter, but the Court of Justice founded its decision on a general principle of law which was common to the legal systems of the Member States.[66]

As a result, the development of general principles of law in the constitutional and administrative law of the Member States has been encouraged by the case law of the European courts. It is important to note that this case law shows a high degree of consistency and started to develop in the early years of the European integration process. A 1957 judgment by the Court of Justice in a staff case set the tone. Considering whether an unlawful decision by the administration could be retroactively revoked, the Court of Justice held that this was a well-known problem of administrative law which was not covered by Treaty provisions and should therefore be solved on the basis of principles adopted in the legal systems of the Member States.[67] The development of general principles of law is a matter for the courts, not for the political institutions.

The third point, judicial creativity, is harder to explain. EC law may provide the less complicated illustration, as the Court of Justice was faced with the necessity of developing a legal system ('the law', in the terminology of the Treaty) on the basis of provisions which did not give much of a clue. The Court had to feel its way. It did so by deriving some basic rules from the multiplicity of technical provisions, by interpreting these rules in the light of the aims of the Treaty, and by slowly developing a system of case law on that foundation. Thus, the Treaty provisions on the abolition of customs duties and import restrictions in intra-Community trade were considered as the expression of the basic rule of free movement of goods, which is one of the elements of the concept of 'customs union', and it is such a union that the Treaty intends to establish. The rule of free movement of goods affects not only national measures with a protectionist character, said the Court: it strikes 'any' trade regulation which has the effect of restricting or hampering trade between Member States. This implied, for example, that imports from other Member States cannot be prohibited for failing to observe technical standards imposed by the importing country (such as manufacturing rules, provisions on the form and presentation of the product, the percentage of alcohol in liquors etc.). The importing Member State will have to recognise the standards applied by the exporting Member

---

[66] Case 155/79, *AM&S* [1982] ECR 1575.
[67] Cases 7/56 and 3-7/57, *Algera* [1957–58] ECR 55.

State, subject to certain limited exceptions permitted by the Treaty (for example, on grounds of public health).[68] On this basis, German rules on 'purity' of beer, requiring that beer could be manufactured only using four specific ingredients, could not be applied to beer manufactured in another Member State in accordance with the standards in force in that State.[69] By combining disparate details, the Court of Justice managed to develop basic rules which led to the emergence of a coherent set of standards governing intra-Community trade. It is judge-made law.

For the European Court of Human Rights, the problem was somewhat different. The provisions of the European Convention are not very technical, but rather general and vague. In order to make these provisions workable, the European Court had to break them up into three or four 'sub-standards' which were practicable and which could, in their turn, lead to further ramifications. In that way, the requirement of 'fair trial' gave rise to the sub-standard of 'equality of arms' between the parties (again an American expression), which is particularly important in criminal proceedings. The European Court then went on to formulate, on the basis of equality of arms, rules to be respected in criminal cases, for example, with regard to the interrogation of anonymous witnesses (important in drugs cases).[70] There is a kind of dynamism in this case law which recalls American developments.[71]

That parallelism is reinforced by the European Court's admission that terms and expressions used by the European Convention may acquire a different meaning as time goes by. In a case concerning the application of the equality principle to the distinction between legitimate and illegitimate children in the Belgian law of succession, the Court acknowledged its awareness that such a distinction was generally accepted at the time the Convention was concluded (1950); but, said the Court, notions used by the Convention must be interpreted 'in the light of present-day conditions'. For that reason, legal evolution in the European States should be taken into consideration.[72] The European Court thereby explicitly accepted the idea of legal evolution in the area of human rights protection, and the role of the judiciary in drawing conclusions from it. That attitude may have

---

[68] Case 120/78, *Cassis de Dijon* ('*Rewe*') [1979] ECR 649.

[69] Case 178/84, *Reinheitsgebot (Commission v. Federal Republic of Germany: 'purity of beer')* [1987] ECR 1227.

[70] ECHR 20-11-1989, *Kostovski v. the Netherlands*, Series A no. 166.

[71] See ch. 3.3 and 3.4.   [72] ECHR 13-6-1979, *Marckx v. Belgium*, Series A no. 31.

contributed to the more or less activist character of much of the European Court's case law.[73]

The European courts may together have set an example to national courts. In a situation where written provisions failed to give a clear guidance to the judge, both courts have been able to develop law, by adhering to a purpose-oriented view and by using their imagination. As situations of such a kind are becoming more and more frequent, national courts may find their inspiration in this approach.[74]

4.5. Courts and parliaments

The growth of judicial power in constitutional matters rebounds on the powers of the legislature. After having examined the practice of judicial review, or the lack of it, in some of the major legal systems, we shall therefore briefly engage in a general discussion of the respective advantages and disadvantages of decision-making by the judiciary and by the representative bodies.

It is not difficult to gain the impression, from the above survey, that decision-making may indeed constitute an important dimension of the problematic relationship between the courts and the political institutions. The controversial abortion cases in the United States and Germany raised many issues, about womens rights, the concept of privacy, the protection of human life, the scope and meaning of human rights, and so on.[75] They also, however, raised a more or less formal issue: who should decide on the liberalization of abortion, and according to what kind of procedure? Politically speaking, that was one of the main issues. Some of the anger and irritation provoked by these cases was due to the lack of democratic process. In Germany, the federal constitutional court seemed to repeat the debate that had already taken place in the Bundestag; only the outcome was different. In the United States, the *Roe* judgment gave rise to a passionate debate on abortion, with the result that the discussion took place after the matter had been decided, instead of the other way round.

For a problem like abortion, legislative bodies can mobilize resources which are not available to courts. Governments can ask for advice from

---

[73] See also ECHR 27-10-1994, *Kroon*, Series A no. 297-C.
[74] See also J. H. H. Weiler, *The Constitution of Europe* (Cambridge, 1999), ch. 5.
[75] See *Roe* v. *Wade* (ch. 3. 4); *Schwangerschaftsabbruch* I (ch. 4.1).

medical and psychological experts, and consult with religious and political organizations or groups, before introducing a bill. Once the bill is pending, newspapers and professional journals will give their comments; individuals and associations can send their observations to members of parliament or parliamentary committees. This may have a pacifying effect. Experience in France provides an illustration. After intense debates in both chambers, a statute authorizing abortion subject to certain conditions was promulgated in 1975. It carried liberalization less far than the American Supreme Court had done.[76] However, the American decision produced irreducible and sometimes violent opposition (under the battle-cry 'pro-life') whereas, in France, passions seemed to simmer down after the statute had been adopted. This is striking in a country like France, with a Catholic past. The Conseil constitutionnel declared in a very brief ruling that the statute was not incompatible with the Constitution.[77] Important changes of the law often need a basis in society; such a basis is more easily obtained when the representative bodies decide.

The political institutions are also in a strong position as far as accessibility of information is concerned. Courts are bound by the laws of evidence. In civil litigation, which habitually respects the autonomy of the parties, the evidence available to the courts concerns the facts the parties have thought fit to produce. The administrative courts, such as exist in France and Germany, are in a somewhat stronger position: they can ask for documents and other information on their own initiative, and the public authority which is party to the proceedings will usually comply. Governments and parliamentary committees have, however, an entirely free hand in collecting every kind of information they consider as relevant. They can also organize fact-finding missions, for example by committees of experts, when they want to uncover hidden practices (such as prison brutalities or police corruption).

The common law countries developed a device intended to broaden the information available to the courts: the presence of an *amicus curiae*. In English law, a barrister can be invited to submit arguments representing interests or points of view which are not those of a party to the proceedings, for example the general interest, or the ideas of a public authority or a professional group which is only indirectly concerned. As a result, the court

---

[76] Text of the 1975 statute in Mary-Ann Glendon, *Abortion and Divorce in Western Law* (Cambridge, Mass., and London, 1987), appendix c.

[77] CC 15-1-1975, *Interruption volontaire de la grossesse*, *Rec.* 19. English translation in Cappelletti and Cohen, *Comparative Constitutional Law*, ch. 12-B.

will, in its decision, also consider other circumstances or arguments than those developed by the parties.[78] Before the US Supreme Court, this procedural mechanism has flourished during the last fifty years, particularly in important constitutional cases. In race-related cases, associations aspiring for racial equality or interested in civil liberties present their arguments to the court; in other cases, federal or state departments or agencies such as the federal ministry of Justice, the attorney general of Tennessee or the Federal Trade Commission, sometimes appear as *amicus curiae*. In 1963, the US Supreme Court struck down a Virginia statute curbing the activities of the NAACP (National Association for the Advancement of Colored People); that association had, as the Court acknowledged in its judgment, the precise aim of intervening in litigation in order to vindicate the rights of the black community.[79] In the agitated 1970s this practice was criticized for transforming the courtroom into a political forum, but criticism petered out when quieter times returned. The possibility of *amicus curiae* briefs tends to assist common law courts in overcoming the constraints imposed by the rules governing procedure and evidence in civil litigation.

Apart from elements like consultation and information, the political process also implies an element of accountability, which has no equivalent in judicial decision-making. If the decision ultimately turns out to have been incorrect, or even bad or dangerous, the political decision-makers, or their political party, will have to face the distress or rage of the electorate. The representative system ensures that they suffer the consequences of what they have done, or ill-done. In extreme cases, parliamentary committees may be set up to investigate how matters went wrong; that is not a pleasant experience for the politicians who are held reponsible. In judicial decision making, the judgment of the final appellate court closes the argument.

There are, however, also important arguments in favour of decision-making by judges. Governments may rush legislation through the representative bodies, in particular in those parliamentary regimes where the government can rely on a stable majority in parliament. British political practice provides an eloquent example in the ill-considered abolition of local government in the great cities during the Thatcher years. In the Netherlands, the *Harmonisatiewet* case showed how rushed-through statutes can cause unexpected harm.[80] Courts will rarely, if ever, indulge in behaviour of this

---

[78] See *Allen* v. *McAlpine* [1968] 2 QB 229.   [79] *NAACP* v. *Button*, 371 US 415 (1963).
[80] See, respectively, ch. 2.5 and ch. 4.3.

kind: they are restrained by their professional attitudes. Judges are profes-
sionally trained to consider every argument, however curious, and to balance different arguments against each other. Normally they will give reasons
for their decisions, thereby enabling others to reconstruct the court's line
of thought.

A further advantage of judicial decision-making is that those who decide
have no personal interest in the result. They are more unprejudiced than
politicians, who are more frequently linked to the business community or to
interest groups, or to single-issue movements such as anti-hunting lobbies
or environmental groups. Sometimes, it is argued that judges will be less
inclined to prejudice than politicians because they have no political or ideological preconceptions. That seems very doubtful to me. The situation is,
from this point of view, not entirely comparable in the different countries.
We have seen that judges of the US Supreme Court are sometimes openly
nominated and appointed because of their political opinions.[81] In England,
the judges have often been accused of a kind of inborn conservatism which
makes them blind to the idea of social progress, particularly in cases concerning the right to strike or the position of trade unions. These reproaches
have diminished recent years, but they have not quite vanished.[82] Recently,
members of the Labour government and newspaper articles have stressed
the insensitivity of many judges to problems of racial discrimination in the
British Isles.

There may be a more general difficulty. From force of habit, judges take
individualistic positions. They see social problems in terms of the rights of
individuals rather than of the organization society. In cases on urban planning, city authorities will, for example, focus on how to build new residential
areas, but the judge is primarily concerned with the rights of neighbouring
property-owners. To that extent the judiciary certainly has some kind of
professional bias, but it is one which may occasionally counteract the usual
prejudices of administrators and politicians.[83]

A bias may also be present when values are in issue which have a natural
appeal to lawyers, for example, procedural guarantees (*ne bis in idem*, *audi et
alteram partem*, presumption of innocence). Concepts such as 'due process

---

[81] See ch. 3.5.

[82] See J. A. G. Griffiths, *The Politics of the Judiciary*, 5th edn (London, 1997); David Pannick, *Judges* (Oxford, 1987), ch. 5.

[83] See also Stephen Sedley, 'Governments, constitutions and judges', in Genevra Richardson and Hazel Genn (eds.), *Administrative Law and Government Action* (Oxford, 1994), p. 35.

of law' and *Rechtsstaat* embody values which are, because of their place in the American and German constitution respectively, primarily under judicial tutelage.[84] Consequently, these notions are probably higher up in the courts' scale of values than in that of political institutions. English courts, less prone to abstract discourse, will avoid speaking in terms of values; but a study of English case law will soon reveal certain value-orientations, most notably with regard to things which have been important in the evolution of the common law of England. As an example, I quote three sentences from a 1966 judgment by Lord Denning in the Court of Appeal:[85]

> Let it not be supposed that this court is in any way opposed to trial by jury. It has been the bulwark of our liberties too long for any of us to seek to alter it. Whenever a man is on trial for a serious crime, or when in a civil case a man's honour or integrity is at stake, or when one or other party must be deliberately lying, then trial by jury has no equal.

This proposition is more likely to be based on preconception than on a serious study of comparative law.

Carrying the debate to a yet more abstract level, we meet the argument that judicial decisions lack 'democratic legitimacy'; for that reason, really important decisions should always be made by representative bodies. The argument is appealing, but cannot stand up to analysis. First, it assumes that for important decisions a democratic basis is always necessary; but that is highly questionable. The British Crown Prosecution Service, the French inspector of taxes, the German and American anti-trust authorities, take very important decisions within the limits traced by the applicable rules of law; like the judges, they are bodies established to uphold the rule of law. Liberal democracies are founded not only on the concept of democracy, but also on the rule of law. It is true that the two ideas have an intimate connection: it is the rule of law which protects minorities, and without such a protection democracy cannot prosper. Nevertheless, the two ideas express different conceptions of the way a country should be run: they are based on different political theories which have each their own merits and emphasize dissimilar elements.

The second weakness of the argument for democratic legitimacy is that democratic processes can only function properly when independent courts are able to prevent those processes from being distorted. The representative

---

[84] See, respectively, ch. 3.3 and ch. 4.1.   [85] *Ward v. James* [1966] 1 QB 273.

system presupposes that all citizens can participate in the political process. They should therefore be able to exercise rights such as voting rights and freedom of expression.[86] If individuals or groups are excluded from participation, courts will have to restore equality. The American desegregation cases prove the point. In the words of an American author: some 'policing' of the representative process may be necessary.[87]

These considerations show that it is not wise to be satisfied with general statements. Much depends on the nature of the problem to be solved and the context in which the decision is to be taken. Every society carries its own dead weights: each is burdened with the undigested consequences of its own past. The radicalism of the US Supreme Court's desegregation decisions can only be understood as a reaction to an entire century of tacit acceptance of racial segregation and, ultimately, against the background of more than two centuries of black slavery. It changed the balance of power between the judiciary and Congress, but it did so because of this radicalism, not for any particular institutional reason.

History also explains why things may be usual in one country which seem repulsive in another. Persons appointed to the supreme appellate court of the United Kingdom, the House of Lords, are granted a life peerage upon their appointment. Because that makes them 'lords' in the full sense of the word, and not only 'law lords', they can also participate in the activities of the House in its legislative capacity. Usually, the law lords only make themselves heard in debates which are of particular interest for the administration of justice, such as bills on civil or criminal procedure (just as the Anglican bishops, also members of the House, will only intervene in matters of morality and in legislation concerning marriage and divorce).[88] The 1998 reform of the House of Lords left all these particularities untouched. In a country like France, where constitutional thinking is still influenced by the ideas of the French Revolution, combinations such as these would be inconceivable.

I should perhaps add that the European Court of Human Rights once declared that decisions by judges who have also been advising the legislative bodies of the State on the same matter they are judging amounts to a violation of Article 6 of the Convention (fair trial).[89] The case concerned

---

[86] See Lijphart, *Patterns of Democracy*, ch. 4.   [87] Ely, *Democracy and Distrust*, ch. 4.
[88] See de Smith and Brazier, *Constitutional and Administrative Law*, ch. 15.
[89] ECHR 28-9-1995, *Procola*, Series A no. 326.

the Council of State of the Grand Duchy of Luxembourg, a body whose task is precisely to be an adviser to the government as well as an administrative court. The European Court held that there should be no doubt on the 'structural impartiality' of a judicial body. That may have some consequences for the position of the law lords in the future. The present system still has some strange anomalies: for example, the Lord Chancellor, who is also a cabinet minister, can sit as a judge in the appellate committee of the House of Lords, at his own discretion. The House of Lords in its judicial capacity is, however, held in high esteem by lawyers in the entire English-speaking world, and beyond.

5

The limits of judicial review

5.1. The political question

Now and then courts refuse to examine a case because they feel it should be dealt with by the political institutions. The US Supreme Court describes such cases as 'non-justiciable'. That view is not directly founded on the text of the American Constitution, which rather implies that the judicial power extends to 'all' cases and controversies.[1] The nature of the case may be such, however, that judicial intervention would not be appropriate.

An early example of this conception is the interpretation of the 'guarantee clause' of the Constitution. It provides that the United States shall 'guarantee to every state in this Union a republican form of government' and protect each of them against invasion.[2] In 1842, when there were two rival governments in the state of Rhode Island, the courts refused to determine which of the two was the lawful government of the state. The US Supreme Court finally held that action by the President of the United States had shown that the decision had been committed to other branches of the federal government.[3] In 1912, the Supreme Court refused to adjudicate a claim that the initiative and referendum procedure instituted by the state of Oregon violated the guarantee clause. Justiciability of the clause would involve an 'inconceivable expansion of judicial power', said the Court, 'and the ruinous destruction of legislative authority in matters purely political'.[4] Strong language indeed.

In its later case law the Court broadened its view by developing what is commonly called the 'doctrine of the political question'. It would nevertheless be going too far to state that this doctrine identifies the area of non-justiciability. There has always been much uncertainty about the limits

---

[1] Art. III s.2 US Constitution.   [2] Art. IV s.4 US Constitution.
[3] *Luther* v. *Borden*, 48 US 1 (1849). The case is described by Justice Brennan in *Baker* v. *Carr*, 369 US 186 (1962).
[4] *Pacific States Tel. & Tel. Co.* v. *Oregon*, 223 US 118 (1912).

of the political question. It is clear that the courts will abstain from deciding whenever the Constitution has committed the issue to another agency
of government than themselves. To that extent, the political question doctrine is a mere consequence of the separation of powers as laid down in the
Constitution. Sometimes, however, the Supreme Court seems tempted to
give a narrow interpretation to the constitutional tasks of other branches
of government. In 1967, the House of Representatives voted a resolution
excluding Adam Clayton Powell from membership on the ground that, before his recent re-election, he had wrongly diverted House funds to his staff
and to himself. According to the Constitution, the House is 'the judge of
the elections, returns and qualifications of its own members'.[5] The Supreme
Court held, however, that these words did not cover Mr Powell's case. The
Constitution, it said, leaves the House without authority to 'exclude' any
person duly elected by his constituents, if he meets the requirements for
membership 'expressly prescribed in the Constitution'.[6] The courts could
therefore grant relief to the excluded Congressman. But in a comparable situation, concerning the exclusion of two state delegations from the
Democratic National Convention of 1972 by the 'credentials committee'
of the Convention (the 'Convention' elects the presidential candidate), the
Supreme Court held that it would not 'interject itself into the deliberative
processes of a national political convention': the political processes should
be free from judicial supervision.[7]

It is not always easy to determine, therefore, when the Court is going to
think that a certain issue is committed to other branches. In the Watergate
tapes litigation, President Nixon invoked notions such as 'executive autonomy' and 'executive privilege' as a pretext for refusing access to tape
recordings of conversations in the White House which might throw some
light on the Watergate scandal (a politically inspired break-in to Watergate,
a building in Washington DC where the Democratic party had its headquarters). The Supreme Court refused to accept these arguments, but its
decisions were heavily criticized.[8]

Closely connected to the idea that certain issues have been committed
to other branches of government is the Court's unwillingness to decide on

[5] Art. 1 s.5(1) US Constitution.   [6] *Powell* v. *McCormack*, 395 US 486 (1969).
[7] *O'Brien* v. *Brown*, 409 US 1 (1972).
[8] See Gerald Gunther, 'Judicial hegemony and legislative autonomy: the Nixon case and the
impeachment process', *UCLA Law Review* 22 (1974), 30.

problems involving the foreign policy of the United States. The Court consistently refuses to examine challenges to the use of military force abroad. In 1979, it held that the question whether the President had power to terminate a treaty with Taiwan without congressional approval was a 'non-justiciable political dispute'.[9] Justice Brennan once cast some doubt on the generality of this view. In one of the reapportionment cases, he said that it was an error to suppose that 'every case or controversy which touches foreign relations lies beyond judicial cognizance'. In this form, the statement sounds like a truism, although the example Justice Brennan gave, the interpretation of treaties, is not very convincing.[10] If the conducting of foreign relations is at stake, the separation of powers as resulting from the American Constitution seems to entrust matters entirely to the political institutions, in particular to the President and the Senate.[11] Ultimately, this role of the political institutions is part and parcel of the representative system and thereby of democracy. It may be true, as Justice Brennan once casually remarked, that 'faith in democracy is one thing, but blind faith is another'[12], but courts should probably stick to the basics.

The Supreme Court has also held that cases can be non-justiciable for 'lack of judicially discoverable and manageable standards'. It is not quite clear whether this concept is part of the political question doctrine or an independent ground of non-justiciability. The leading case concerned a decision by the legislature of the state of Kansas to ratify an amendment to the Constitution, relating to child labour, which had been proposed by Congress thirteen years earlier. The opponents argued that ratification was only possible 'within a reasonable time', which had, they said, elapsed. The Supreme Court stated that it could not find any criteria for judicial determination; the decision depended on the appraisal of a great variety of conditions 'which can hardly be said to be within the appropriate range of evidence receivable in a court of justice'.[13] Justice Harlan relied on this ground in his dissenting opinions in the 1962–4 reapportionment cases, but on that occasion, the majority opinions gave short shrift to the argument.[14]

It is sometimes said that the 'complexity' of a case may constitute a ground for non-justiciability. The Supreme Court referred to it in the case on the Kansas approval of the child labour amendment; however, this complexity

---

[9] *Goldwater* v. *Carter*, 444 US 996 (1979).   [10] *Baker* v. *Carr*, 396 US 186 (1962). See ch. 3.4.
[11] See Art. II s.2(1) and (2) US Constitution.
[12] See Frank F. Michelman, *Brennan and Democracy* (Princeton, N.J., 1999), p. 61.
[13] *Coleman* v. *Miller*, 307 US 433 (1939).   [14] See ch. 3.4.

argument should probably be seen as part of the explanation of why it was hard to find judicially manageable standards, rather than as an independent ground. In later case law, the argument does not reappear. Admittedly, the courts are often called on to decide complex matters, for example, in multi-party tort actions or in cases involving international aspects of patents or trade marks. Foreign policy decisions have a different kind of complexity, however: the relevant facts, the evaluation of risks, the necessary contacts, the responsibility for the consequences, they are all beyond the area of judicial investigation. Looked at in this perspective, the complexity argument could make sense.

The political question doctrine seems to have slowly vanished from the case law of the US Supreme Court since the reapportionment cases of 1962–4. In 1995, the Court was very much divided over the question whether the states could limit the number of terms for federal office holders (it was a 5-4 decision); but the judgment, though quoting Mr Powell's case, avoided any allusion to the 'political question'.[15] It is interesting to observe, though, that broadly similar doctrines have been developed in other constitutional systems. I refer, in particular, to the concept of *acte de gouvernement* (governmental act) as applied by the French administrative courts. The concept has been developed by the supreme administrative court, the Conseil d'Etat; it is even mentioned in some nineteenth-century decisions.

There has always been uncertainty about the exact scope of the concept. In some cases, the Conseil d'Etat held that a certain administrative decision, because of its very nature, did not lend itself to review by a court; in other cases, it said explicitly that the decision constituted an *acte de gouvernement* which could not be subjected to judicial review. Modern commentators agree that the two most important categories of decisions covered by the doctrine are those concerning the relations between government and parliament, for example a decree for the dissolution of the National Assembly, and those involving the foreign policy of the French Republic.[16] When the newly elected President Chirac decided to resume nuclear testing in French Polynesia in 1995, the Conseil d'Etat ruled that this decision could not

---

[15] *US Term Limits* v. *Thornton*, 514 US 779 (1995). See also Lee Epstein and Thomas G. Walker, *Constitutional Law for a Changing America* (Washington, DC, 1998), ch. 3.

[16] See L. Neville Brown and John S. Bell, *French Administrative Law*, 5th edn (Oxford 1998), pp. 161–4, 137–8; Guy Braibant and Bernard Stirn, *Le droit administratif français*, 4th edn (Paris, 1997), pp. 261–4.

be separated from the conduct of international relations, in particular because of the then current negotiations for a new treaty banning nuclear testing. Consequently, the decision could not be challenged before the administrative courts; as the court put it with unbeatable succinctness: 'elle échappe, par suite, à tout contrôle juridictionnel' (thus, it 'escapes' any judicial supervision).[17]

The two categories of decisions I mentioned do not cover all cases where the Conseil d'Etat relies, explicitly or implicitly, on the doctrine of *acte de gouvernement*. In 1962, the court considered that the President's decision to proclaim a state of emergency constituted an *acte de gouvernement*.[18] The background of the case was somewhat peculiar. When President de Gaulle allowed the start of talks with representatives of the Algerian rebels in 1961, a group of French generals in Algiers came out in open revolt against the government. The generals considered that their slogan 'Algérie française!' had helped to bring de Gaulle to power in 1958, and that the President had deceived them by contemplating the granting of independence to the territory. De Gaulle's reaction was swift. He immediately made a televised speech to the soldiers enjoining them, in the strongest terms, not to obey the 'treacherous' generals; and he proclaimed the state of emergency in accordance with Article 16 of the 1958 Constitution. This provision empowers the President to issue such a proclamation under certain conditions (serious and immediate threat to the institutions of the Republic or to the nation's independence, for example), and after having consulted the Prime Minister, the presidents of the Assembly and of the Senate and the Constitutional Council. In a situation of national emergency, the normal distribution of legislative and administrative powers no longer applies: most powers are then concentrated in the hands of the President. One of the President's first decisions was to institute a special military tribunal for acts of treason. Some imprisoned army officers attacked the legality of the emergency situation, alleging that there had been no real emergency and that, anyway, the potential emergency had come to an end very quickly. There was some truth in these allegations, but the Conseil d'Etat held that the decision to apply Article 16 of the Constitution was an *acte de gouvernement*; neither the legality of that decision nor the duration of the emergency situation

---

[17] CE 29-9-1995, *Association Greenpeace France*, *Rec.* 348. See also case note in *Public Law* (1996), 169.

[18] CE 2-3-1962, *Rubin de Servens*, *Rec.* 143; also in Long, Weil and Braibant, *Les grands arrêts de la jurisprudence administrative*, 11th edn (Paris, 1996), no. 96.

could be challenged before the courts.[19] The case gives a vivid illustration of the area of tension between politics and the judiciary in times of crisis.

Like the US Supreme Court, therefore, the French Conseil d'Etat recognises that certain decisions are outside the scope of judicial control because of their political character. No such general view can be found in German case law. The attitude of the Bundesverfassungsgericht is rather that its jurisdiction extends to any statute whatever its nature; but the Court is sometimes inclined to accept that certain assessments have to be made by the political institutions and cannot be supervised by the courts.

An interesting case concerned the fast breeder nuclear reactor at Kalkar in Westphalia.[20] The question before the constitutional court was whether the federal statute providing a licensing system for the construction and operation of nuclear power stations was sufficiently specific and precise. Neighbouring small-holders had argued that parliament was itself under a duty to establish the applicable standards and could not limit its legislative performance to the stipulation that the licensing authority must take every precaution 'in the light of existing scientific knowledge'. The Court saw no reason to annul the statute. On the one hand, it rejected the government's argument that the principle of parliamentary democracy would imply that parliamentary decision-making must prevail over the powers of other branches of government. The Basic Law includes no principle of interpretation in that sense, said the Court:[21] judicial interpretations have to take account of the specific division of powers and competences under the Basic Law. On the other hand, the judgment continues, acceptance of the risks resulting from a new nuclear technology such as the fast breeder involves the political responsibility of the representative bodies for the consequences of their decisions. Only the future can show whether this technology will ultimately present more advantages than dangers. It is not the function of the courts, the judgment concludes, to substitute their assessment of the possible risks for that of the political branches of government. And in a phrase recalling the political question doctrine, the Court adds that it is unable to evaluate the situation in the absence of suitable legal standards.

---

[19] See also Michèle Voisset, *L'article 16 de la Constitution du 4 octobre 1958* (Paris, 1969), in particular pp. 223–94.

[20] BVerfGE 49 no. 6, *Kalkar*, 1978.

[21] On this crucial point, the partial translation of the judgment in Kommers, no. 4.6, is defective.

In later years, judgments illustrating the same approach have been rendered in sensitive areas such as defence and foreign relations. Defence issues are not, as such, excluded from judicial review. However, the federal constitutional court proceeds very cautiously: it examines defence problems with the utmost restraint, always bearing in mind that the assessment of certain situations, and of certain risks, should be left to the political institutions, which will finally be accountable to the electorate.[22]

Although the expression 'political question' seems to have vanished from judicial language, the problems this concept was intended to deal with continue to crop up. Perhaps these problems are too diverse and too complicated to be covered by a single concept. Nevertheless, no better approach has yet been invented.[23] It is sometimes said that some problems are too petty, or flimsy, for judicial interference: *de minimis non curat praetor*. A comparative study of the boundary line between law and politics may show that there are also problems which are too large for the courts. Issues such as the Vietnam War, participation in military operations in former Yougoslavia, nuclear testing in the Pacific and the choice for or against nuclear energy go beyond the scope of a court of justice. To that extent, the political question doctrine remains alive as long as representative bodies have to co-exist with an independent judiciary.

5.2. The counter-majoritarian difficulty

The expression 'counter-majoritarian [or anti-majoritarian] difficulty') was coined in the American literature. It refers to the question of how far the result of judicial decision-making can be removed from what a clear majority of the population thinks right.

This problem occurs in particular in systems that have judicial review of legislation. In Great Britain, a line of case law considered to depart too much from popular feeling can be corrected by Act of Parliament; in the United States or Germany, such a correction is not possible if the controversial case law is founded on the courts' interpretation of the constitution. Changing the constitution for that purpose is not a realistic option because of the

---

[22] See BVerfGE 66 no. 3, *Mittelstreckenraketen*, 1983. See also R. Ergec, 'Le contrôle juridictionnel de l'administration dans les matières qui se rattachent aux rapports internationaux', *RIDC* (1986) 72.

[23] See, for a historical view, Y. S. Zemach, *Political Questions in the Courts* (Detroit, Mich., 1976).

psychological and legal objections such a change would engender. In politics, efforts to overturn judicial decisions by constitutional change form a somewhat risky strategy: the procedures are cumbersome and protracted,[24] and meanwhile, popular unease or disagreement may have shifted to an entirely different matter.

American literature often considers that judicial review is linked to the Constitution, not to public consent, and that judges should therefore occasionally be 'daring enough to defy popular will'.[25] The compatibility of that view with the requirements of democracy has given rise to different theories. The traditional argument goes back to *Marbury*: it considers that democracy requires first and foremost that the Constitution be respected for the very reason that it expresses the will of the people.[26] This view represents, of course, a very abstract way of looking at the problem: it disregards what 'the people' might actually think at a given moment. A second theory avoids this difficulty: it assumes that experience shows that courts may be quicker than representative bodies in anticipating changes in popular opinion. As one author put it, the roots of judicial decisions 'must already be in the nation'.[27] The desegregation cases are often quoted as proof of this evaluation, but later developments, for example with regard to affirmative action, seem rather to belie the claim. In this view, courts must be equipped with a very sensitive antennae for gauging shifts in popular opinion; but the law of evidence is hardly tailored to this particular task. In a third concept, democracy means that the people share the values embodied in the Constitution, but it does not follow that they will be in favour of all the practical consequences resulting from these values. That is probably a correct picture of how things actually happen, but it leaves the main problem, that of legitimacy, unresolved.

In this debate, some caution regarding political terms may be in order. The notion of 'popular will' is elusive. Most of the time, we don't know what the people, or a majority of them, really think. Opinion polls are notoriously unreliable. The results of a general election will sometimes reveal what

---

[24] See Art. v US Constitution; Art. 79 (German) Basic Law.

[25] Laurence Tribe, *American Constitutional Law* 2nd edn (Mineola, N.Y., 1988), pp. 61–6. See also the thoughtful comments of Alexander Bickel in *The Least Dangerous Branch: The Supreme Court at the Bar of Politics* (Indianapolis, Ind., 1963).

[26] See ch. 3.1.

[27] Cox, *The role of the Supreme Court*, ch. v. See also Eugene W. Rostow, 'The democratic character of judicial review', *Harv.L.Rev.* 66 (1952), 193.

kind of ideas a majority of voters had in mind, but that is not necessarily so. Frequently, elections are more about persons than about ideas. Besides, traditional attitudes based on social, religious or regional backgrounds will have a considerable influence on electoral behaviour. There are also occasions when the voters are chiefly out to show that they are fed up with the current political leadership and just want a change. Consequently, elections do not always indicate what the population is thinking about any particular issue.[28]

One of the assumptions underlying the representative system is, however, that the opinions of the majority in parliament roughly correspond to those of the electorate. It must be presumed, therefore, that recent legislation will normally tally with the feelings of large part of the population. The link with popular feeling is bound to be stronger in case of recent legislation than in case of a judicial decision. Justice Frankfurter used this observation as an argument against judicial activism. In a 1958 dissent, he expressed the opinion that the Constitution 'has not authorized the judges to sit in judgment on the wisdom of what Congress and the Executive Branch do'; that assessment falls to the electorate.[29] The case concerned a man who had lost his citizenship after deserting from the American army in Morocco. Although this desertion lasted less than a day, the applicable statute was merciless; and it was a recent statute. The Supreme Court held that this sanction was disproportionate and violated the Eighth Amendment forbidding 'excessive fines' and 'cruel and unusual punishments'. Frankfurter, dissenting, thought the Court was pronouncing policy on the basis of 'its own notions of what is wise or politic'. Justice Brennan, in his concurring opinion, refuted this argument: proportionality is a legal category, not just a matter of wisdom or prudence.

The debate in Germany is less lively than in the United States. The emphasis on *Rechtsstaatlichkeit* is probably strong enough to overcome possible doubts about the democratic character of judicial review. Moreover, distrust of politics is greater than in the United States, particularly among the educated classes. Doubts about the workableness of democracy, very common in the later Weimar years, survived the catastrophic period 1933–45.[30] The idea that judicial review of legislation has the very purpose of restricting

---

[28] See Charles E. Lindblom, *The Policy Making Process* (Englewood Cliffs, N.J., 1968), chs. 6-7.

[29] *Trop* v. *Dulles*, 356 US 86 (1958).

[30] See William E. Scheuerman, *Carl Schmitt, The End of Law* (Lanham, Md., and Oxford, 1999), ch. 4 and Epilogue to part I.

the realization of popular aims, or rather of keeping it within constitutional bounds, flourished in the first years of the Federal Republic. It helped to determine the attitudes of German lawyers.

There is a second element which colours these attitudes: German legal thinking is much more inclined to embrace natural law concepts than American legal doctrine. In such a concept, law is not just the consequence of what legislative bodies lay down in their enactments. Certain legal principles, particularly those embodying human rights and the fundamental guarantees of the rule of law, have a legal value of their own; they are considered as 'supralegal' (*übergesetzlich*). As a result, they cannot be abolished or modified at the whim of whoever happens to be in power. Political institutions may be so obsessed by their policy options on matters like inflation, public health or asylum seekers that they can occasionally forget or disregard these fundamental requirements. Only the judiciary will then be able to recall the limits that supralegal rules impose on politics; its traditional role is indeed to be the guardian of the rule of law. Natural law concepts are perceptible in the Basic Law itself, for example in the provision that certain constitutional rules cannot be changed at all.[31] In the early years of the Federal Republic, the Bundesverfassungsgericht envisaged the possibility that a certain provision of the Basic Law itself might be unconstitutional (*verfassungswidrig*) because of its neglect of supralegal principles. It would be an error to believe, the Court said, that a constitution-maker can do as he likes. Experience with the Nazi regime in Germany had revealed that legislative bodies may enact statutory injustice (*gesetzliches Unrecht*). In extreme cases, highly improbable in a liberal democracy, constitutional courts should fulfil their specific role by giving priority to justice over positive law.[32] In this philosophy, the counter-majoritarian difficulty has vanished; or rather, it has been pushed over the intellectual horizon.

By comparison, politics reigns supreme in France. However, the debate has a particular twist. The counter-majoritarian difficulty is considered as an area of tension not between the courts and the parliament, but between the courts and political leadership (*le pouvoir*) as represented by the President, or the President and the Prime Minister together. In French politics, the expression *gouvernement des juges* is readily used when a judicial decision does not comply with official policy, and it is intended as a reproach. When, for example, new decentralization measures during the

---

[31] See Art. 79 s.(3) Basic Law.

[32] BVerfGE 3 no. 15, *Prozesskosten im Ehescheidungsverfahren*, 1953.

second term of President Mitterrand included a statute concerning the special position of Corsica, the President addressed some angry words at the Constitutional Council after its declaration that a provision mentioning 'the Corsican people' (*le peuple corse*) was unconstitutional. The court found that the 1958 Constitution assimilated the notion *le peuple* to *le peuple français*, and this people consisted of citizens, not of other peoples.[33] One perhaps needs to know something about French history and French politics before being able to understand the emotion aroused by the approval or disapproval of the word *peuple* for the Corsicans. We should remember, however, that since 1791 republican constitutions have explicitly provided that the French Republic is 'one and indivisible'.[34] Moreover, 'la France' is not just a country, a State and a nation, it is also a kind of political myth, to be revered and admired; an entity – or perhaps a being – the people can identify with. De Gaulle, who knew his Frenchmen well, addressed the citizens at difficult moments (for example, during the revolt of the generals in Algiers) by addressing France: 'Eh bien! Mon vieux et cher pays, nous voici donc ensemble, encore une fois face à une lourde épreuve' (Well, my dear old country, there we are together again, once more facing a heavy trial) – as if he were looking Marianne straight in the eyes.[35] Political leaders symbolize this essential link of the citizens with the French nation much more than any judge could ever do.

Summarizing, we could say that American debates on the counter-majoritarian difficulty do not find a true equivalent in Europe: not in Britain, because the majority can always prevail; not in Germany, because the rule of law is considered as more important than majority rule; not in France, because French opinion (legal opinion included) is reluctant to accept that courts can take decisions which are not in conformity with the politics of the Nation.[36] All this does not make the American debate any less interesting.

5.3. The area of discretion

When looking at the German system of judicial review of legislation, we saw that the federal constitutional court considers that it must leave some

---

[33] CC 9-5-1991, *Statut de la Corse*, *Rec.* 50; *Les grandes décisions* no. 476.

[34] Now Art. 2 Constitution 1958. Already Art. 1 title III Constitution 1791.

[35] See Charles Debbasch and Jean-Marie Pontier, *La société française*, 2nd edn (Paris, 1991), pp. 3–8; Jean Lacouture, *Citations du président de Gaulle* (Paris, 1968), p. 23.

[36] See, generally, Stone, *The birth of judicial politics in France*, chs. 4 and 9.

leeway to political institutions in some situations. Even when bound by constitutional rules or principles, the legislature should have some room to do things in its own way. Thus, courts cannot exercise complete control over how statutes have shaped the principle of equality: within certain margins, legislative bodies have the freedom to mould the form equality will take in a given situation (*Gestaltungsraum*).[37] Similarly, the federal constitutional court considers that some concepts in the Basic Law are primarily intended as a general guideline to be further elaborated by the legislative bodies. Thus, the Court held that the notion of 'social state' (*Sozialstaat*) sets a task for the political institutions but does not describe how this task should be achieved: politics will have to fill in the details.[38] Other solutions, the Court added, would be contrary to the requirements of democracy. In other words, room is left to the political institutions to give, within certain limits, their own definition of the concept of *Sozialstaat*.

That view recalls one of the recurring themes in the case law of the European Court of Human Rights. Although the European Court sometimes curbs actions of national authorities which may affect human rights and fundamental freedoms, it recognises that, in certain areas, these authorities have a 'margin of appreciation' free from judicial interference. In an Austrian case concerning rent control – disputed by property owners as violating their right to peaceful enjoyment of their possessions – the European Court ruled, for example, that the legislature should have 'a wide margin of appreciation, both with regard to the existence of a problem of public concern warranting measures of control and as to the choice of the detailed rules for the implementation of such measures'. That decision is very characteristic of the European Court's views.[39]

These findings raise a somewhat wider question: perhaps there are, more generally, certain subjects or certain issues that courts leave, or should leave, to the care of the legislature, or the government, or public administration, because the problem is typically outside the scope of their judicial tasks and responsibilities. The mere fact that Mr X has been appointed as Home Secretary (or Minister of Justice) seems to imply that it is up to him to decide whether separate prisons should be built for dangerous or violent criminals and, if so, where. He will be accountable to Parliament in a parliamentary

---

[37] See ch. 4.1.   [38] BVerfGE 59 no. 12, *Westdeutsche Rundfunk*, 1982.
[39] ECHR 19-12-1989, *Mellacher v. Austria*, Series A no. 169. See also P. Van Dijk and G. G. H. van Hoof, *Theory and Practice of the European Convention on Human Rights* 3rd edn (The Hague and London, 1998), pp. 82–95.

regime, or to the President under the US Constitution, but the choice is his and cannot be corrected by the courts. To put it differently: the very nature of some problems excludes judicial scrutiny, not because these problems are too political for the courts to handle, but simply because the courts do not exist in order to solve them. It is not difficult to find literature on this general question, but it usually concerns administrative law: to what extent is the administration free to act according to its own views, without being exposed to the possibility of judicial correction?[40] Once the observer has identified this question as a separate problem, he will find it back in most legal systems. Nevertheless, it is hard to find a theory which will help the courts to apply the correct criteria. More often than not, legal literature follows the courts' case law, rather than guiding it. German literature has, however, elaborated a theoretical framework, the theory of *Ermessen* (discretion). I shall try to explain this on the basis of relevant books and articles.

A pure example of *Ermessen* is the situation in which statutory provisions stipulate that an administrative body 'can' do something, without laying down any standard or guideline for the use of this power. Thus, a statute may provide that the Minister of Economic Affairs 'can' decide to grant subsidies to the ship-building industry, without any further provision as to when such subsidies would be appropriate.[41] In a second category of cases, the statute fixes some standards, but puts the assessment of them entirely in the hands of the public authorities. The mayor of a city may, for example, forbid a demonstration if it could, in his view, present a danger to public safety. In a third category, the statutes are completely silent. A town council decides to have a sculpture erected in honour of a once famous local pop-group, but a number of citizens prefer one in honour of Mozart, who passed two nights in the local inn in 1793. The main legal question is then if, and to what extent, the dissatisfied ship-builder, action group or Mozart lover can challenge the decision before the courts.[42]

German theory provides a coherent answer to this question. The court will first have to determine whether the contested decision is truly within the area of discretion. A discretionary power is not recognised for the sole reason that the applicable statute uses indeterminate concepts which need

---

[40] See, generally, Schwarze, *European Administrative Law*, ch. 3-3-1 (in particular: I, II and IV).

[41] It is a somewhat outdated example, as the matter is presently covered, in Europe, by EC regulation 1540/98, establishing new rules on aid to ship-building (*Official Journal* L no. 202/1).

[42] See Ernst Forsthoff, *Lehrbuch des Verwaltungsrechts*, vol. I, *Allgemeiner Teil*, 10th edn (Munich, 1973), par. 5.

further clarification or interpretation before they can be applied; there is room for different concepts in such a case, but the choice is not necessarily left to the administration. If, for example, such an open concept requires an 'evaluative judgment' (*wertende Beurteilung*), the administrative practice is submitted to judicial review. Notions like 'reasonable care' or 'acting fairly' illustrate the point; their interpretation ultimately falls within the competence of the courts. Judicial review is also possible if the authority believed that it was acting within the scope of its discretion but, according to the courts, it was not. If the authority goes beyond the limits of its discretion (*Ermessensüberschreitung*), the decision is reviewable.[43] The classic example is the case where a body such as a county or city council is free to issue, or not, a licence to pursue certain otherwise forbidden activities, for example, to discharge industrial waste into an important waterway, but the courts consider that this does not imply the freedom to impose a financial contribution on the licensee. If the decision remains within the limits of administrative discretion, the court still has two tasks to fulfil. The first is to check whether formal requirements have been respected: there may, for example, be rules on the written form of the decision, or on the duty to proceed to certain consultations, or on time-limits. The second task concerns the substance of the decision. There is room for judicial intervention if the administration has misused its discretionary powers (*Ermessensmissbrauch*). That is particularly the case if these powers have been used for a purpose which is foreign to the aims of the statutory provision on which the powers are based.[44] Such a situation occurs, for example, when local authorities change traffic regulations in the inner city in order to compel a polluting factory to relocate its activities, or cut off the water supply to certain buildings in order to get rid of squatters. Administrative powers are then deflected from the purpose for which they have been granted and that must be considered as illegal by the courts.[45]

There is an infinite variety of situations administrative decisions will have to deal with, and the intensity of judicial control will vary accordingly. The theory of *Ermessen* provides, however, an analytical framework which allows for these variations. It is perhaps for that reason that it also helps

---

[43] See, on terminology, Howard A. Fisher, *The German Legal System and Legal Language*, 2nd edn (London and Sidney, 1999), p. 130.

[44] See Hartmut Maurer, *Allgemeines Verwaltungsrecht*, 12th edn (Munich, 1999), par. 7.

[45] The expression 'misuse of powers' is used in this sense in Art. 230 EC Treaty (ex 173). See case 78/74, *Deuka* [1975] ECR 421.

to understand developments in other countries apart from Germany. In the case law of the French Conseil d'Etat, no general view comparable to the theory of *Ermessen* can be discovered. Nevertheless, the court usually leaves certain assessments entirely to the administration, or submits them only to a light form of supervision. For example, it has developed the view that the administrative courts should respect 'technical' judgments made by the administration. Thus, the question whether materials used for manufacturing a hair lotion were poisonous, or the judgment that a certain Bordeaux wine merits an *appellation contrôlée*, are left entirely to the wisdom of the decision-makers.[46] As in German theory, however, the vague or open character of notions used in the applicable legislation does not secure decisions against judicial review. Normally, the courts will examine whether the facts on which the decision is founded have been correctly established and, moreover, whether these facts can be considered as covered by the vague notion in question. Thus, the court will itself determine whether certain press publications present a 'danger for young people', or whether it is 'absolutely urgent' to expel immediately a certain foreigner.[47] Even in sensitive areas such as public security, the Conseil d'Etat relies on its own definitions and interpretations.

The Conseil d'Etat recognises, however, that there are areas of discretion where the applicable legislation gives the administration complete freedom: it can decide or refrain from deciding, and if it decides, it can freely choose between different solutions. As one commentator put it, the law sometimes leaves freedom of decision, of action and of judgment; that characterizes true discretionary powers.[48] Gradually, however, the Conseil d'Etat started to bring these powers under a certain form of judicial control. In cases where the statute only said that the Secretary of State 'can' refuse to issue a passport, or 'can' admit certain students to a competitive examination, the court found it had to annul decisions when they violated general principles of law. In a 1954 case, five students had been refused admission to an important examination for entry to the Ecole Nationale d'Administration on the ground (they believed, on the basis of rumours circulating in Paris) that they were communists; the Secretary of State argued that he had simply exercised the complete discretion given him by the applicable statute. The

---

[46] CE 27-4-1951, *Société Toni, Rec.* 236; CE 14-10-1960, *Syndicat agricole et viticole de Lalande-de-Pomerol, Rec.* 529.

[47] CE 5-12-1956, *Thibault, Rec.* 463; CE 13-11-1985, *Lujna Gorostiola, Rec.* 325.

[48] Braibant and Stirn, *Le droit administratif français*, p. 238.

Conseil d'Etat, though recognising that the Secretary of State could take account of evidence of the unsuitability of candidates for public service, held that the refusal to admit the students could not be based exclusively on their political opinions, because that would violate the general principle of equal access of all Frenchmen to public functions; therefore, the Secretary of State had to show that there were other reasons for his decision.[49]

A second step followed when the Conseil d'Etat ruled that the administration's freedom of appreciation could not be unlimited. In particular, administrative courts are required to examine whether the decision is based on a manifest error of judgment ('erreur manifeste d'appréciation'). The intensity of this form of judicial supervision varies according to the kind of decision which is at issue; it is, however, always slight, and there are cases where the courts forgo any form of control. The Conseil d'Etat refused to examine the merits of candidates for a decoration, even when it was alleged that the minister's error of judgment had been manifest. In most cases, however, that minimal control is exercised.[50]

A gradual extension of judicial control over the exercise of discretionary powers can also be found in the common law countries. Initially, the courts adhered to the view that they should abstain, because the way discretion was used could be more adequately supervised by the representative bodies. In England, this tendency was more perceptible than in the United States.[51] Very slowly, the general philosophy of the judges seemed to change. First, they started to monitor procedural elements, considering that procedure was not within the area of discretion. Secondly, courts started to fix the limits of the area of discretion, with the result that decisions going beyond these limits were *ultra vires* and therefore void. Finally, a serious error of judgment was considered as a sufficient ground for judicial interference. The US Supreme Court summarized its attitude in a 1971 judgment. The case concerned the construction of an interstate highway which had to cross a public park in Memphis, Tennessee. Lower courts had refused to examine the complaint of a citizens' association that the administration, though free to trace the route of the highway, could not base its judgment on incorrect findings of fact. The courts, said the Supreme Court, would have to verify whether the necessary procedural requirements had been

---

[49] CE 28-5-1954, *Barel*, *Rec.* 308; also in *Les grands arrêts* no. 86.
[50] Example: CE 2-11-1973, *Librairie François Maspero*, *Rec.* 611; also in *Les grands arrêts* no. 104.
[51] See Cane, *Introduction to Administrative Law*, ch. 7.

followed, whether the decision-making body was acting within the scope of its authority, whether it had actually considered the relevant facts and whether its decision suffered from 'a clear error of judgment'.[52]

English legal history illustrates the difficulties courts experience when faced with discretionary powers. There are some old decisions, some of them dating back to Elizabethan times (late sixteenth century), holding that however extensive the powers granted to public authorities, this cannot justify an unreasonable exercise of those powers. When interpreting the enabling provisions of Acts of Parliament, courts would state that Parliament could never have intended to allow public authorities to act unreasonably. For a long time, it was not entirely clear how to apply this standard. At first, courts hesitated to adopt it if the public body in question had unlimited discretion. And secondly, it was not clear how the reasonableness test should be construed: should judges substitute their view as to what was reasonable in a given situation for the view of a minister, a city council, or the board of a nationalized industry? In 1948, the Court of Appeal gave a somewhat restricted scope to the reasonableness test: in the *Wednesbury* case it decided that 'unreasonableness' could only be established if 'the Court considers it a decision that no reasonable body could have come to'.[53] Lord Greene, Master of the Rolls, explained that 'there may be something so absurd that no sensible person could ever dream that it lay within the powers of the authority'.

Since then, this test of '*Wednesbury* unreasonableness' has become a ground of review in its own right. It is no longer necessary to attack the decision indirectly, by alleging that the enabling clauses of a statute cannot be taken to permit an unreasonable exercise of powers: the unreasonableness test stands on its own feet. As a general ground of review, it retains, however, the narrow meaning ascribed to it by the Court of Appeal.[54] Narrow though it is, however, it leaves room for differences of opinion. In a 1986 House of Lords judgment, the issue was whether doctors employed by an area health authority could lawfully give contraceptive advice or treatment to a girl under sixteen years of age without the consent of her parents. The court considered that prevailing social attitudes were marked by a great divide. 'Some doctors approve and some doctors disapprove of the idea that a

---

[52] *Citizens to preserve Overton Park* v. *Volpe*, 401 US 402 (1971). See also Martin Shapiro, 'Administrative discretion: the next stage', *The Yale Law Journal* 92 (1983), 1487.

[53] *Associated Provincial Picture Houses Ltd.* v. *Wednesbury* [1948] 1 KB 233.

[54] See G. L. Peiris, 'Wednesbury unreasonableness: the expanding canvas', *CLJ* 46 (1987), 53.

doctor may decide to provide contraception for a girl under sixteen without the knowledge of the parents. Some parents agree and some parents disagree with the proposition that the decision must depend on the judgment of the doctor.'[55] Under those circumstances there could be no *Wednesbury* unreasonableness, said the court; but one of the law lords disagreed.

A second limit to the exercise of discretionary powers exists when the enabling clause uses broad and indefinite terms and so leaves room for judicial interpretation. The question whether a certain lay-out of the landscape could be considered as a 'park' in the sense of the applicable statute was fully reviewed by the court.[56] Like the French administrative courts, English courts determine the meaning of a legal characterization by deciding if certain facts are covered by it or not. The discretion stops where legal interpretation starts.

For judicial control of unlimited discretion, new standards have been developed since the late 1960s and early 1970s. After the end of the Second World War, more and more wide administrative powers had been established, in particular under welfare state legislation. That situation led to increasing recourse to the courts, as it became apparent that political control by the representative bodies was not always effective; this was most notably the case when a great many decisions had to be taken every day, for example, in social security matters. As Lord Woolf put it in a recent essay, there is more reason for judicial assertiveness when the other checks on government are not operating as effectively as they usually do.[57] The new developments have encouraged a redefinition of the applicable standards in a way which seems familiar to the student of comparative law.

The first sign of a changing view on matters of discretion appeared in 1968 when the House of Lords quashed a ministerial decision which was entirely based on full discretion. The applicable statute provided that complaints by milk producers about the actions of the Milk Marketing Board had to be referred to a committee of investigation 'if the Minister in any case so directs'. The court held, however, that real complaints should be examined and that the 'permissive language' of the statute did not imply that the minister's discretion to refuse investigation was unfettered. The minister should act lawfully, 'and that is a matter to be determined by looking at the Act and

---

[55] *Gillick* v. *West Norfolk and Wisbech Area Health Authority* [1986] AC 112.

[56] *White and Collins* v. *Minister of Health* [1939] 2 KB 838.

[57] Harry Woolf, 'Judicial review – the tension between the executive and the judiciary', *LQR* 114 (1998), 591.

its scope and object in conferring a discretion upon the Minister'.[58] The court feels free, therefore, to define the purpose of the statute in question; discretionary powers do not authorize the executive bodies to disregard, as the Court of Appeal once put it, 'the policy of Parliament'.[59]

Further inroads into discretionary powers were made by cases where decisions given under such powers might lead to a restriction to the exercise of a human right or fundamental freedom. The courts will then examine whether such a restriction is justified by an 'important competing public interest'. Wide discretionary powers granted to the government under the Broadcasting Act 1981, used to prevent the broadcasting of statements by representatives of organizations prohibited under the Prevention of Terrorism Act (particularly the IRA), could not mean that the courts were 'powerless to prevent the exercise by the executive of administrative discretion... in a way which infringes fundamental human rights'. That would even be the case when such discretion had been conferred 'in terms which are on their face unlimited'.[60] It is not clear, however, how far the courts are willing to proceed on this road towards greater judicial interference. The right to life can certainly be considered as a human right, but the courts are nevertheless very reluctant to decide claims about what priorities health authorities are to observe with regard to terminally ill patients. In one such sad case, the Court of Appeal quite openly said that health authorities had to make 'difficult and agonizing judgments' when allocating a limited budget to the maximum advantage of their patients, and that this was 'not a judgment which the court can make'.[61]

In a third category of cases, the courts insist that the administrative body must state the reasons for its decisions even when the statute confers unlimited discretion. If it is alleged, for example, that the administration has misused its powers, or acted beyond the limits of its discretion, the court should be in a position to examine such an allegation; and it can only properly do so when it is told what the reasons for the decision have been.[62] This line of case law tallies with the general tendency of English

---

58 *Padfield v. Minister of Agriculture, Fisheries and Food* [1968] AC 997.
59 *Laker Airways Ltd. v. Department of Trade* [1977] QB 643. See also *R v. Tower Hamlets LBC ex p Chetnic Developments Ltd.* [1988] AC 858.
60 *R v. Secretary of State for the Home Department* ex p *Brind* [1991] 1 All ER 720.
61 *R v. Cambridge District Health Authority* ex p *B* [1995] FLR 1055.
62 *AG v. Ryan* [1980] AC 718; *R v. Secretary of State for the Home Department* ex p *Fayed* [1997] 1 All ER 228.

courts to subject procedural requirements to full review. More generally, we can conclude that nowadays the courts can examine both the substance of discretionary decisions and the procedure under which they have been made; but while review of procedural elements tends to develop into full review, the courts' scrutiny of substantive elements is very much influenced by the character of the decision and the nature of the arguments against it. There is, perhaps, more pragmatism in this particular area of the law than anywhere else.[63]

A final question is whether the study of the area of discretion actually helps in understanding problems of judicial review of legislation. My 'yes' to this question is based on three considerations. First, discretionary powers raise general issues. It may be true that they are more conspicuous in the field of administrative law; but they arise wherever judicial control extends to what public authorities have decided. Secondly, developments in European Community law show how administrative law techniques can be used to solve questions of constitutional and international law. In cases on economic law, the EC Court of Justice uses the same reasoning in its scrutiny of regulations and of individual decisions.[64] Thirdly, study of constitutional cases often reminds the comparative lawyer of standards developed in administrative law. When constitutional courts, or the US Supreme Court, leave matters of economic legislation largely to the political institutions, but exercise a strict scrutiny over legislation on the rights of prisoners, aliens, women or workers, the theory of discretion, or the practice of administrative courts with regard to the use of discretionary powers, may help to explain those differences.

5.4. Methods of interpretation

Cases where the terms of a statute represent a straightforward violation of the constitution are relatively rare. Judicial review of legislation often concerns situations where a particular application of a statute might lead to an infringement of constitutional provisions, for example, on protection of human rights and fundamental freedoms. That situation may occur with regard to legislation on matters of public security, such as anti-terrorism laws or statutes on the powers of the police. Constitutional courts will

---

[63] See also Wade and Forsyth, *Administrative Law*, chs. 11-12.
[64] Case 114/76, *Bela-Mühle* [1977] ECR 1211; case C-350/88, *Delacre* [1990] ECR I-395.

then have to make a choice: either the possibility of an unconstitutional application means that the statute itself, which opens this possibility, is incompatible with the constitution; or the court considers that the statute is to be interpreted in such a way that it is compatible with the constitution, so that the possibility of an unconstitutional application cannot be recognised and should therefore be disregarded.

In Germany, the federal constitutional court tends to opt for the second alternative. In a very early case, it held that a possible misuse of certain provisions of a statute could not justify a judgment of unconstitutionality. The court explained that the persons or institutions responsible for the implementation of these provisions had to apply the statute 'loyally' and 'within the limits of reasonableness' ('in vernünftigen Grenzen').[65] In other words, for every piece of legislation it is assumed that its implementation agrees with the provisions of the Basic Law. In its later case law, the constitutional court developed a method of interpretation known as *verfassungskonforme Auslegung* (interpretation in agreement with the constitution). The expression has been poetically translated as 'constitutionally faithful interpretation',[66] but somehow this does not sound like a legal expression in English. Under whatever designation, the concept is a persistent element in the case law of the German courts.

There has been a parallel development in American case law, but it seems to have slowly vanished from constitutional usage in the United States. In a 1936 case, Justice Brandeis – one of the great reformers in the American judiciary – formulated seven 'rules' the Supreme Court should adopt when examining the constitutionality of legislation (the '*Ashwander* rules').[67] The first rule asked the Court to resist appeals against political decisions; persons or groups defeated in the legislature should not be able to transfer their battle to the courts under the guise of an inquiry into the constitutionality of the legislative act. I quote rule 7 in full:

(7) When the validity of an Act of Congress is drawn in question, and even if serious doubt of constitutionality is raised, it is a cardinal principle that this Court will first ascertain whether a construction of the statute is fairly possible by which the question may be avoided.

---

[65] BVerfGE 1 no. 27, *Parlementarische Geschäftsordnung*, 1952.
[66] See Schwarze, *European Administrative Law*, pp. 690–1.
[67] Justice Brandeis, concurring, in *Ashwander v. TVA*, 297 US 288 (1936).

This 'cardinal principle' looks very much like the (later) German doctrine of *verfassungskonforme Auslegung*. It has often been quoted and discussed in American legal literature, but it has never explicitly been adopted by the Supreme Court.

In the 1960s and 1970s, when the Supreme Court began to emphasize the importance of civil liberties, even in politically sensitive areas,[68] the idea of interpretation in conformity with the Constitution was abandoned. If several applications of a statute are possible, and some of them would violate constitutionally protected rights, the Court considered that the statute was 'overbroad' and therefore unconstitutional. In a 1964 case Justice Harlan, speaking for the Court, said that even legitimate aims which the legislature had in mind when formulating rules of conduct 'may not be achieved by means which sweep unnecessarily broadly and thereby invade the area of protected freedom'.[69] This concept of 'overbroadness' (or 'overbreadth') has since become an important standard for the Court's scrutiny of the constitutionality of state or federal legislation. It applies in particular if the aim of the statute could also have been achieved by narrower provisions. When a man had been convicted of contravening a Georgia statute prohibiting 'opprobrious words or abusive language' tending to cause a breach of the peace (he had shouted 'white son of a bitch' to a policeman in a scuffle), the Court held that the statute violated the First Amendment: to prevent a breach of the peace, it was not necessary to put the prohibition in terms broad enough to suppress the people's right to show their opinions.[70] That is a far cry from the seventh *Ashwander* rule.

In the culture of debate which characterizes the US Supreme Court's decision-making process, it is rare to find the Court adhering to any hard and fast rule on interpretation. The attitudes of individual justices depend very much on the subject matter and the kind of discussion they have lately been involved in. A good example can be found in the Court's case law on the rights of American citizens to travel abroad. In a first case, the administation refused to issue a passport to a person who had failed to swear that he was not and had never been a communist, as required by State Department regulations at the time. In its majority opinion, the Court said 'we do not reach the question of constitutionality', as it found a narrower ground for

---

[68] See ch. 3.3.   [69] *NAACP* v. *Alabama*, ex rel. *Flowers*, 377 US 288 (1964).
[70] *Gooding* v. *Wilson*, 405 US 518 (1972).

granting relief to the challenger (no valid delegation of powers). However, Justice Douglas, delivering the majority opinion, went out of his way to emphasize that American citizens had a right to travel, a right which was part of the 'liberty' they could not be deprived of without due process of law.[71] In a later case, the Court seemed to rely squarely on the citizens' right to travel abroad as if the earlier case had been decided on that ground. The protection of such a right was, however, short-lived: since the 1980s, the Court has accepted prohibitions on travel to Cuba, even when they are not supported by Congressional authorization.[72] Ultimately, the question of constitutionality seems to have been settled by implication.

A very strict way of imposing an interpretation of statutes which is in conformity with the Constitution has been developed by the French Constitutional Council. When a bill is referred to it for a declaration of conformity with the Constitution,[73] it sometimes gives such a declaration in a half-hearted kind of way: it rules that the bill will be in conformity with the Constitution if it is interpreted in the way the Council indicates (*conformité sous réserve*). In 1984 the Council had to examine the constitutionality of a very controversial bill concerning mergers of publishing firms. The bill introduced a special competition regime for the publishing world and it was, according to its opponents, aimed at a great publishing house whose newspapers were continually harassing the then governing socialists. The constitutional issue was whether this specific piece of competition law violated the freedom of the press, and the answer of the Constitutional Council was essentially that it could only avoid unconstitutional consequences if certain strict conditions were met.[74] Two years later, this approach was further developed: a bill on the electoral system, which empowered the government to set, by decree, the exact boundaries between the constituencies, was declared in conformity with the Constitution, 'under the strict reservations of interpretation' formulated in the judgment. In fact, the Council told the government exactly how it should use its powers.[75] By adopting this stratagem, the Constitutional Council may have been able to limit the number of cases in which it has to refuse a declaration of conformity; but

---

[71] *Kent v. Dulles*, 357 US 116 (1958). The due process clause Justice Douglas referred to is part of the Fifth Amendment.

[72] Respectively: *Aptheker v. Secretary of State*, 378 US 500 (1964); *Regan v. Wald*, 468 US 222 (1984).

[73] See ch. 4.2.

[74] CC 11-10-1984, *Entreprises de presse*, Rec. 73; also in *Les grandes décisions* no. 38.

[75] CC 2-7-1986, *Découpage électoral*, Rec. 78; also in *Les grandes décisions* no. 42-1.

there is little doubt that it has also been treading somewhat heavily on ground hitherto allotted to the political institutions. The Council's method of imposing its interpretation on the future application of the statute did not, however, give rise to substantial objections among French lawyers or in French public opinion.[76]

A comparison between *verfassungskonforme Auslegung*, the *Ashwander* rules and *conformité sous réserve* illustrates that courts have been looking for concepts and methods permitting them to limit the number of rulings on unconstitutionality. The reasons for this are not always evident. It is true that constitutional provisions use open and indeterminate notions, such as 'due process of law', much more frequently than do ordinary statutes or the provisions of Civil and Commercial Codes do; and in the United States, the advanced age of the Constitution aggravates the difficulty. As Justice Jackson once complained: 'Just what our forefathers did envision, or would have envisioned had they foreseen modern conditions, must be divined from materials as enigmatic as the dreams Joseph was called upon to interpret for Pharaoh.'[77] Meanings ascribed to expressions, or even to words, change as society develops. The American Supreme Court once referred to 'the evolving standards of decency that mark the progress of a maturing society'.[78] That is well said; but the problem is, of course, that legislative bodies may have their own opinion on the way standards of decency have evolved, and this idea does not necessarily coincide with that of the judges. In systems based on judicial review of legislation, the courts are the ultimate interpreters of the Constitution; but representative bodies can perhaps claim that they are the ultimate interpreters of the evolution of standards of decency in society. In a democracy, that contradiction cannot easily be resolved. Awareness of it may help, though, to suggest prudence to the main actors.

Judicial prudence may also be in order because the ordinary methods of interpretation, commonly used for determining the meaning of legal provisions in statutes or codes, are not always applicable to constitutional rules or principles. Legislative history may, for example, help to interpret an article of the new Dutch Civil Code; the history of a provision of the US

---

[76] See *Le Monde*, 20 November 1986 (Kajman); *Le Figaro*, 17 and 19 November 1986 (Favoreu). A detailed analysis is given by Thierry di Manno, *Le juge constitutionnel et la technique des décisions interprétatives en France et en Italie* (Paris, 1997).

[77] Justice Jackson, concurring, in *Youngstown Sheet and Tube Co.* v. *Sawyer*, 343 US 579 (1952).

[78] *Rhodes* v. *Chapman*, 452 US 337 (1981).

Constitution, if it can be traced at all, doesn't really help to understand the present meaning of the rule. As Professor Tribe recently said, a construction of what the framers of the US Constitution had in mind can yield little more than 'a faded snapshot of a bygone age'.[79] Similarly, the search for the system underlying individual legal provisions will be rewarding when the meaning of Civil Code rules on transfer of ownership has to be established, linked as these rules are to the property regime in general and its relationship to the law of obligations. The due process clause and the guarantee clause of the American Constitution cannot be explained on such a basis.

Interpreting constitutional texts and interpreting ordinary statute law are, therefore, different intellectual operations.[80] The traditional methods of interpretation discussed in legal literature do not always apply in constitutional matters. That does not necessarily mean that constitutional interpretation is more difficult. Many concepts used in constitutions or in constitutional debates go back to very old traditions and have been discussed for centuries. The couple 'rule of law' and *Rechtsstaat* provides a perfect illustration. Both concepts may be open-ended, but the hard core of their purport is determined by legal tradition, as witnessed by an ample literature in the fields of philosophy, law and politics, as well as by a long series of judicial decisions. The real problem, which does not exist to the same degree for concepts such as patent or bankruptcy or mortgage, is the direction of legal evolution.

From that point of view, the American debate is very characteristic. Equal protection simply cannot retain the same meaning after the abolition of slavery and after the massive waves of immigration that brought people from all over the world to the United States. As the European Court of Human Rights once explicitly said, in a case concerning the legal position of illegitimate children, human rights 'must be interpreted in the light of present-day conditions', with the result that distinctions once regarded as permissible and normal in many countries must now be considered as discriminatory.[81] This is very much the attitude adopted in the US Supreme Court's case law on equal protection. That is indeed one of the concepts

---

[79] Laurence H. Tribe, in Antonin Scalia, *A Matter of Interpretation – Federal Courts and the Law* (Princeton, N.J., 1997), p. 81.

[80] In a different sense (but as part of the 'activism debate' in the USA): Scalia, *A Matter of Interpretation*, pp. 37–44.

[81] ECHR 13-6-1979, *Marckx*, Series A vol. 31.

which has areas of penumbra around its hard-core meaning; sometimes different courses are open. The question who is to choose a new line of development presents an uncomfortable problem: new ideas may develop in society; governments or parliaments may want to break new ground; courts will try to slowly develop their case law. These three elements of legal evolution do not always take the same path.[82] And courts are not always able to impose their interpretations on an unwilling society.

That can help to explain the modesty which occasionally characterizes judicial attitudes in constitutional matters.

5.5. Preserving democracy

Courts do not exist in order to sustain democracy. In a sense, there is even a contradiction between the concepts of democracy and the rule of law: the former is based on majority rule, the latter on protection of the individual. From an analytical point of view this is not the same thing; majorities are perfectly able to oppress individual citizens.

Historical evidence suggests, however, that democracy goes hand in hand with the rule of law; where one of the two disappears, the other is in danger of being abandoned. The reason is probably that majority rule, in the democratic sense of the word, implies that different political opinions can compete for the voters' favour. Every opinion must have a chance to become more generally accepted, so that the minority of today can be the majority of tomorrow. Freedom of expression and protection of minority feelings are part of the prerequisites of democratic government.[83] Conversely, authoritarian rulers will normally start their reign by silencing political opponents and trying to control public opinion. Empirically speaking, democracy and the rule of law cannot be dissociated.

Under these conditions, there must also be a link between the evolution of case law and the development of democratic institutions. We have already seen some instances of this correlation. The US Supreme Court once made a kind of policy declaration, in the 'Carolene Products footnote', which called for a more assertive judicial attitude in cases where the ordinary political

---

[82] See Wolfgang Friedmann, *Law in a Changing Society*, 2nd edn (Harmondsworth, 1972), ch. 15-16.
[83] See Robert A. Dahl, *On democracy* (New Haven, Conn., and London, 1998), ch. 5.

processes were menaced or failed to work well.[84] In a somewhat similar way, the interpretation of the doctrine of political question, or of discretionary powers, is often inspired by considerations concerning the role of political decision-making in a system of representative government.[85]

Political developments in Britain show this correlation quite clearly: failure of democratic processes to work efficiently has led to a growth of judicial interference. Majority rule in a two-party system like the British one means that the parliamentary majority, i.e. the majority party in the House of Commons, controls legislation; very often, however, this majority itself is tightly controlled by its political leadership. Recent political leaders of importance, like Thatcher or Blair, have acted like generals commanding their troops. That affects the accountability of cabinet ministers to Parliament. Members of Parliament who belong to the majority party, but who are not themselves part of the government ('back-benchers'), can always put questions, raise issues or attack government practices during parliamentary debates and question time; but as soon as the position of the government is threatened, or that of any of its members still in favour with the Prime Minister, the British practice of party discipline will prevail. Members of Parliament need the support of their party if they want to get re-elected; and the 'whips', who secure party discipline in the House of Commons, know that they do. In the English literature it is taken for granted that the Prime Minister can rely on his parliamentary majority as long as there are no major splits in the cabinet.[86] The cohesion of the majority party necessarily reduces the role of ministerial accountability as a check on government. As a result, dissatisfied citizens turn to the courts instead of writing to their MPs.

A second reduction of the role of ministerial accountability is due to the scattering of former departmental responsibilities over different more or less autonomous agencies. Efforts directed at 'decentralizing' and 'debureaucratizing' the Westminister administration have actually led to a thick forest of offices, services and agencies.[87] That means, however, that the

---

[84] *United States* v. *Carolene Products Co.*, 304 US 144 (1938); see ch. 3.4.

[85] See ch. 5.1 and 5.3.

[86] See Simon James, *British Cabinet Government*, 2nd edn (London and New York, 1999), ch. 4; James Barber, *The Prime Minister since 1945* (Oxford, 1991), ch. 6.

[87] See Gavin Drewry, 'The new public management', in Jowell and Oliver (eds.), *The Changing Constitution*, ch. 7; John F. McEldowney, *Public Law*, 2nd edn (London, 1998), chs. 10 and 13.

boundary lines of ministerial responsibility are often blurred. Supervision will then be entrusted to the Audit Office or the courts, rather than to members of Parliament or parliamentary committees. Judicial forms of supervision seem to prosper as political supervision becomes less effective.[88] It is, perhaps, not mere coincidence that the introduction of a general remedy for judicial review of administrative action in English law, in 1977, occurred at the very moment when ministerial accountability was beginning to show signs of wear.[89]

British experience shows, therefore, that there is a complex relationship between the representative system and the administration of justice. It has a dialectics of its own. The result may be that things will never get completely settled. New developments, or ongoing processes of change, in one area will have consequences in other areas. The boundary lines between the activities of courts and political institutions will vary accordingly.

This finding raises a somewhat different question: does a similar correlation between courts and politics exist when the people do not act through their elected representatives but directly, i.e. by means of a referendum? In constitutional systems founded on the sovereignty of the people the answer must surely be no: when the people itself has expressed its opinion, there is little more a court can do. That statement indeed represents the legal situation in France but, oddly enough, not in the United States.

In France, the Constitution states that national sovereignty belongs to the people, who exercises it through their representatives or by referendum.[90] In 1962, the Constitutional Council ruled that it had no power to examine the constitutionality of measures adopted by referendum. The decision concerned a case in which the President of the Republic submitted a proposal to change the Constitution (instituting direct election of the President) directly to a referendum.[91] The difficulty was that the Constitution itself fixed two ways of changing constitutional provisions, one by a joint session of the houses of parliament and one by referendum, but only after parliamentary

[88] See Mike Radford, 'Mitigating the democratic deficit? Judicial review and ministerial accountability', in Peter Leyland and Terry Woods (eds.), *Administrative Law Facing the Future* (London, 1997), p. 40. See also Lord Woolf's article on this point (quoted note 57).

[89] The remedy is now laid down in Supreme Court Act 1981, s.31. See, on the declining role of ministerial responsibility, Lord Denning, MR, in *Gouriet v. Union of Post Office Workers* [1977] QB 729.

[90] Art. 3 Constitution 1958.

[91] CC 6-11-1962, *Loi référendaire, Rec.* 27; also in *Les grandes décisions* no. 14.

approval of the proposed modification, which had not been obtained in the 1962 case. The President's advisers thought, however, that a constitution adopted by referendum could also be modified by referendum. Whatever the rights and wrongs of that argument, the Constitutional Council refused to examine the problem, and the French literature accepted, albeit grudgingly, the validity of the new constitutional provisions.[92]

The American attitude is different: the courts examine the compatibility of acts adopted by referendum with the US Constitution. Already in 1868, the US Supreme Court ruled that secession of a state from the Union was contrary to the Constitution, even if that secession had been decided by referendum.[93] One should be aware, of course, that this judgment took place immediately after the end of the Civil War, in which the secession of the Southern states had been subdued by force of arms. Almost a century later, the Supreme Court ruled that a California referendum could not make changes to the state constitution which violated the equal protection clause of the federal Constitution. The proposal submitted to referendum concerned the freedom of California citizens to sell property to persons of their choice. The court considered that this proposal 'was intended to authorize, and did authorize, racial discrimination in the housing market'.[94] The state legislature had passed anti-discrimination statutes barring racially restrictive covenants in real estate transactions, and this legislation was opposed by many property owners, who organized a movement to change the state constitution by referendum. Even so, it appeared that they could not circumvent the constitutional barriers.

In both cases, the referendum touched upon an extremely sensitive area of American public life. Later case law confirms, however, that the two cases express the present state of American constitutional law. In a case involving the organization of referendums in a city in Ohio, the Court held that there could be no unconstitutional 'delegation' of legislative power to the people, as the people had 'reserved' the power to deal directly with matters in the state constitution. Nevertheless, the Court examined whether or not a referendum intended to correct zoning decisions in urban planning was contrary to the due process clause of the Fourteenth Amendment.[95]

---

[92] See *RDP* (1962) 931 and 936 (G. Berlia and P. Lampue); *Recueil Dalloz* 1963, p. 399 (L. Hamon).
[93] *Texas* v. *White*, 74 US 700 (1868).
[94] *Reitman* v. *Mulkey*, 387 US 369 (1967).
[95] *City of Eastlake* v. *Forest Enterprises Inc.*, 426 US 668 (1975).

The German situation is less ambiguous. It is true that, according to the Basic Law, all public authority 'emanates from the people' and shall be exercised by the people 'through elections and referendums and by specific legislative, executive and judicial bodies'.[96] Nevertheless, there is no real practice of the referendum at the federal level, and only a very limited use of it by the *Länder*. The Basic Law was not adopted by referendum and it cannot be changed by referendum.[97] It does provide for a compulsory referendum on one particular point: changes of the frontiers between the *Länder* are brought about by federal statute which must be confirmed by referendum.[98] This subject is, however, of no real significance, either politically or legally, in present-day Germany. The *Länder* have sometimes toyed with the idea of organizing a referendum in order to show their opposition to decisions of the federal authorities. This happened in particular with regard to the federal policy on nuclear energy, a subject which occasioned an important rift in public opinion during the late 1970s and early 1980s. The federal constitutional court holds, however, that a referendum organized by one of the *Länder* violates the Basic Law when it concerns matters which are under federal jurisdiction. Institutions of the *Land* cannot legislate on federal matters, said the Court, even if the institution concerned is a popular referendum.[99]

On the basis of this short comparative survey, it would be interesting to speculate about the use of the concepts of 'the people' and 'the sovereignty of the people'. That would, however, take us too far away from our main theme.[100] For the moment, we conclude that there is an area of friction between democracy, representative institutions and popular power on the one hand, and the rule of law and the role of the courts on the other. The boundaries of that area are not always the same in different constitutional systems, and they are subject to change within any given constitutional system. Courts sometimes do, and sometimes don't, recognise the importance of respecting the requirements of democracy in their decisions. On this point, the US Supreme Court has a much more straightforward way of reasoning than its European counterparts. It recognises, as Justice Brennan

---

[96] Art. 20 s.(2) Basic Law.   [97] See, respectively, preamble and Art. 79 s.(1)-(2) Basic Law.

[98] Art. 29 s.(2)-(6) and Art. 118 Basic Law.

[99] BVerfGE 8 no. 14, *Volksbefragung über Atomwaffen*, 1958; BVerfGE 60 no. 14, *Startbahn West*, 1982.

[100] But see Geoffrey I. Benn and Richard S. Peters, *Social Principles and the Democratic State* (London, 1969), esp. ch. 15; Weiler, *The Constitution of Europe*, ch. 8.

once put it, that an interpretation of the Constitution is often 'a statement about the proper role of government in the society which we have shaped for ourselves'[101], and it discusses such a statement quite openly. We know something of American Justices' concept of democracy; we cannot say the same of the concepts of the law lords, or those of the *neuf sages* (nine wise men) of the French Constitutional Council.

[101] Justice Brennan, dissenting, in *Marsh* v. *Chambers*, 463 US 783 (1983).

The legality of administrative action

6.1. The model of separation

From the viewpoint of comparative law, the existence, or absence of judicial review of legislation is certainly an important aspect of the position of the courts vis-à-vis the political institutions. Other elements of the constitutional system, however, may have a comparable impact on the politico-judicial relationship. It is to these other elements that we shall now turn.

I shall first examine judicial review of administrative action. In general, problems of administrative law are less spectacular than those that occasionally emerge in constitutional jurisprudence, but their influence should not be underestimated. First, judicial activities in this field raise some of the same questions as we encountered when looking at judicial control of constitutionality. Here also, a modest and hesitant beginning has progressively led to a more comprehensive review and to a more assertive tone of judgment. The theory and practice of the supervision of discretionary powers has already provided us with some examples.[1] Secondly, administrative decisions are produced on a scale, and in a quantity, which have no parallel in legislation. Most people are more directly affected by the powers of government and its bureaucracy than by formal enactments. Frequently these powers have a direct bearing on the life and happiness of large numbers of citizens, for example administrative decisions concerning social security benefits, or the admission and expulsion of aliens, or granting or refusal of building permission. Moreover, government decisions may also be of paramount importance to society as a whole: involvement in armed conflict and the use of police powers are in the hands of governments rather than parliaments. In most countries, the exercise of those powers is currently subject to a certain form of judicial supervision; but often it took a long time before it was accepted that courts could play a role in such matters.

---

[1] See ch. 5.3.

Resistance to judicial intervention in matters of government and administration was predominantly founded on two entirely different considerations. In some countries, particularly Great Britain, government powers covered practically the whole area of administration, but the correct use of those powers was regarded as the very heart of the debate between government and Parliament. Initially, courts were only inclined to interfere in exceptional cases, such as government actions devoid of any legal basis. In a country like Germany, where the position of the representative bodies was weak during the entire nineteenth century, judicial remedies against administrative action were available. However, some areas of government, such as public order and the police, were considered so much part of the exercise of sovereign powers that any check on it, judicial or otherwise, was excluded. That view was strengthened by the conviction, held by most German authors until quite recently, that the work of the administration was of such a nature that its contents could not be dictated by legislative bodies or by judicial decisions. This independence was based on the idea that the administration was not created simply in order to execute and implement the decisions of the legislature: it also has the task of developing and specifying policies, translating general guidelines into practical action and thus giving shape to the purposes of the State ('Konkretisierung der Staatszwecke').[2] Somehow, judicial intervention did not quite fit into this general picture. The consequence was that attitudes towards judicial protection against administrative action remained ambivalent for a long time.

By a curious irony of history, it was France which first achieved the subjection of government action to judicial control. That subjection, practically completed in the first half of the nineteenth century, was the consequence of legislation which was pursuing exactly the opposite result. In the early years of the French Revolution, legislation was passed to produce a total separation between the courts and the government administration. The new revolutionary governments were very suspicious of the judiciary, which was still manned by the aristocracy at the time. In their view, courts might try to counteract the measures of the revolutionary institutions; therefore, the judiciary should be prevented from 'troubling' the operations of the government administration. In 1790 a statute was adopted providing that

---

[2] See Hans Peters, *Lehrbuch der Verwaltung* (Berlin, 1949), ch. 1-II-2; Walter Jellinek, *Verwaltungsrecht* (Bad Homburg and Berlin, 1966), s.1-III and s. 2-II.

'judicial functions are distinct and will always remain separate from administrative functions'.[3] Henceforth it was to be a criminal offence for judges to take cognizance of administrative acts 'of any kind'. Other statutes of the same period confirmed these prohibitions and regulated the consequences. Citizens could complain about the *incompétence* (lack of jurisdiction) of administrative institutions, but these complaints should be addressed to the King as *chef de l'administration générale*. Problems occasioned by the activities of the administration should be solved within the administration itself.

Thus the French version of the *séparation des pouvoirs* was born.[4] The independence of the administration with regard to the courts was its principal motive. In this concept, administrative actions are performed in the public interest; their operation should therefore not be frustrated by others, courts included. Only when the administration acted in excess of its powers could the King annul the decision, a power later exercised by the republican governments or, in Napoleon's days, by the Emperor. Under Napoleon – when he was still the 'first consul' Bonaparte the new system began to take shape: he established the Conseil d'Etat as the supreme advisory body, which had also the task of drafting decisions on the complaints submitted to the government ('sur les affaires contentieuses').[5] For that purpose, a 'section du contentieux' was set up within the Conseil d'Etat. This 'section', however, dealt with the citizens' complaints as if it were a court: it heard the parties, examined the documents, asked for additional information and formulated a decision based on legal rather than political considerations. Such decisions only had the status of advice to the government, but the Emperor never departed from them and thereby set the trend for future events. By the early nineteenth century, the Conseil d'Etat had developed into an institution which actually settled conflicts between citizens and the administration, and it did so with complete independence. Formally, it could only advise the government to annul or confirm the contested decision, but the advice was always followed in practice.[6] In 1872, when the

---

[3] Loi des 6–24 août 1790, titre 2 art.13.

[4] See, for its historical roots in the *ancien régime*, Alexis de Tocqueville, *L'ancien régime et la révolution* (1856, reprint Paris, 1964), bk. II chs. 4-5.

[5] Arrêté du 5 nivôse an VIII (1799). See also Brown and Bell, *French Administrative Law*, ch. 3.2.

[6] A stylized but somewhat overstated description of this evolution is given by John H. Merryman, 'The French deviation', in *Scintillae iuris, Studi in memoria di Gino Gorla* (Milan, 1994), vol. I, p. 617.

Third Republic had been established, new legislation determining the institutional structure of the Republic laid down that the Conseil d'Etat was to act as an administrative court: it was not part of the judiciary but it was to decide independently whether administrative decisions were to be annulled for *incompétence*.[7]

Later developments extended the jurisdiction of the Conseil d'Etat. In the second half of the nineteenth century, the court began to give a wide interpretation to the concept of *incompétence*. The question whether an administrative body had acted within its powers, said the court, was not merely a matter of looking at the enabling provisions of the applicable statute; the administration could also act in excess of its powers by disregarding procedural requirements (*vice de forme*) or by misusing its powers (*détournement de pouvoir*).[8] Ultimately, other violations of the law were also included in the concept of *incompétence*.[9]

By gradually developing its own case law, the Conseil d'Etat created a general remedy, the *recours pour excès de pouvoir* or *recours en annulation*. Any decision of the administration, government ministers included, can be attacked by any interested citizen or business corporation for *excès de pouvoir*; it makes no difference whether the contested decision is an individual one, or a general decision such as a regulation. The culmination of this development came in 1950, when the Conseil d'Etat ruled that the *recours pour excès de pouvoir* was a general remedy, always available in order to enforce respect for legality. The case concerned concessions for the use of abandoned and uncultivated plots of land, and the applicable statute provided that the granting of such concessions could not be disputed by means of any administrative or judicial remedy. The Conseil d'Etat held, however, that this provision did not exclude the *recours pour excès de pouvoir* before the Conseil d'Etat, 'which can be brought against any administrative decision, even without any legal provision to that effect'.[10] After the Second World War new legislation established a hierarchy of administrative courts, the Conseil d'Etat acting as an appeal court except in certain cases involving, in particular, government regulations, where it still acts as a court of first (and only) instance.[11]

---

[7] See Cappelletti, *The Judicial Process in Comparative Perspective*, ch. 3-1-c.

[8] On this see ch. 5.3.

[9] See Georges Vedel and Pierre Delvolvé, *Droit administratif*, 12th edn (Paris, 1992), part III ch. 5.

[10] CE 17-2-1950, *Dame Lamotte*, *Rec.* 110, *Les grands arrêts* no. 74.

[11] Further details in Brown and Bell, *French Administrative Law*, ch. 3.3.

The model of separation had, therefore, the practical result of subjecting the entire field of administrative action to a control of legality by a body which, though formally part of the administration, acted *de facto* as a court. The judicial character of this control was emphasized when the administrative courts of first instance, and later also administrative courts of appeal, were introduced: they were called *tribunaux* and *cours d'appel*, just like their civil and criminal law counterparts. The judicial role of the administrative courts was enhanced when litigation concerning the liability of public bodies was referred to these courts. Apart from the general *recours en annulation*, a remedy called *recours de pleine juridiction* can now be brought before the administrative courts. By this remedy, the petitioner does not ask for the annulment of a decision, but rather seeks certain benefits, or a certain form of behaviour, from the public body, for example, observance of a contract, damages for tort, or restitution of what has been unduly paid. In these cases, the jurisdiction of the administrative courts is founded on a purely formal criterion: if the respondent in the action is a public body, the case is referred to the administrative and not the ordinary civil courts. A leading nineteenth-century case on government liability concerned injuries suffered by a child who had been knocked down by a small truck belonging to the State tobacco company.[12] In that case already, it was held that issues of State liability for tort are not governed by the Civil Code, but by principles of administrative law to be developed by the administrative courts – which can, however, seek inspiration in the practice of private law.

This formal criterion, though clear enough in tort law, can lead to difficulties in the law of contract. There seems to be no reason not to apply ordinary rules of private law when a local authority buys furniture for classrooms or wine for a reception. The Conseil d'Etat decided in this way in the early twentieth century, in a case where the city of Lille had purchased some granite to improve its pavements.[13] The ordinary courts have jurisdiction when the public authorities act in exactly the same way as any private person would do; the link with the exercise of public powers is then severed. In order to avoid conflicts of jurisdiction, the 1872 Act established a 'Tribunal des Conflits' to decide in the event that the ordinary courts and the administrative courts both claim jurisdiction, or both deny it. Thus it is always possible to gain certainty about the exact borderline between the two

---

[12] Tribunal des Conflits 8-2-1873, *Blanco*, *Les grands arrêts* no. 1.
[13] CE 31-7-1912, *Société des granits porphyroïdes des Vosges*, *Rec.* 909, *Les grands arrêts* no. 29.

areas of jurisdiction. Under French law, jurisdiction determines substance: if administrative courts take the case, administrative law will be applied.

As a result, administrative law has become a completely separate part of French law. To that extent the revolutionary lawgivers of the late eighteenth century have been more successful than many observers and commentators originally predicted. The separation does not just concern legal practice, it also governs the academic world.[14] There is in French law an area of *droit public* with its own standards, concepts and principles but also with its own reviews, conferences and university chairs. Although this strict separation is occasionally criticized in the French literature,[15] it remains an important aspect of French legal practice and legal thinking.

The French system has a certain aesthetic quality, because of the spotless logic which seems to have guided its construction. When one takes a closer look at it, however, gaps and overlaps appear; but as a whole, it is a well-arranged system founded on clear and practicable standards. The logic of the construction may, however, also lead to results which are far from satisfactory. One of the most subtle theories developed by the Conseil d'Etat is that of the *voie de fait* (purely factual behaviour). There is *voie de fait* when the action of the authorities is so irregular that it can in no way be related to any administrative power whatsoever; therefore it cannot be considered as an administrative act, so it must be 'factual conduct' to be examined only by the ordinary civil courts. The standard example is the seizure by the police of films belonging to a private person quietly taking pictures of Chartres cathedral.[16] The theory fits with what the French call 'the logic of the system', but the practical result is that the victim must go through the expensive and laborious procedure before the civil courts when the administration has acted in such an outrageous way that its activities lack even the bare appearance of being within its powers.

Digressing slightly, I should perhaps add that the rigid distinction between public and private law has a quality which seems to appeal to the French mind. According to French literature, *clarté* (clarity) is the chief virtue of French legal thinking, and there is no better method of promoting

---

[14] See Braibant and Stirn, *Le droit administratif français*, Introduction (in particular nos. II and IV).

[15] See François Testu, 'La distinction du droit public et du droit privé est-elle idéologique?', *Recueil Dalloz* (1998), Chr. 37; Laurent Cohen-Tanugy, *La métamorphose de la démocratie* (Paris, 1989), ch. 5.

[16] CE 18-11-1949, *Carlier, Rec.* 490.

such clarity than by distinguishing clearly among the different characteristics of the materials to be examined – preferably dividing them into
two groups.[17] Problems of classification have an importance here which
they don't necessarily have elsewhere. Experience teaches, however, that
complicated matters can indeed be made accessible by means of simple
dichotomies.

6.2. The Conseil d'Etat

Right across the vicissitudes of French political history, the Conseil d'Etat
has been an element of stability for nearly two centuries. After Napoleon's
fall, it continued to exercise its advisory and quasi-judicial functions during
the Restoration; it survived the 1848 revolution and found its place in the
short-lived Second Republic and the Second Empire of Napoleon III. In the
early years of the Third Republic, its *Section du Contentieux* was recognised
as what it had already been for a long time, namely a court. Nowadays it is
impossible to imagine the French legal and political landscape without the
the Conseil d'Etat.

The importance of the Conseil d'Etat's role has increased because of the
gradual growth in the tasks of public authorities. In 1750, Montesquieu
could still write that the executive power 'makes peace or war, sends or re-
ceives embassies, establishes security and prevents invasions'[18]. That seems
to echo an almost arcadian past, long since swept away by the emergence of
the modern state with its responsibilities for infrastructure, urban planning,
education, public health, social security, economic policy, protection of the
environment, and so on. Legal evolution has been profoundly influenced
by the extension of government tasks and by the development of a modern
administration. One of the most conspicuous consequences has been the
growing significance of public law.[19] However, that development did not
take the French lawyers completely by surprise. When the modern welfare
state began to be established, in the middle of the twentieth century, the
Conseil d'Etat had already created a conceptual framework that enabled
the lawyers to fix the limits of the legality of administrative action. It is

---

[17] See Daniel Mornet, *Histoire de la clarté française, ses origines, son évolution, sa valeur* (Paris,
1929), part III ch. 3; Henri Mazeaud, *Nouveau guide des exercices pratiques* (Paris, 1966), ch. 4.

[18] Montesquieu, *L'esprit des lois*, book XI ch. 6 (ed. L'Intégrale, p. 586).

[19] See Friedmann, *Law in a Changing Society*, chs. 10-12.

true that the huge expansion of the administration and its activities faced the administrative courts with new problems, but in France, the novelty of these problems presented differences of degree, not of kind. Countries without a developed system of administrative courts were less prepared to meet the new challenges.

Historically speaking, that situation represents a strange paradox: the French model of separation was instituted for the very purpose of protecting the administration against judicial intervention. English authors were quick to point out that this had the effect of putting the administrative bodies 'above the law', thereby exempting from the power of the laws those persons 'who ought to be the most entirely submitted to them'. Edmund Burke, who wrote these words in 1793, thought that the revolutionary leaders would thus be able to use the administration as 'the great instrument' for gaining their sinister objectives.[20] However that may have been, what happened in fact was exactly the opposite: administrative action was entirely subjected to an independent control of legality at a time when the common law courts were still keeping aloof from issues of government and administration. Dicey's famous book on the law of the constitution, although published in 1885, repeated Burke's scathing remarks about the *droit administratif* in France as if nothing had happened in the intervening ninety years. Only the tenth edition of the work, published in 1959, made a serious comparison between the British and French systems.[21]

Some distinctive features of French society may have helped to develop and consolidate the particular position of the Conseil d'Etat. There is a high degree of centralization in French politics and administration, but also in the economy and in communications, media and culture: Paris is 'la métropole' in the true sense of the word. Many things affecting the whole country, from the final examinations in secondary education to the supply of water and electricity, are determined and managed in Paris. This is generally done by a highly competent and very devoted bureaucracy. As there is a weak parliamentary tradition, the position of the bureaucracy is relatively powerful, even in times when there is strong political leadership.[22] The general availability of the *recours en annulation* fits nicely in this picture.

---

[20] Edmund Burke, *Reflections on the Revolution in France* (1790, new edn 1793). The quotations are from part II (Everyman edn, pp. 204–5).

[21] Dicey's *Introduction*, ch. XII.

[22] See Alain Peyrefitte, *Le mal français* (Paris, 1976), chs. XI-XXII.

And as this remedy can only lead to annulment, the courts, though able to trace the limits of what the bureaucracy can do, cannot impose their own views as to how things should actually be done. To that extent the *recours en annulation* appears to reconcile the autonomy of administrative action with the necessity of legal controls.

Another element may have contributed to the strong position of the Conseil d'Etat: the administration does not see the court as a kind of hostile power. The members of the Conseil are viewed as being themselves part of the administration, with the corresponding attitudes and mentality. They may have been civil servants, or trained as administrators, for example at one of the famous *grandes écoles* specifically established for the education of future leaders of the public administration, such as the Ecole Nationale d'Administration. Moreover, the *conseillers d'Etat* are sometimes made available, on a kind of loan, to one of the ministries, to do temporary jobs requiring experienced trouble-shooters: they may, for example, spend some time investigating the defects of the prison regime, or the legal aspects of space travel.[23] When a bill is sent for scrutiny by the Conseil d'Etat the government is obliged to ask its advice – the draftsmen are invited to a frank discussion with a committee of *conseillers d'Etat*, who pit their experience in drafting against the expertise of the ministry's agents in the relevant subject matter. There is, therefore, a kind of fellow-feeling between the members of the Conseil d'Etat and the representatives of the administration; their idiosyncracies are not dissimilar. The government bureaucracy knows that the members of the Conseil d'Etat have acquired a wisdom in matters of administration which can only be beneficial for the management of public service. As a result, there is mutual confidence. That circumstance may have facilitated the pragmatic way in which the Conseil d'Etat has always dealt with the problems caused by the discretionary powers of the administration.[24]

The peculiarity of the French system is that this amicable relationship between the Conseil d'Etat and the administration in no way affects the independence of the Conseil when acting as a court. A spectacular demonstration of this independence occurred in 1962, when the Conseil annulled an *ordonnance* (regulatory decree) of President de Gaulle instituting a special military court for the trial of the army officers who had staged the military coup in Algiers in protest against government negotiations with

---

[23] See also Brown and Bell, *French Administrative Law*, ch. 4.   [24] See ch. 5.3.

the Algerian rebels.[25] The enabling statute had been adopted by referendum, after a government declaration of March 1962 formally announcing the conclusion of the agreements which were to end the military operations in Algeria. According to the statute, the President had power to take, by way of *ordonnance*, all legislative or regulatory measures necessary to the implementation of this declaration. The Conseil d'Etat recognised that the statute conferred very wide powers on the President, and that those powers included the institution of special courts. Neither the wording nor the objective of the statute could, however, justify organizing those courts in such a way as to disregard the fundamental rights of the defence. That could only be justified if it were indispensable to the implementation of the government declaration of March 1962. The procedural rules provided by the *ordonnance*, particularly the exclusion of any form of appeal, did not satisfy this test of necessity, with the result that the President's decree must be considered as illegal.

The President and his allies were scandalized by this judgment. It gave rise to a legal and a political debate. The legal problem was that the three petitioners, ex-army officers, had been sentenced to death by the military court, and two of them had already been shot. The government rapidly submitted a bill to Parliament in order to regularize what had happened, and this bill was duly adopted and promulgated, since the Gaullists had a comfortable majority in Parliament at the time. It was only many years later that retroactive validation of administrative decisions was ruled unconstitutional by the Conseil constitutionnel. It was, said the Constitutional Council in 1980, contrary to the independence of the administrative courts, which had specific functions that must not be encroached upon by the legislature or the government.[26] That doctrine had not yet been developed in the 1960s, and retroactive validation had been practised before. However, the whole episode left a bad taste.

The political problem was that President de Gaulle regarded the judgment as a personal defeat. He had bitterly resented the revolt of 'his' generals, and he felt that the result of the referendum showed that the French people were behind him. The intensity of these feelings was stimulated by a series of bomb attacks carried out by the scattered remains of the

---

[25] CE 19-10-1962, *Canal, Robin et Godot, Rec.* 552, *Les grands arrêts* no. 97.
[26] CC 22-7-1980, *Validation, Rec.* 46, *Les grandes décisions* no. 31.

military rebels and their handful of supporters, which kept the country on the alert for quite a while. The courageous judgment of the Conseil d'Etat occurred, therefore, at an awkward moment. De Gaulle saw it as a challenge to his leadership; he immediately announced a drastic reform of the Conseil d'Etat. Traditions have their own resistance, however: a committee sat on the problem until quieter times had returned, and the reform finally adopted did little more than introduce some minor changes in the working procedures of the Conseil.[27] This outcome emphasized how much the independence of the administrative courts had become part of French constitutional tradition.

Over the years, the Conseil d'Etat has shown an impressive degree of ingenuity and resourcefulness. Standards have been refined or adjusted as the nature of administrative problems has changed. One of the most striking examples of such an adjustment is the way the court has been able to develop the concept of general principles of law ('principes généraux du droit'). Respect for legality does not only mean that statutory rules are to be observed, it also implies the obligation not to violate general principles of law. The expression itself appears for the first time in a 1945 judgment;[28] commentators agree, however, that this judgment merely gave a name to a phenomenon which had already existed for nearly a century. As one observer put it: 'la notion a précédé la terminologie' (the concept preceded the terminology).[29] At the first stage, the court held that French legislation, for example the Civil Code, was based on certain assumptions and that administrative bodies were not free to depart from them. One of the oldest examples is the freedom of trade which, according to the Conseil d'Etat, characterized French commercial and business legislation. Assumptions of this kind were considered as principles: the legislative bodies were not bound by them when enacting a statute, but other authorities could not disregard them. At the second stage, the Conseil d'Etat developed a series of procedural requirements to be met by administrative authorities even if the applicable statute did not refer to them. Most important among these requirements are the rights of the defence (*droits de la défense*); they include the right to be heard. In the absence of statutory provisions to

---

[27] See Georges Maleville, *Conseiller d'Etat, témoignage* (Paris, 1979), pp. 142–54; Olivier Dupeyroux, 'L'indépendance du Conseil d'Etat statuant au contentieux', *RDP* 99 (1983), 565.

[28] CE 26-10-1945, *Aramu, Rec.* 213.

[29] Braibant and Stirn, *Le droit administratif français*, p. 218.

the contrary, said the Conseil d'Etat, administrative authorities are free to revoke an earlier decision, such as a concession to have a news-stand in a public place; but they can do so only after having given the interested person the opportunity to state his or her opinion. That also applies if the applicable legislation is silent on the matter, because general principles of law, to be respected by the administration, include the rights of the defence.[30]

A third category of general principles of law has become more and more important for the evolution of the court's case law. These principles embody traditional legal values which have resulted from a legal evolution spanning several centuries. Legal certainty and equal protection are the most obvious examples. In France, these general principles of law are founded not only on tradition but also on certain written texts, in particular the *Déclaration des droits de l'homme et du citoyen* of 1789, to which the preamble of the Constitution refers.[31] The Conseil d'Etat does not always explicitly identify the general principle of law it is invoking; some turns of phrase appear and reappear in its case law which, though based on a general principle of law, are used as if they were self-evident. An early example occurred in 1933, when the mayor of the city of Nevers prohibited a public meeting because demonstrations against the main speaker – a well-known right-wing agitator – had been announced by trade unions and socialist organizations.[32] The Conseil d'Etat held that the mayor had the power to take the measures necessary for protecting public order, but must reconcile the exercise of this power with the freedom of assembly guaranteed under French constitutional law. It emerged, however, from the evidence that the mayor would have been able to protect public order by ordinary police measures, so that there was no need to prohibit the meeting. Similar expressions reappear in later case law.[33] Legally speaking, the court applies the principle of proportionality in these cases: administrative measures should not be excessive. A certain balance is required between the prohibitions or restrictions to be imposed and the end to be achieved. In particular, where civil liberties or free movement of persons are concerned, the administration, even when pursuing a legitimate aim such as traffic regulation or the protection of

---

[30] CE 5-5-1944, *Veuve Trompier-Gravier, Rec.* 133; CE 9-5-1980, *Etablissements Cruse, Rec.* 217.
[31] See ch. 4.2.
[32] CE 19-5-1933, *Benjamin, Rec.* 541, *Les grands arrêts* no. 52.
[33] CE 23-1-1953, *Naud, Rec.* 32; CE 8-12-1972, *Ville de Dieppe, Rec.* 794.

public order, will have to opt for measures which cause as little hindrance as possible to the exercise of these rights.

As we have already seen, this method of applying general principles of law as part of the 'legality' has been taken up by the Court of Justice of the European Communities and also, to a certain extent, by the European Court of Human Rights.[34] The Conseil d'Etat probably showed the way.

It is necessary to add, however, that the principle of proportionality has some peculiarities when compared to other general principles of law. Because it imposes limits on the exercise of government powers, it has an important constitutional dimension.[35] Its application may have the effect of censuring government policies. A famous example concerned the law of expropriation. Under French law, the procedure for expropriating land for public works (motorways, airports, military installations etc.) cannot start until the government has formally declared that the works are in the public interest ('d'utilité publique'). Such a declaration can, of course, be challenged by means of a *recours en annulation*, but until the 1970s judicial supervision was limited to questions of form and procedure (problems of 'external legality', in French legal parlance). In later case law, however, the Conseil d'Etat began to apply the principle of proportionality, thereby also calling in question the justification for the measure in question. An operation can only be declared 'd'utilité publique', the court held, if the cost, the encroachment on private property and the other possible inconveniences it causes, for example to local communities in the neighbourhood (noise, environmental damage), are not excessive in comparison to the public interest served. Therefore, for example, the extension of a motorway in the direction of the Swiss frontier south of Lake Geneva was held not to be in the public interest, since the Swiss authorities had declined to connect it to the Swiss motorway network on their side of the frontier. The Minister's contention that even without such a connection the work was an important part of French road planning was not accepted by the court.[36]

Decisions of this kind can cut deep into the policy of public authorities. That may be the reason why the English courts have been very reluctant

---

[34] See ch. 4. 4.

[35] See also Walter van Gerven, 'The effect of proportionality on the actions of Member States', in Evelyn Ellis (ed.), *The Principle of Proportionality in the Laws of Europe* (Oxford, 1999), 37 (at p. 62).

[36] CE 28-3-1997, *Autoroute du Chablais*, Rec. 120.

to apply the principle of proportionality.[37] It threatens to bring the courts into the heart of problems already settled by the political institutions.

6.3. French practice

The development of a distinct body of administrative law in France is not only the result of the generality of the *recours en annulation*. The complete separation from civil and commercial law has been helped by the creation of separate rules and principles concerning the liability of public bodies and administrative contracts. That creation is largely due to the Conseil d'Etat.

Liability in tort is entirely based on case law. Initially, its scope and character were very close to liability for *faute* ('fault' or negligence) under the French Civil Code.[38] Public bodies were held responsible for a *faute de service* committed by one of their authorities, servants or agents. If the fault had not been committed in the exercise of the public service, it was to be regarded as a personal fault of the tort-feasor, so that the victim could only bring an action before the ordinary civil courts. Progressively, however, the administrative courts accepted that personal faults might also amount to a *faute de service*. Wrongful conduct of servants or agents now constitutes such a fault when, owing to the circumstances of the case, it cannot be dissociated from the public service or, as the Conseil d'Etat puts it, cannot be regarded as devoid of any link with the service ('comme dépourvu de tout lien avec le service').[39] As a result, the exclusive jurisdiction of the civil courts is limited to a few particular cases, for example those where a government agent intentionally causes harm to a personal enemy. In such a case, there cannot be any connection with the exercise of public power.[40]

A new chapter of tort liability was opened when the Conseil d'Etat accepted no-fault liability (*responsabilité sans faute*) as a special form of liability of public bodies. The leading case concerned the refusal of local authorities to expel squatters from lands they were unlawfully occupying. A court order obtained by the owner was of no avail, because the authorities feared that the execution of the order might lead to grave disturbance. The Conseil d'Etat accepted that the administration could refuse to help

---

[37] See *R* v. *Secretary of State for the Home Office* ex p. *Brind* [1991] 1 All ER 720.
[38] Art. 1382 Code civil.
[39] CE 18-11-1949, *Demoiselle Mimeur*, *Rec.* 492, *Les grands arrêts* no. 73.
[40] See Michel Paillet, *La faute du service public en droit administratif* (Paris, 1980), nos. 24–5.

the owner enforce the court order, on grounds of public security, but in that case it should offer him financial compensation.[41] A second step followed some years later, when damage had resulted from the application of legislation which was itself silent on financial compensation. In order to protect the dairy industry, a statute had prohibited the production and sale of a commodity resembling cream but not made exclusively from milk. A company alleging that it was the only producer of this non-dairy cream had to wind up its business. The Conseil d'Etat noted that the product had not been forbidden for reasons of health protection. Under these circumstances, it said, Parliament could not have intended that the company should bear the loss alone; it should be borne by society as a whole.[42]

This line of case law led to an important new doctrine, that of the equality with regard to public burdens ('égalité devant les charges publiques'). Put in its simplest terms, it associates no-fault liability with the application of general principles of law, in particular the equality principle as expressed in the 1789 Declaration. Equal protection implies, said the Conseil d'Etat, that citizens should be treated equally with regard to charges resulting from public burdens. The administrative courts accept that the activities of the public service can cause loss and annoyance, of a financial or other nature, to the citizens; in principle, there can be no tort action for damage occasioned by the lawful exercise of public functions. However, if the loss caused by a certain measure is suffered only by a particular individual or company, or group of individuals or companies, they are entitled to compensation, because that loss, though the necessary consequence of a measure taken in the public interest, should be borne by the collectivity, not just by a limited group. The technical expression is then that this individual or group has suffered a *dommage spécial*, as opposed to the general damage suffered by the citizenry in general. Some judgments use the notion of *dommage anormal*. A picturesque example occurred in 1963, when the local authorities of a small town in the Pyrenees decided that one of the two country roads leading to the top of a hill (with a famous and beautiful view) would henceforth be accessible to only donkeys and their drivers, in order to prevent collisions between donkeys and pedestrians. A newsagent selling picture postcards and little souvenirs to tourists had his shop on this road, and as asinine interest in postcards is limited, he had to shut up shop. The measure in

---

[41] CE 30-11-1923, *Couitéas*, *Rec.* 789, *Les grands arrêts* no. 45.
[42] CE 14-1-1938, *La Fleurette*, *Rec.* 25, *Les grands arrêts* no. 57.

question was lawful, said the Conseil d'Etat, since it was founded on the need to ensure the safety of road users; but the damage suffered by the shopkeeper was an 'abnormal' damage and had to be compensated.[43]

Gradually, and more problematically, a similar reasoning has begun to be applied in cases involving economic regulations and measures. When the prefect of a department on the Mediterranean coast issued a temporary prohibition on unloading wine in one of the local ports because of violent action by wine producers against shipments of Italian wines, the Conseil d'Etat held that, in the circumstances of the case, such a decision was lawful under French law, but wine importers who had entered into contracts with suppliers of Italian wine should be compensated. Public order should not be enforced at the sole expense of a certain group of businesses.[44] In some of these cases, the courts start from the assumption that businessmen and other entrepreneurs know that economic life involves certain risks. These risks include the possibility that economic legislation may be modified to their disadvantage, or measures of economic policy turn out to cause them losses. They have to accept these risks. Some losses, however, go beyond the economic risks inherent in the entrepreneur's activities. If he is part of a specific group of entrepreneurs faced with risks one cannot reasonably expect in ordinary business life, he may be entitled to compensation. That approach has been further developed in the case law of the EC Court of Justice on Community liability for economic regulations.[45] It can also be found in some national legal systems outside France. When, for example, a certain method of feeding animals raised for meat is prohibited on grounds of public health, such as fear of swine fever or mad cow disease (BSE), the farmers will have to bear the consequences, at least as far as the courts are concerned (the government can always decide to subsidize the sector for reasons of public interest). If, however, specific farmers or groups of farmers suffer an abnormal damage because, unlike others, they have no other choice but to cease production completely, they may be entitled to compensation.[46]

---

[43] CE 22-2-1963, *Commune de Gavarnie*, *Rec.* 113.

[44] CE 7-12-1979, *Les Fils de Henri Ramel*, *Rec.* 456. Further materials in Roger Errera, 'The scope and meaning of no-fault liability in French administrative law', 39 *Current Legal Problems* (1986) 157.

[45] Examples: cases 64 and 113/76, *Dumortier Frères* [1979] ECR 3091; joined cases c-104/89 and 37/90, *Mulder and others* v. *Council and Commission* (*Mulder* II) [1992] ECR I-3061.

[46] This is a Dutch example: HR 18-1-1991, *Leffers*, *Ned.Jur.* (1992), 638.

In matters of contract the scope of administrative law is not as wide as in tort. It is not sufficient that one of the parties is a public body, because contracts are within the jurisdiction of the ordinary courts if their subject matter shows that similar contracts might have been concluded by private persons. There is, however, always a *contrat administratif* when the clauses of the contract concern things which would not be found in a contract between private parties. That may be the case if the task to be performed under the contract could never have been agreed upon by private parties (for example a concession to run a bus service), or if some of the terms of the contract would not be freely entered into between private persons or companies, for example the possibility of unilateral cancellation of the contract on grounds of public interest.

The provisions of the Civil Code are not binding on the parties to an administrative contract, but they can be applied by analogy. As a result, the public law of contract presents certain peculiarities, some of which later found their way to ordinary contract law. That is especially true of the doctrine of *imprévision* (unforeseen circumstances), developed by the Conseil d'Etat with regard to concessions but later also applied to other administrative contracts.[47] The doctrine concerns the situation where the implementation of the contract becomes particularly burdensome for the private party as a result of events nobody could have foreseen when the contract was concluded. An example is a steep rise in energy prices in times of war or sudden international crisis. The concession holder, for example a bus or tram service or a distributor of gas or electricity, will be unable to make any profit and would normally have to cease its activities; but the continuity of the public service requires that these activities be continued. The Conseil d'Etat holds that such a problem cannot be solved on the basis of the terms of the agreement between the parties. The disadvantage resulting from the increased burdens should partially be borne by the administration, which is, after all, primarily responsible for the continuity of the services rendered. Therefore, a 'reasonable part' of the increased burden will be shifted to the administration, whether the contact includes this possibility or not.[48]

From the point of view of the relationship between the courts and the political institutions, which is what mainly interests us, the review jurisdiction

---

[47] CE 30-3-1916, *Gaz de Bordeaux*, *Rec.* 125, *Les grands arrêts* no. 34; CE 9-12-1932, *Tramways de Cherbourg*, *Rec.* 1050, *Les grands arrêts* no. 50.

[48] See also Brown and Bell, *French Administrative Law*, pp. 208–10.

embodied in the *recours en annulation* remains the most important element of French administrative law. Questions of liability in tort or contract may lead to differences of opinion with the ordinary court hierarchy or with distinguished professors of civil law; the annulment of an important government measure will often irritate or even anger political leaders or heads of government departments. From a legal point of view, it is, however, impossible to make a strict separation between the different parts of the creative work performed by the Conseil d'Etat. But politically and psychologically, the administrative courts derive their chief importance from the fact that they offer a generalized supervision of legality. That, at least, is what French lawyers tend to think. According to René Cassin, one of France's great jurists, and himself once vice-president of the Conseil d'Etat,[49] the mere existence of this body keeps alive the awareness of a watchdog among the administrators and encourages confidence in law and liberty among the citizens.[50] There is something noble about these proud words. The experience of the last ten or twenty years suggests, however, that the confidence of citizens in their government and in the law depends on a lot more than the working of courts or other institutional arrangements.[51]

From a comparative point of view, it is interesting to note that judicial supervision of legality in France shows some similarities to judicial review of legislation in the United States. The wide *pouvoir réglementaire* of the French government, in particular in the Fifth Republic, on the one hand, the large conception of legality developed by the Conseil d'Etat on the other, ensure that the scope of review is often comparable. A similar remark could be made with regard to the methods used by both courts. Just as the American Supreme Court developed a set of coherent standards for assessing the constitutionality of legislation by inventively interpreting vague concepts such as equal protection and due process of law, so the Conseil d'Etat has been discovering similar standards for judging the legality of administrative regulations and measures, by defining general principles of law and by establishing general guidelines for good administration. When, in the early years of the Fifth Republic, the Constitutional Council started to review

---

[49] The vice-president acts as chairman. The President of the Republic is formally president of the Conseil d'Etat.

[50] In *Etudes et documents* (official publication of the Conseil d'Etat) 1949, p. 19.

[51] Further reflections in B. Stirn, *Le Conseil d'Etat, son rôle, sa jurisprudence*, 2nd edn (Paris, 1994).

the constitutionality of legislation under certain conditions, it found much of its inspiration in the case law of the Conseil d'Etat. The latter had, for example, shown the way in matters of human rights protection by founding general principles of law on the 1789 Declaration, via the preambles to the 1946 and 1958 constitutions.[52]

There is, however, an important difference between the ways the Constitutional Council and the Conseil d'Etat invoke general principles of law. In the view of the Conseil d'Etat, whose review jurisdiction is limited to administrative acts, general principles are binding upon the administration, but legislative bodies are free to depart from them, provided they do so clearly and explicitly. For the Constitutional Council, which reviews legislation, the situation is not the same. Some general principles of law such as human rights protection and the independence of the courts are considered as 'fundamental principles recognised by the laws of the Republic', which cannot be disregarded by new statutes.[53] Other principles, like proportionality, which are not rooted in the text of the Constitution, its preamble or the 1789 Declaration, are not included in the Constitutional Council's supervision of constitutionality. They are not part of what the experts call 'le bloc de constitutionnalité'. The administrative courts exercise a tighter scrutiny. Not only are there formal reasons for this difference: it can also be justified on grounds of democracy. Supervision of the administration, even in the very wide definition of that term as used in French law and practice, is not the same as supervision of a democratically elected national parliament.[54]

6.4. Semi-separation: Germany

There is a separate body of administrative law in Germany, and there are separate administrative courts; but the German legal system has not the same rigorous distinctions as the French. The main difference between the two countries is probably that the impact of the Constitution, and its

---

[52] See CE 9-3-1951, *Concerts du conservatoire*, *Rec.* 151, *Les grands arrêts* no. 77; CE 26-6-1959, *Syndicat général des ingénieurs-conseils*, *Rec.* 394, *Les grands arrêts* no. 92. See also ch. 4.2.

[53] The term is used in the preamble to the 1946 Constitution.

[54] See Louis Favoreu, 'Le droit constitutionnel: droit de la Constitution et constitution du droit', *RFDC* (1990), 71; Bruno Genevois, 'Continuité et convergence des juridictions constitutionnelle et administrative', *RFDA* (1990), 143.

interpretation by the constitutional court, is much more clearly perceptible in Germany. The judgments of the ordinary and administrative courts
show the direct influence of the case law of the Federal Constitutional Court.
Sometimes they merely translate general rulings of the constitutional court,
for example on the interpretation of human rights, into detailed standards
to be applied within their own area of jurisdiction. In France, of course,
the constitutional court only examines bills, legislation once promulgated
being immune from attacks on constitutional grounds. In Germany, on the
contrary, every judgment of the supreme administrative court can be challenged by a constitutional complaint from the private party that lost the
case.[55] Thus procedural elements strengthen the influence of constitutional
thinking in the evolution of German case law. There are, however, also constitutional provisions directly affecting the position of the administrative
courts.

First, the Basic Law provides that the tortious liability of public authorities ('liability for violation of an official duty') shall be within the jurisdiction of the ordinary civil courts.[56] These courts apply the provisions of the
German Civil Code (BGB or Bürgerliches Gesetzbuch) and the concepts
developed in private law. As a consequence, the scope of administrative law
is less extensive than in France. This is also true because the notion of administrative contract is unknown in German law. Contract is a private law
concept, and contract cases are heard by the ordinary courts. In German
thinking the administration, acting as such, acts unilaterally.

Secondly, another provision of the Basic Law guarantees access to justice
(Rechtsweggarantie). If a person's rights are violated by public authority he
or she can have recourse to the courts. If no other remedy has been established by statute, the ordinary courts will have jurisdiction.[57] This residual
jurisdiction of the civil courts has no great importance in actual practice: liability problems are within their jurisdiction because of a specific
constitutional provision, while supervising the legality of administrative
decisions is in the hands of the administrative courts on the basis of the
general statute governing their jurisdiction.[58] According to some authors,
however, the Rechtsweggarantie has a meaning that goes beyond mere procedural matters. By creating remedies for the protection of citizens' rights,
the Basic Law must be assumed to require a full review of administrative

---

[55] See ch. 4.1 and 4.2.   [56] Art. 34 Basic Law.   [57] Art. 19 s.(4) Basic Law.
[58] Verwaltungsgerichtsordnung; see in particular s. 40.

decisions by the courts. Some older judgments of the federal constitutional court adhere to this theory, which also seems to have influenced the case law of the administrative courts.[59]

As problems of State liability are part of ordinary tort law, they are usually examined in literature on private law. The ground rule is laid down in one of the tort provisions in the Civil Code: if an official intentionally or negligently violates his official duty, he is liable (*Amtshaftung*). A number of enactments, now codified in the Basic Law, have shifted the responsibility of the official to the State, or to any other public body on whose behalf the official was acting.[60] The limits of the liability are, however, fixed by the Civil Code: no-fault liability, as developed by the Conseil d'Etat in France, has no equivalent in German law. The limitation to culpable breach of official duty makes sense in a system of individual responsibility based on fault, which is the one adopted by the BGB. It is more difficult to see whether it also makes sense if applied to the liability of the modern State with its many ramifications. The civil courts have reacted to this dilemma by significantly raising the standards of care to be observed by officials. That device helps to extend liability to situations not covered by traditional notions of negligence, but it cannot do so when the official has been acting within the proper limits of his authority. As officials are not personally liable for damage or loss resulting from the exercise of discretionary powers, the State will not be liable for it either.[61]

Judicial review of administrative action is closer to the French model, but with some important differences. Under German administrative law, only individual decisions (*Entscheidungen*) can be attacked for lack of a legal basis, not regulations or decisions with a regulatory character (*Verordnungen*). The philosophy behind this distinction – unknown in France – is that the regulatory activities of administrative authorities should be under the direct supervision of the representative bodies: regulations are fewer in number than individual decisions, and they are more closely connected to the legislative process. Government accountability to parliament is therefore also regarded as a check on illegal behaviour. As a consequence, the scope of judicial review of administrative action is more restricted than in France.

---

[59] See Ernst Forsthoff, *Verwaltungsrecht*, vol. I, 10th edn (Munich, 1973), p. 90.

[60] BGB s. 839; Art. 34 Basic Law.

[61] See B. S. Markesinis, *The German Law of Torts, a Comparative Introduction*, revised 3rd edn (Oxford, 1997), pp. 902–5.

The general statute on the administrative courts enumerates the various remedies. Most important are the *Anfechtungsklage*, by which a petitioner asks for the annulment of a certain decision (more or less in the same way as in the *recours en annulation* in French law), and the *Feststellungsklage*, by which the petitioner asks the court to determine authoritatively what the legal situation actually is (more or less like the action for a 'declaration' in English law). The action for annulment is available only to those who allege that their 'rights' have been violated by the decision.[62] The courts have been inclined to give a wide interpretation to the notion of 'rights', so that in fact many interests can be protected by means of an action for annulment.

Since the 1960s, the *Anfechtungsklage* has also become an important instrument for promoting political views and attempting to correct policy decisions. Environmental groups and pacifist organizations have tried to block government activities on matters like the construction of nuclear power plants or military airports, by challenging the legality of every decision taken for that purpose. The administrative courts found these actions admissible, since the petitioners could invoke such constitutional rights as the right to life, the right to live in peace, and the right to a clean environment.[63] As regards substance, the tendency of the administrative courts has been to uphold decisions which are founded on a clear legislative mandate, but to submit them to very strict scrutiny when the applicable statute offers various possibilities, thereby leaving the real choice to the administration. In general, German courts dislike vague statutory provisions which do not embody the actual policy decision; this may be because between 1933 and 1945 the Nazi regime tried to pervert legal provisions in such a way as to provide a specious legal basis for their criminal activities. The Bundesverfassungsgericht held in 1958 that statutes conferring powers upon the administration to impose burdens on citizens should be 'determinate' (*Bestimmtheitsgebot*).[64] Such provisions ought to be determinate and limited in their object, aim and extent; only thus, the Court said, would citizens be in a position to foresee and assess the charges they would have to face. Later case law made it clear that this ruling did not exclude the use of indeterminate notions in legislation; in particular cases, for example in economic law, the administration will have a margin of discretion (*Ermessen*), which can only be defined in imprecise terms.[65] The administrative courts

---

[62] See *Verwaltungsgerichtsordnung*, ss. 42–3.
[63] See Art. 2 s.(2), Art. 1 s.(2) and Art. 20a Basic Law.
[64] BVerfGE 8 no. 34, *Preisgesetz*, 1958.   [65] See ch. 5.3.

consider this *Bestimmtheitsgebot* to be inspired by a concern to protect the interests of individual citizens and, therefore, as an admonition to the courts to submit the exercise of powers based on vague concepts to close investigation.

That consideration brings us to one of the main points of discussion in German administrative law: the relation between discretionary powers on the one hand, and vague or indeterminate notions ('unbestimmte Rechts-begriffe') on the other. Initially, there was a tendency to blend these two concepts into one. The courts acted on the assumption that the legisla-tive bodies must have used vague notions intentionally, i.e. they must have intended to confer discretionary powers upon the administration. That sim-plistic view could not be maintained, however. Expressions such as 'public order' or 'public security' are vague because they are meant to cover dif ferent situations that cannot always be foreseen in advance – not because they intend to grant discretion to the administration. The limits of judicial control in these cases give rise to specific problems, for example with regard to the assessment of facts characterized as dangerous to public order. These problems are not the same, however, as those caused by misuse or excess of discretionary powers.[66]

The next point in the discussion was the extent of judicial supervision: should the courts respect the assessments made by the administration or proceed to a complete and independent check on the interpretation of vague concepts? Sometimes, the courts held, the expression used may be vague, but it nevertheless implies that only one application is correct in the given situation. That would be the case with regard to 'empirical' con-cepts, where the facts have a decisive influence on the choice to be made. The same would not apply to concepts requiring a 'value judgment' to be made by the administration. In the latter case, only a limited supervi-sion would be allowed (procedure, form, excess of power). This distinction between empirical and value judgments does not make things any easier; frequently, both aspects will be present. The question, for example, whether the introduction of a new pharmaceutical product on to the market is a danger to public health will probably be made on the basis of a care-ful analysis of the product concerned ('empirical') as well as on the basis of gauging the risks society is willing to accept in its efforts to improve health standards ('evaluative'). When the administrative courts discovered

---

[66] An important contribution to the debate was Horst Ehmke, *Ermessen und unbestimmte Rechts-begriffe im Verwaltungsrecht* (Tübingen, 1960).

that the distinction did not always work, they were inclined to subject the interpretation of vague concepts to a full reassessment.

This attitude again highlighted the difference from discretionary powers, and it is hard to find a clear distinction between the two concepts in most of the case law of the administrative courts. It is clear, however, that certain assessments made by the administration will hardly, if ever, be re-examined by the courts. Examples are questions relating to the qualifications of a certain person for a certain job, purely technical problems and the judgment of which of two or more competing interests is to prevail. The courts feel free, however, to follow their own assessment with regard to most vague concepts. They did so, for example, with regard to the question whether a certain publication 'glorified war', and whether this glorification was of such a nature as to expose young persons to moral corruption.[67]

This broad concept of the judicial task has, however, been severely criticized in the German literature. Policy-making is not a judicial function, according to many authors, and the courts should therefore respect the administration's power to 'shape' or 'mould' (gestalten) its policy on the basis of its vision of developments in society. If the statutory provision permits two or more possible interpretations of the same notion, the statute is normally assumed to have intended to leave the choice to the administration. Some judgments of the federal administrative court followed this idea, but the case law never entirely stabilized on this point. Often, the courts seem to be trying to weigh the need to protect the individual against the administration's policy considerations. The frontier between 'normative concepts', to be interpreted by the courts, and provisions leaving a margin of discretion to the administration remains elusive.

Traditionally, academics have had a strong influence on legal evolution in Germany. Law dons have a higher social status there than elsewhere in the Western world; they are often consulted when new legislation is in preparation; their opinions are cited in judgments, for example those of the federal administrative court. Learned debates find their way into case law, with the result that judgments may examine such abstract questions as the need for 'optimal' rather than 'maximum' legal protection. There is no parallel to the pragmatic approach characterizing the case law of the French Conseil d'Etat. However, the German courts also have a much fuller and more comprehensible way of reasoning: the grounds for the judgments

[67] BVerwGE 23 no. 23, *Die Saga vom Sturmbataillon*, 1966.

of the federal administrative court enable the reader to understand the thinking of the court and to follow the evolution of its case law over a longer period of time. The grounds for the French judgments, though beautifully expressed, are usually too concise to reveal what was going on in the mind of the court, or of its individual judges.[68]

The view that the administrative courts are the branch of the judiciary which specializes in annulment and assessment of legality, while questions of liability remain within the jurisdiction of the ordinary courts, is not limited to Germany. Some countries which have a French-style Council of State, such as Italy and Belgium, and to a certain extent the Netherlands, consider State liability as part of the law of tort, governed by private law and subject to the jurisdiction of the civil courts. Sometimes, however, the application of general tort law leads to the same results as the specific administrative regime existing in France. In Italy and the Benelux countries, the constitutions say nothing about liability for tort, and the civil codes very little. The codes formulate some broad principles, and case law does the rest. In most of continental Europe, tort law is judge-made law, and that is also true for matters of State liability. English authors sometimes tend to overestimate the importance of codification in continental Europe. The French Civil Code has five provisions on tortious liability; the BGB, introduced nearly a century later, not many more. In both countries, most rules on traffic liability, unfair competition, medical liability, liability for professional negligence, responsibility for dangerous commodities, for nuisance, for air, water or soil pollution, are to be found in court judgments. There may be statutory provisions giving detailed rules on a specific subject, such as motor car accidents, but most of tort law, and the general system of tortious liability, have been elaborated by the courts. In so far, State liability is not in a special position.[69]

6.5. The common law systems

Until quite recently, English judges used to say that English law did not have a separate system of administrative law.[70] This statement was based

---

[68] See, generally, on this subject: Hein Kötz, 'Über den Stil höchstrichterlicher Entscheidungen', *Rabelszeitschr.* 37 (1973), 245; Markesinis, *The German Law of Torts*, pp. 8–12.

[69] See also Zweigert and Kötz, *An Introduction to Comparative Law*, ch. 40-IV.

[70] Example: Lord Reid in *Ridge* v. *Baldwin* [1964] *AC* 40.

on two assumptions concerning the main characteristics of English law: first, the law was supposed to have no special rules for the activities of the government, or the administration, or the State; and secondly, there were no special administrative courts, the ordinary courts having jurisdiction over all cases, whoever the defendant and whatever the subject.

Both assumptions were only partially correct. There were no special rules for the public sector, but the Crown has traditionally enjoyed a special position in English law; and constitutionally speaking, the Crown is the central government. On the basis of the maxim 'the King can do no wrong', the Crown could not be held liable in tort for acts or omissions of its agents or officials. And while there were no special administrative courts, welfare state legislation instituted many 'tribunals' to adjudicate complaints on specific issues, such as social security benefits, data protection, immigration and value added tax. As time went by, these tribunals gradually began to act as if they were courts of law.

The complete immunity of the Crown ended in 1947, when the Crown Proceedings Act opened the possibility of suing the Crown for breach of contract and in tort. There were, however, two important restrictions. The statute provided explicitly that the courts could not grant an injunction against the Crown, and that money judgments could not be executed against the Crown; these provisions are still on the statute book.[71] Furthermore, the statute did not affect the Crown's privilege of refusing to produce documents in evidence if it would be contrary to the public interest. Before 1968, the Attorney-General (who represents the Crown before the courts) only had to invoke 'freedom of communication with and within the public service' as grounds for refusing to disclose certain documents. But in that year, the House of Lords began to consider this position untenable. It held that such documents must be shown to the court, on a confidential basis, so that it could consider whether the grounds of public interest alleged on behalf of the Crown should outweigh the public interest in the proper administration of justice.[72] English courts are, nevertheless, still extremely cautious in their assessments of the confidential or sensitive nature of government information. In a 1985 case, the House of Lords accepted that membership of unions could be banned for employees of a government information centre on grounds of national security. The legitimate expectations of the unions might have been violated (the unions had been engaged in negotiations on

---

[71] Crown Proceedings Act, 1947, ss. 21 and 25.   [72] *Conway* v. *Rimmer* [1968] *AC* 910.

the matter), said their lordships, but (unspecified) government concerns about national security had to prevail.[73]

Usually, tribunals are instituted by the statute governing the subject matter in question: rent tribunals by the Housing Act, social security tribunals by social security legislation and so on. Most of these statutes provide for an appeal from a decision of the tribunal to the ordinary courts ('statutory appeal'). Sometimes, the statute institutes an 'appeal tribunal': from decisions of the employment tribunals, which have jurisdiction in labour cases, an appeal lies to the Employment Appeal Tribunal, chaired by a High Court judge; a further appeal is then possible to the Court of Appeal. If no statutory appeal of any kind has been provided for, the courts consider that the decisions of the tribunals can be submitted to judicial review in the same way as administrative decisions. There is, however, little uniformity in the remedies against tribunal decisions, and English authors occasionally complain that it is a patchwork rather than a system of remedies.[74]

Initially, the tribunals were considered as mere administrative bodies. The rules of civil procedure did not apply, and different statutes gave different rules on matters like publicity of hearings, legal aid, evidence and so on. In 1958, the first Tribunals and Inquiries Act was established with the purpose of streamlining the organization of the tribunals. The Act provided, *inter alia*, that all tribunals were obliged to give reasons for their decisions. It also instituted a supervisory body, the Council on Tribunals, which was to report regularly to the government on the working of the tribunals and on changes of legislation it thought desirable. Later legislation tended to strengthen procedural guarantees, traditionally one of the weak points of the tribunal system.[75] As a consequence of this legislation, a certain 'judicialization' of the work of the tribunals took place. From a formal point of view, however, these bodies are not courts: they remain part of the administration in a certain specialized branch.

The normal way to have an administrative decision submitted to judicial review is to apply to the ordinary courts. The general application for judicial review has only been introduced in the 1970s. In earlier days, the petitioner had to choose between different actions with medieval names ('*mandamus*',

---

[73] *Council of Civil Service Unions* v. *Minister for the Civil Service* (GCHQ case) [1985] AC 374.

[74] Cane, *An Introduction to Administrative Law*, ch. 19. See also Wade and Forsyth, *Administrative Law*, ch. 24.

[75] Tribunals and Inquiries Act, 1971; Tribunals and Inquiries Act, 1992.

'prohibition', '*certiorari*'), which each had a different purpose and a different procedural regime (standing, time limits, formalities, evidence, etc.). In medieval times, these ancient actions were part of the centralization efforts of the Norman kings. Initially, they were used by the royal courts of law to keep other courts, such as ecclesiastical courts and local or regional courts (often of Anglo-Saxon origin), within the proper bounds of their specific jurisdiction. If they had acted *ultra vires*, their decisions were quashed. In the course of time, when the medieval structure gave way to a centralized system of courts and modern government started to develop, the ancient actions were used to check whether public bodies such as local authorities, boards, agencies and tribunals had acted within their jurisdiction. Nowadays, an application for judicial review must be brought before a special section of the High Court ('divisional court', normally sitting with two judges); the court then gives 'leave' to initiate proceedings, after having established that the applicant has a 'sufficient interest' in challenging the administrative decision under one of the ancient actions (the court makes the choice for the applicant).[76] This procedure is exclusive in the sense that administrative decisions cannot be challenged by any of the ordinary remedies, for example an action for a declaration, without previous leave for judicial review.[77] There is therefore a special kind of action for challenging the legality of administrative decisions, but it is heard by the ordinary courts and does not have the same comprehensive character as the French action for annulment.

It is difficult to say whether these procedural eccentricities make any difference as far as the grounds for review are concerned. Sometimes, the concept of jurisdiction has been interpreted in a fairly extensive way. A decision is, for example, always considered *ultra vires* when it violates 'principles of natural justice'. These principles cannot be compared to the general principles of law in French administrative law: 'natural justice' concerns only procedural guarantees, in particular the right to a hearing and the rule that the decision-makers must not have any particular interest in the decision ('rule against bias'). Principles of natural justice constitute, therefore, a method for the courts to supervise the regularity of the administrative proceedings that gave rise to the decision. In general, English administrative law is much more concerned about procedural matters than about the

---

[76] See Supreme Court Act, 1981, s. 31. The 'supreme court' consists of the High Court plus the Court of Appeal.
[77] *O'Reilly* v. *Mackman* [1983] 2 AC 237; *Avon County Council* v. *Buscott* [1988] QB 656.

substantive aspects of the decision. Until 1969, errors made within the jurisdiction of the administrative body could not lead to annulment. If the minister, or the local authority, or any other public body, had observed the limits of his or its jurisdiction, the courts refused to examine whether the decision was correct, or reasonable.

In *Anisminic*, 1969, the House of Lords settled two important issues.[78] First, it interpreted a statute explicitly providing that the decision of a certain tribunal 'shall not be questioned in any court of law' in the sense that it only affected judicial supervision of errors 'within the jurisdiction'. The 'ouster clause' could not prevent the court from quashing decisions that were *ultra vires*. Secondly, the court gave a wide interpretation to the supervision of jurisdiction. A tribunal, the Foreign Compensation Commission, had excluded certain persons from compensation for damage suffered because of nationalizations in foreign countries, on the ground that they were not British citizens. The House of Lords did not agree: 'upon a true construction of the statute', it held, a requirement as to nationality could not be imposed. And the court continued to find that, on this ground, the Commission had acted outside the limits of its jurisdiction. Since, there have been more cases where a tribunal was found to have acted *ultra vires* because it had applied the wrong legal test. Some judgments suggest, however, that the same rule, though applicable to all tribunal decisions, does not apply to decisions by government ministers or local authorities: errors of law committed by the administration cannot be reviewed if they do not concern the definition of the authorities' jurisdiction.[79]

This line of case law is not entirely compatible with one slightly different line of argument. Some judgments have somewhat qualified the rule that errors of law within the jurisdiction cannnot be corrected by the courts. This rule, it was held, does not apply in case of 'manifest' errors of law, which can be discovered by a mere glance at the case file ('error on the face of the record'). The leading judgment concerned a decision by a tribunal, but it is couched in general terms.[80] It would appear that these different elements of the case law on errors of law are not entirely in harmony. The lack of uniformity is perhaps due to the particular way the common law of England develops: new solutions to problems are rarely derived from

[78] *Anisminic Ltd.* v. *Foreign Compensation Commission* [1969] 2 AC 147.
[79] Example: *R* v. *Hull University Visitor*, ex p *Page* [1993] AC 682.
[80] *R* v. *Northumberland Compensation Appeal Tribunal*, ex p *Shaw* [1952] 1 KB 338.

pre-existing rules or principles. They are found by applying precedents or, contrarily, by distinguishing the case and not applying the apparent precedent. As a result, English courts are case-oriented, and not very much given to thinking in terms of the cohesion of rules in the legal system. The English legal evolution as a whole seems to somewhat lack consistency when compared to the situation in France or Germany.[81]

The concept of jurisdiction returns in the law of State liability. When an administrative decision embodies a choice of policy, the courts tend to respect that choice when it is made within the jurisdiction; they will then normally consider that the administrative body has exercised its discretionary powers.[82] If, however, the act occurs in an operational context not implying policy, the courts will examine whether the administration has disregarded a duty of care, in the private law sense of the expression, with regard to the person or persons suffering the damage. This liability for negligence is mainly relevant for cases concerning factual behaviour by government officials that has caused property damage or personal injury. Here again, the borderline between different liability regimes is not entirely clear.[83] Cases involving liability for actions by central government are extremely rare; and the courts are not very generous in allowing damages for negligence in such cases.[84] It appears that a more liberal judicial attitude may have been emerging these last years under the influence of developments in European Community law.[85]

Nowadays, English authors admit that administrative law is a well-developed branch of English law; books are now being published on the subject of 'administrative law'.[86] This subject is often described as the law relating to judicial supervision of government power, a definition that must probably be taken to include supervision of the powers of local authorities and other administrative bodies that are not part of central government (such as river, police or educational authorities). In that sense, administrative law existed in England long before the expression was used. When Dr Bentley, a troublesome Cambridge don, was summarily dismissed by

---

[81] See Zweigert and Kötz, *Introduction to Comparative Law*, ch. 18. See also B. S. Markesinis, 'Conceptualism, pragmatism and courage: a common lawyer looks at some judgments of the German Federal Court', *AmJCompL* 34 (1986), 359.
[82] See ch. 5.3.   [83] See *X v. Bedfordshire County Council* [1995] 2 AC 633.
[84] Example: *Bourgoin S.A. v. Ministry of Agriculture* [1986] QB 716.
[85] Further materials in P. P. Craig, *Administrative Law*, 4th edn (London, 1999), ch. 26 s.11–12.
[86] Examples can be found in earlier footnotes.

the Chancellor of the University in 1723, the decision was annulled because the victim had not been given the opportunity to present his own view. The learned judge said that 'even God himself did not pass sentence upon Adam', after the fatal bite from the apple, 'before he was called upon to make his defence'. 'Adam, says God, where art thou? Hast thou not eaten of the tree whereof I commanded thee that thou shouldst not eat?'[87] This judgment is very typical of the development of the common law in the seventeenth and eighteenth centuries: elementary principles of justice such as the right to a hearing were established by the courts in the shape of simple rules of law, but these rules were the same for officials and for private persons. Nevertheless, part of modern English administrative law has been built on that basis.

The basic structure of American administrative law reveals its English ancestry: the common law applies to the governors as well as to the governed, and the ordinary courts have jurisdiction over matters touching the administration of the country. Some specialized courts have been established by federal statute, for example tax courts; but an appeal against their decisions can be brought before the ordinary courts. If the applicable statute is silent on the possibility of appeals, the US Supreme Court assumes that the decisions can be reviewed by the courts; there is a presumption of 'reviewability'.[88]

The administrative landscape of the United States has one important characteristic which distinguishes it from its European counterparts. Over more than a century, wide powers with regard to specific sectors of economic, social and cultural life have been conferred, by federal statute, on 'federal agencies'. The Interstate Commerce Commission was established as far back as 1877 to monitor railroad tariffs, after ruinous competition had brought some railway companies to the brink of bankruptcy. At present the ICC has wide powers with regard to the transport of goods by rail and road, on inland waterways and by pipeline. Other important agencies are the Federal Trade Commission, which enforces anti-trust law, and the Securities and Exchange Commission, which supervises participation in limited liability companies.[89] There are probably more than fifty such agencies, some of them more important than others.

---

[87] The text can be found, with further references, in Wade and Forsyth, *Administrative Law*, p. 470.

[88] *Abbot Laboratories v. Gardner*, 387 US 136 (1967).

[89] Historical survey in Stephen G. Breyer and Richard B. Stewart, *Administrative Law and Regulatory Policy* (Boston, 1979), pp. 20–35.

These agencies are independent. Their tasks and their powers are fixed by statute, and neither the President nor Congress can tell them how to exercise those tasks and powers. When President Franklin D. Roosevelt dismissed a member of the Federal Trade Commission in 1933, on the ground that the man's ideas on economic policy did not agree with those of the new government, the courts annulled the decision.[90] The independence of the agency was one of the main grounds for the decision.

Within their area of jurisdiction, most agencies perform a number of functions. They may, for example, have the power to impose rules of behaviour: the ICC fixes safety rules for the road transport of inflammable or explosive goods. Agencies may sometimes grant licences. They may also investigate certain practices of enterprises and prosecute offenders; occasionally they can impose fines themselves. Other agencies may issue 'cease and desist orders' if they come across unfair practices, for example unfair labour practices or unfair competition. In case of statutory review, all questions of law will be reconsidered by the court; but matters of fact are usually left to the wisdom of the agency, unless it has acted unreasonably. On procedural issues, however, the agencies are subject to strict judicial scrutiny. As a result, agency proceedings have been more or less 'judicialized'. In 1946, a federal statute established uniform rules on agency proceedings. It fixed detailed provisions on matters such as previous notice of the intention to decide on a certain subject, time limits for filing grievances or complaints, public hearings, legal aid and reporting.[91] This process of assimilating agency proceedings to litigation before the courts was strengthened when the US Supreme Court began to protect procedural guarantees on constitutional grounds, for example with regard to legal aid. These guarantees were made applicable to agency proceedings. Nowadays, private citizens and business corporations are usually represented by lawyers at agency hearings.

However, the federal agencies cannot be considered as courts. Many of them combine, in a single body, the rule-giving, executive and judicial (or quasi-judicial) functions that the US Constitution so carefully distinguishes. That gives American administrative law its particular flavour.

It is, finally, interesting to note that it is the federal agencies, rather than the federal government, which conduct day-to-day economic policy. The

---

[90] *Humphrey's Executor* v. *United States*, 295 US 602 (1935).
[91] Federal Administrative Procedures Act, 1946. Extracts in Breyer and Stewart, *Administrative Law*, p. 1087.

growth of agency government in the days of F. D. Roosevelt's 'New Deal' contributed to this development, but it started much earlier. In Britain, as in France or Germany, it would be difficult to envisage such a situation: not only for political reasons, as the confidence of European politicians in independent bodies is limited, but also because constitutional systems based on accountability of ministers to Parliament make the representative bodies feel they should be able to supervise economic policy as thoroughly as possible.

Courts and governments

7.1. Separation of powers

Separation of powers, in the American sense of the expression, hardly exists in countries with a parliamentary regime of government: although the judiciary is independent, the other two powers are intertwined. The government can only remain in power as long as a parliamentary majority is willing to support it; ministers are accountable to Parliament; and statutes are made – in fact, if not always in law – by the government and the Parliament acting together.

That is particularly true for Great Britain, where the development of cabinet government under a two-party system has tended to establish a clear distinction between the government and its parliamentary majority on the one hand, the opposition party on the other. This distinction characterizes the debates in the House of Commons, the directly elected house, where most decisions of political importance are discussed. The parliamentary debates illustrate that the executive is not independent, or 'separate' from the legislative bodies. Cabinet ministers participate in these debates as members of Parliament, from the government 'front bench'. The opposition party has its own 'front bench', or 'shadow cabinet'. Bills are usually introduced by government ministers; it is also possible for any MP to introduce a 'private member's bill', but such a bill will only be examined if it is compatible with the parliamentary timetable.

With hindsight, it is difficult to understand why Montesquieu's famous book on 'the spirit of the laws' explained its ideas on separation of powers in a chapter called 'De la constitution d'Angleterre'.[1] By the middle of the eighteenth century, when the book was written, the British system of cabinet government was already beginning to take shape. The cabinet depended less and less on the opinions and the whims of the King, and more and more on

---

[1] *L'esprit des lois*, book xi ch. 6 (ed. L'intégrale, p. 586).

its working relationship with both Houses of Parliament.[2] The concept of separation of powers is rarely invoked in British debates on constitutional issues.

In the continental countries of Western Europe, the situation is not as clear-cut as in Britain. There is no two-party system: after general elections, coalitions between different parties will be formed, sometimes after lengthy negotiations, in order to get a parliamentary majority backing the government. Usually, ministers are not themselves members of the representative bodies. Moreover, the national constitution will impose limits on the extent of legislative and executive power, particularly in Germany, where, for example, delegation of legislative power is only permitted within narrowly defined limits.[3] The main rules of the parliamentary regime continue, however, to apply.

In France, that application is not as influential as in Italy, Germany or the Benelux countries. French ministers, although supported by a parliamentary majority, have to collaborate at the same time with the President, who has been directly elected by the population since 1962. In political terms, the French President has his own 'legitimacy'. From a constitutional point of view, it is relevant that he can exercise certain powers without the assent of his Prime Minister: he can, for example, proclaim a state of emergency (but only under certain conditions laid down in the Constitution), or proceed to a referendum (but only on issues enumerated by the Constitution).[4] In the early years of the Fifth Republic, the President always had the same political colour as the parliamentary majority, but since 1986 there have been several occasions where the 'majorité présidentielle' and the 'majorité parlementaire' have not coincided. In such a situation, called 'cohabitation' in modern French (a kind of political concubinage), the Prime Minister has to perform some tricky balancing acts.

Whatever the variations among the constitutional systems in Western Europe, these systems share one very important characteristic: the political debate will normally determine the respective powers and tasks of the representative bodies and the government. For matters not explicitly mentioned in the Constitution, it is not necessary to know whether the government has acted within its 'executive' powers or not, as long as a parliamentary

---

[2] See Robert Blake, *The Office of Prime Minister* (Oxford, 1975), ch. II.

[3] See David P. Currie, 'Separation of powers in the Federal Republic of Germany', *AmJCompL* 41 (1993), 201.

[4] See Art. 16 and Art. 11 Constitution 1958.

majority is prepared to accept what the government did. In American constitutional law, however, it is not the political debate but the legal meaning of the concept of 'executive power' which settles questions concerning the limits of the President's authority. American courts determine whether the President, in taking a certain decision, has remained within the boundaries of his 'executive power' and, conversely, whether Congress, by adopting a certain statute, was still acting in its 'legislative' capacity, rather than intruding upon the executive power reserved to the President. Both problems have given rise to interesting judgments, which have no equivalent in Western Europe.

The concept of executive power is notoriously vague. It cannot simply mean that the President is only allowed to 'execute' the rules adopted by the legislative power. If that were the case, many government acts would not be covered by any of the three concepts used in the Constitution to divide government powers among the different institutions. Some decisions would be in a constitutional no-man's land, which is patently absurd. The US Supreme Court was faced with this problem as far back as 1928, when it had to decide who was to exercise voting rights based on company shares belonging to the United States.[5] The Court seemed to accept that the executive power of the President encompassed every act of government administration that has no legislative or judicial character and is not explicitly mentioned elsewhere in the Constitution. Such a general approach leaves room for doubt, however.

That was illustrated in the 'steel seizure case' of 1952, probably one of the most interesting judgments ever rendered on a topic of constitutional law.[6] A collective bargaining agreement between the employers in the steel industry and the steelworkers' trade unions had expired, and new negotiations had ended in deadlock. The unions then announced a nation-wide strike in the steel industry. President Truman feared that such a strike might jeopardize American defence efforts (this was during the Korean War), because steel was indispensable for the production of war materials. When mediation organized by the President failed to end the crisis, probably owing to ill will on the part of the employers, the President came to the conclusion that the only way to ensure continued availability of steel was to order a governmental seizure of the steelworks. A few hours before the strike was to

[5] *Springer v. Philippine Islands*, 277 US 189 (1928).
[6] *Youngstown Sheet and Tube Co. v. Sawyer*, 343 US 579 (1952).

begin, he issued an 'executive order' directing the Secretary of Commerce to take possession of the most important steelworks and keep them running. The Secretary of Commerce acted accordingly, by taking the administrative measures necessary to seizing the works, and by ordering the chairmen of the steel companies to keep production going as operating managers for the United States. The companies complied, but asked for an injunction restraining the Secretary from continuing to seize the plants. The day after issuing the 'executive order', the President sent a message to Congress explaining what he had done; Congress took no action.

There was no statutory basis for the President's decision. A majority in the Supreme Court considered that a seizure of this nature could only have been ordered by an Act of Congress, or on the basis of such an Act. It was 'law making', Justice Black said speaking for the majority, not part of any 'executive' function. The President's argument that he had been forced to act in a state of emergency was rejected by the majority opinion. The three dissenting judges found that argument convincing: in time of war, they thought, the President had to display the leadership required by the situation; he had to prevent national disasters from happening. In an emergency, executive inaction would be foreign to the 'energy and initiative' in the executive envisaged by the Constitution.

Two concurring opinions expressed a more subtle view. Justice Frankfurter said that the areas of the three authorities of government could not be defined on the basis of an abstract analysis: these areas are 'partly interacting, not wholly disjointed'. For that reason, it was necessary to examine 'the way the framework has consistently operated', since an unbroken executive practice can be treated as 'a gloss' on the executive power vested in the President.[7] He was not satisfied, however, that such an unbroken practice had been sufficiently demonstrated by the evidence before the Court. Justice Jackson constructed a similar argument. He agreed with Frankfurter that presidential powers 'are not fixed but fluctuate, depending upon their disjunction or conjunction with those of Congress'. He then made a distinction between three hypothetical situations: the President acts pursuant to an express or implied authorization of Congress; or he takes measures incompatible with the express or implied will of Congress; or he acts in the absence either of a congressional grant or of a denial of authority. In the latter situation, 'there is a zone of twilight, in which he and Congress

---

[7] See also ch. 1.1.

may have concurrent authority, or in which its distribution is uncertain'. Congressional inertia or quiescence might then entitle the President to act on his own responsibility. However, the present situation was, in Jackson's opinion, not covered by this hypothesis. Congress had not left seizure of private property an open field; in particular, congressional labour legislation had never envisaged this type of measure as a response to strikes. All in all, the steel seizure judgment includes some interesting lessons in constitutional law.[8]

In recent years, there has been more case law on the opposite problem: can Congress enact laws that infringe the executive power of the President? It is important to recall, in this context, that Congress has been trying to reassert its authority after the Nixon years, which brought presidential authority and prestige to a low ebb. How far can Congress go in this direction? In 1983, the Supreme Court examined the constitutionality of the so-called legislative veto on administrative decisions.[9] In enacting various laws, Congress had delegated authority to administrative agencies, but it had retained the right of each of its two Houses to veto administrative decisions with which it disagreed. The majority of the Court held that the legislative veto provision of the Immigration and Naturalization Act violated the doctrine of separation of powers. A veto could be constitutional only when considered as a legislative act, Chief Justice Burger said for the majority; therefore, it would require passage by a majority of both Houses of Congress and the signature of the President. Justice White, dissenting, expressed the view that the legislative veto was an important political invention, which had been indispensable against the background of the delegation of considerable law-making powers to independent agencies. If Congress could delegate these powers under Article 1 of the Constitution, it was difficult to understand why that same provision should prohibit Congress from reserving a check on the exercise of these powers. Justice White's opinion also cited a long list of statutes containing a legislative veto provision, but that did not deter the majority from deciding the case in general terms.

A similar problem arose when Congress, in its efforts to reduce budget deficits, imposed a maximum deficit on federal spending for each of the coming years. It assigned to the Comptroller General of the United States

---

[8] Further materials in Alan W. Westin, *The Anatomy of a Constitutional Law Case. The Steel Seizure Decision* (New York, 1968, reissue 1991).

[9] *Immigration and Naturalization Service* v. *Chadha*, 462 US 919 (1983).

the responsibility of reporting to the President what spending reductions were needed to reduce the deficit to the target amount. The Supreme Court recalled that the Comptroller General was subservient to Congress, as he could only be removed at its initiative. The powers assigned to him by the statute were, however, executive in nature. By placing the responsibility for the execution of the statute in the hands of an officer who was subject to removal by it, Congress retained control over such execution, in violation of the doctrine of separation of powers.[10]

American courts do interfere, therefore, in how the distribution of powers between Congress and the executive is organized. As a result, the political debate in Washington is often coupled with a legal one. When, in 2000, a bill was introduced in the Senate to regulate the procedure for granting pardons or reprieves to convicted offenders, it was generally considered as an attempt to curb the powers of Mrs Reno, President Clinton's Attorney-General (in the USA this is the cabinet minister responsible for the Justice department); the Republican Senate majority regarded her as the kind of unrepentant 'liberal' they abhorred. Immediately, however, the question was raised whether Congress had the authority to legislate on subjects allotted to the executive branch by the American Constitution.[11]

There is little doubt that the Westminster Parliament would be entirely free to enact measures of this kind; but then, the British cabinet has a command over its parliamentary majority which the American President usually lacks. The difference between the two systems is mainly due to the fact that in Britain there is no separation of powers between the cabinet and the Parliament, but a necessity for close collaboration between these two bodies. However, the difference can also be explained by the way the two-party system operates in each of the two countries. In Westminster, the Prime Minister is the party leader and, by the same token, the leader of the 'parliamentary party' in the House of Commons. This group of MPs is well organized, and guided by the cabinet minister appointed as the 'leader of the House of Commons'. In important debates, party 'whips' will uphold party discipline: they will ensure that their colleagues vote with the government. The whips may even threaten unwilling MPs with de-selection as their party's candidate. Normally, the opposition party will also have

---

[10] *Bowsher* v. *Synar*, 478 US 714 (1986).
[11] See Art. II s.2(1) US Constitution. The bill in question was published as S. 2042, 106th Congress, 2nd Session.

whips to enforce the party line in the House of Commons. The rules of 'the club' – the metaphor goes back to the nineteenth-century novelist Anthony Trollope – apply, and they leave no room for intervention by outsiders, judges included.[12]

By comparison, members of the American Congress, particularly senators, are very independent personalities, who would not submit to being directed or admonished by a cabinet minister or a party whip. If a new President has a legislative program of his own, he will have to cajole Congressmen or senators into proposing the necessary bills. Occasionally, a strong President may have a great influence on the legislative work of Congress. That happened, for example, under Franklin D. Roosevelt, a forceful personality with a new and original political program, when first elected, and under Lyndon B. Johnson, who knew exactly how to bully senators into submission by a combination of flattery, promises and threats. In the USA, however, such a situation can last only for a limited time.[13] Moreover, as soon as a bill has been launched, it will be examined in accordance with congressional procedures: there will, for example, be committee hearings at which committee witnesses will be interrogated. Cabinet ministers may be heard, but their position in these legislative proceedings is identical to that of interested individuals or representatives of organized interest groups.[14]

In other words: separation of powers is not only a constitutional scheme in the USA, it is also part of political practice.

7.2. Federalism

Many books and learned articles have been written about federalism in general; even for federalism in the United States alone, the output is considerable. We shall, however, limit our inquiry to one particular problem: the influence of a federal form of government on the respective powers of courts and political institutions.

Here again, American constitutional law provides us with valuable insights. The US Constitution is very precise in its delimitation of federal

---

[12] See Peter G. Richards, *Mackintosh's The Government and Politics of Britain*, 6th edn (London and Melbourne, 1984), chs. 6 and 10.

[13] See also Richard M. Pious, *The American Presidency* (New York, 1979), ch. 6; Grant, *The American Political Process*, ch. 2.

[14] See William J. Keefe, *The American Legislative Process. Congress and the States* (Englewood Cliffs, N.J., 1993), chs. 6–7.

powers; at least, this seems to be so at first sight. Article 1, on the legislative power, enumerates the eighteen matters that come under federal authority ('Congress shall have power . . .' etc.).[15] Some of these items have a slightly eighteenth-century ring ('to establish post offices and post roads', for example), but other powers are still extremely important nowadays (example: 'to coin money, regulate the value thereof, and of foreign coin, and fix the standards of weights and measures'). Legislative powers not attributed to Congress remain in the hands of the individual states.[16] Some of the later amendments to the Constitution, however, give Congress the power to 'enforce', by appropriate legislation, the new constitutional rules or principles they define. That happened, in particular, with regard to the abolition of slavery and the introduction of the due process and equal protection clauses in the aftermath of the Civil War.[17]

Measures of economic policy are not mentioned among the federal legislative powers. They are usually based on the 'interstate commerce clause', part of the power of Congress 'to regulate commerce with foreign nations, and among the several states, and with the Indian tribes'. In the early twentieth century, the US Supreme Court gave a narrow interpretation to the concept of 'interstate commerce'; that was one of the reasons for its collision with President Franklin D. Roosevelt in the 1930s.[18] Since 1937, however, the Court has mended its ways. When, for example, a farmer in Ohio attacked marketing quota provisions for wheat, laid down in a federal statute, the Court upheld the legislation in question. It recognised the importance of the economic effects of the measure. Questions of federal power, said Justice Jackson for the Court, could not be decided by finding that the activities affected by the measure were production rather than trade, or that an individual wheat grower intended his supplies for the local market and not for interstate shipping. The wheat market as a whole was a national market.[19]

The wide interpretation of the interstate commerce clause broadened the scope of federal powers. Federal statutes on non-economic issues could also be founded on this interpretation. The Civil Rights Act, 1964, was adopted in order to eradicate racial discrimination from American society, but it was ultimately based on the commerce clause. The possibility of founding the Act on the enforcement clause of the Fourteenth Amendment had been envisaged; but the Attorney-General was not sure that the Fourteenth

---

[15] Art. 1 s.8 US Constitution.   [16] Tenth Amendment, US Constitution.
[17] Thirteenth Amendment, s.2, and Fourteenth Amendment, s.5, US Constitution.
[18] See ch. 3.5.   [19] *Wickard* v. *Filburn*, 317 US 111 (1942).

Amendment could justify all the elements of the Act, and considered that relying on the commerce clause would exclude any possible doubt as to the constitutionality.[20] The Supreme Court accepted this view in two 1964 judgments.[21]

The second of these judgments concerned a local restaurant in Alabama, 'Ollie's Barbecue', which had a 'take-out service for Negroes' but did not admit blacks to the restaurant. The district court had held that there was no demonstrable connection between food purchased in interstate commerce and discrimination in a restaurant. The Supreme Court reversed the decision: the courts should also consider, it said, the effect of discrimination on the interstate travel of blacks. The concurring opinions recognised that the Civil Rights Act was not about economics but about human dignity, and that not every remote or possible effect on commerce could be accepted as an adequate constitutional ground for uprooting traditional distinctions between local problems governed by state laws and questions of national interest subject to federal laws. What the Court had to consider, however, was not an isolated local event but the aggregate effect of discriminatory practices. Some of the Justices were reluctant to accept this justification. Justice Douglas said that the right of the people to be free from discrimination occupied a higher position in American constitutional law than the movement of cattle or fruit across the state lines. The decision reached by the Court would be more acceptable, he thought, under the Fourteenth Amendment. In a later case, the Court held that an isolated amusement park in Arkansas was covered by the Civil Rights Act because it was open to interstate travellers and served food, a substantial portion of which had moved in interstate commerce.[22] After that judgment, it was difficult to imagine any kind of economic activity that was *not* covered by the notion of interstate commerce.

In political terms, this case law paved the way for a centralizing tendency, which indeed characterized American developments until the 1980s. The large scope for federal legislative powers reduced the role of the states as politically relevant entities. In a somewhat curious way, this centralizing tendency was reinforced by the Supreme Court's activist attitude to human

---

[20] Hearings before the Senate Committee on Commerce, S.1732, 88th Congress, 1st Session, parts 1 and 2.

[21] *Heart of Atlanta Motel* v. *United States*, 379 US 241 (1964); *Katzenbach* v. *McClung*, 384 US 294 (1964).

[22] *Daniel* v. *Paul*, 395 US 298 (1969).

rights protection. As the scope of the rights embodied in the federal Bill of Rights increased, state powers were more and more affected. When the Supreme Court decided that the prohibition of unauthorized searches and seizures, as laid down in the Fourth Amendment, implied that materials seized during an unlawful search of the suspect's home could not be used as evidence against him (the so-called exclusionary rule), it upset many state systems of criminal procedure.[23] When the first judgments in this sense were rendered, about half the states adhered to common law principles, which do not recognise the exclusionary rule. This line of case law led to much dissatisfaction: the state authorities feared it might impede the 'war against crime' they had announced. In 1968, the Senate discussed a bill that sought to limit the jurisdiction of federal courts in order to leave states free to adopt whatever rules on evidence they thought fit; but these efforts finally failed.

The Court itself, however, gradually narrowed down the exclusionary rule in later years. When police officers had acted in good faith, it ruled, the convictions could be upheld.[24] In the 1990s the Court seemed inclined to adopt, in general, a less libertarian view and to emphasize the rights of the prosecution. It limited, for example, the use of *habeas corpus* by prisoners, and it broadened the powers of the police to search motorcars; other decisions in the same vein followed.[25] At about the same time, the Court began to restrict its wide interpretation of the commerce power. In 1995, it held that the power of Congress under the commerce clause was limited to activities that 'substantially affect' interstate commerce.[26] As a result, federal legislation cannot be based on the commerce clause unless an adequate connection to interstate commerce can be established.

The rediscovery of the importance of the states was not limited to the courts. Public opinion had begun to manifest its discontent with a creeping process of centralization it found, or thought it could find, in the acts of the federal institutions, President and Congress as well as the Supreme Court. In electoral campaigns, Republican candidates found that their new emphasis on 'states' rights' was a vote winner. When the Republicans acquired a majority in Congress, they tried to cut federal spending on the ground that more leeway should be left to the states. Academics began to devote more

---

[23] *Mapp* v. *Ohio*, 367 US 643 (1961). See also *Miranda* v. *Arizona*, 384 US 436 (1966).
[24] *Massachusetts* v. *Sheppard*, 468 US 981 (1984).
[25] See Schwartz, *A History of the Supreme Court*, pp. 372–5.
[26] *United States* v. *Lopez*, 514 US 549 (1995).

attention to state constitutions; these constitutions were more attuned to the particular needs of society, they thought, than the federal Constitution, but conferred no less expansive liberties on the citizens.[27] Authors and journalists began to proclaim a 'new federalism' as a new and more adequate constitutional theory, which was to embody a new balance between federal and state powers.[28] The process is still going on.

Summarizing, we could say that the role of the courts in delimiting the extent of federal powers has been very important, but developments in the interpretation of the relevant constitutional concepts show an intimate link with the evolution of political opinion in American society. The rise of economic interventionism under the Democratic Presidents, from Franklin D. Roosevelt to Lyndon B. Johnson, and of the civil rights movements of the 1960s and the 1970s, coincided with the wide interpretation of federal powers and federally protected rights by the Supreme Court (albeit after some initial skirmishes in the 1930s). The Court began to retreat, step by step, when the aversion to 'big government' gained the upper hand in public opinion.[29]

Germany is a federal republic like the United States, but the role of the courts in tracing the boundary line between federal and state powers has been less marked. One of the reasons for this difference is the way the German Basic Law organizes the distribution of powers. It enumerates a relatively small number of 'exclusive' federal legislative powers, but it gives a long list of subjects for 'concurrent' legislation.[30] This list contains some very important items for the legislative agenda, such as civil and criminal law and measures of economic policy. On matters covered by this list, the *Länder* have power to legislate as long as, and to the extent that, the federation (*Bund*) has not exercised its legislative power by enacting a statute.[31] In this significant area of legislation, the constitution leaves the political bodies free to decide whether matters will be left to the *Länder* or governed by federal rules.

---

[27] See Shirley S. Abrahamson, 'Divided we stand: state constitutions in a more perfect union', *Hastings Constitutional Law Review* 18 (1991), 723.

[28] See Kathleen M. Sullivan and Alan Brinkley, *New Federalist Papers, Essays in Defense of the Constitution* (New York and London, 1997), chs. 1 and 2. See, for a detailed analysis, David L. Shapiro, *Federalism, A Dialogue* (Evanston, Ill., 1995).

[29] See also Cass R. Sunstein, *Legal Reasoning and Political Conflict* (Oxford and New York, 1996), chs. 7 and 8.

[30] Art. 73 and Art. 74 s.(1) Basic Law.   [31] Art. 72 s.(1) Basic Law.

In spite of this flexible arrangement, some matters are firmly entrenched in the autonomy of the *Länder*. Matters relating to education, including the school system, and culture are not listed among federal or concurrent powers (with a few exceptions), and the *Länder* jealously guard their authority in these matters. The federal government is aware that it must respect the 'Kulturhoheit' of the *Länder* (something like 'cultural sovereignty'). In European Union negotiations on educational or cultural matters, for example on vocational training, the German delegates will usually have to postpone decisions until representatives of the *Länder* have given their approval.

The notion of *Kulturhoheit* has a pleasing kind of limpidity, but it is not always easy to fix its limits. When a spelling reform of the German language was proposed in 1992, after orthographic experts had arrived at an agreement with their colleagues in Austria and Switzerland, the decision-making process was organized by a conference of culture ministers of the *Länder*. After definitive adoption of the reform by the experts, this conference decided that the *Länder* would introduce the new spelling in all schools, provided the Prime Ministers of the *Länder* and the federal government would give their consent. The reform proved very unpopular: newspapers refused to follow it, action committees were formed to oppose it, and disgruntled parents brought actions against schools and *Land* governments alleging violation of their children's rights to free development of their personality.[32] Finally, the *Bundestag* (federal diet) became alarmed. It decided to debate the uncertainty caused by the reform and the reactions it had provoked. The debate led to a resolution, in which the *Bundestag* acknowledged that the evolution of language could not be imposed by decree but had to be left to grow naturally. In its operative part, however, the resolution did little else than 'invite' the ministers of culture of the *Länder* to organize a procedure for reconsidering the reform, and to 'ask' the federal government to monitor that procedure.[33] After fresh discussions, the conference of culture ministers decided not to make any change to the new spelling rules for the moment; but a new committee of experts was set up, which this time included authors and journalists, to consider whether the new rules should be clarified or further developed.

---

[32] Art. 2 s.(1) Basic Law. See BVerfGE 98 no. 12, *Rechtschreibreform*, 1998.
[33] Bundestag Drucksache 13/10183, 1998.

The spelling episode reveals a typical problem of federalism. For issues of national concern, it is difficult to entrust matters entirely to decentralized government. Popular anxiety will focus on the national government and the national parliament, whatever the constitutional distribution of powers. The German solution to this puzzle is to damp down possible conflicts by striving for a consensus. From this point of view, political culture is different from that in the USA; it also leaves less room for interesting court decisions on the limits of federal powers.

France and Britain are unitary states. Britain is, however, in a somewhat peculiar position. Since the Union of 1707, Scotland has been part of Great Britain, but it retained, as it still does, its own legal system and its own established church (the 'Kirk').[34] Northern Ireland is not part of Great Britain, but it belongs to the 'United Kingdom of Great Britain and Northern Ireland'; in practice it has been less autonomous than Scotland, at least since the 'troubles' started in the 1970s. Some of the dependent territories, such as the Channel Islands and the Isle of Man, are not part of the United Kingdom; but the British government exercises some supervisory powers, and is responsible for the defence and foreign affairs of these territories.[35] This list could be extended to other, and sometimes more colourful, situations, for example Gibraltar and the Falkland Islands. The United Kingdom and its dependencies seem to form a 'composite monarchy' – a term sometimes used by historians to describe Austria before 1918.

The devolution laws of 1998 (the Scotland Act, 1998 and the Government of Wales Act, 1998) did not abolish or change this layered construction of the United Kingdom; they merely added new layers. For Scotland, the powers devolved to the Scottish Parliament seem to amount to prolonging the traditional autonomy of Scotland in certain matters. For Wales, however, the powers of the Assembly are entirely new. For all practical purposes, the country has been part of England since medieval days: English law applies, and the Anglican church, once the established church as in England, has an important presence. There is a Welsh language (a Celtic language), but it is only spoken by a minority of Welshmen.

The future of this complicated structure is uncertain. Many Scots want more autonomy, some even complete independence; the status of Northern Ireland is the subject of a lingering conflict; Spain contests British rule over Gibraltar, Argentina that over the Falklands. Legally speaking, Scotland

---

[34] Further materials in J. D. B. Mitchell, *Constitutional Law*, 2nd edn (Edinburgh, 1968), ch. 5.
[35] See De Smith and Brazier, *Constitutional and Administrative Law*, ch. 3.

presents the most interesting topic, as the Scotland Act attributes important powers to the Scottish Parliament (the Welsh Assembly only exercises powers of legislation specifically delegated to it by the Parliament in
Westminister). For the moment, though, courts can only examine whether
an Act of the Scottish Parliament is within the legislative competence of that
Parliament. Acts of the Parliament in Westminster are still immune from
judicial scrutiny.[36]

7.3. The imperial presidency

The separation between the legislative, executive and judicial branches of
government was laid down in the initial text of the US Constitution, as it had
been adopted by the 'constitutional convention' which met in Philadelphia
in 1787. Obviously, the country was not the same then as it is nowadays:
the thirteen states establishing the US consisted principally of rural communities, all situated near the Atlantic seaboard. In the eyes of the drafters
of the Constitution (the 'founding fathers'), state powers were to remain
more important than federal powers; and none of the three departments of
government would be more powerful than the others. The President of the
United States could not be compared to a monarch such as the British King,
Hamilton wrote in the Federalist papers: his powers were limited by law,
he was to be elected for only four years, and he would be no more than a
magistrate, without 'supercilious pomp of majesty'. There would be a closer
analogy, Hamilton thought, between the President and the Governor of New
York.[37] The early Presidents conformed more or less to this image, except
the first President, George Washington, who was venerated as a war hero.

The proper balance between the three powers which the 'founding fathers' had in mind was inspired by the view that the liberty of the citizens
would be better assured if none of the federal institutions was strong enough
to impose arbitrary or authoritarian decisions. This theory had ancient
roots. It had been advocated very forcefully by Montesquieu: in his view,
constitutions should be arranged in such a way that one power can always
stop the other ('il faut que, par la disposition des choses, le pouvoir arrête
le pouvoir').[38] However, good theories, even if laid down in a constitution,

---

[36] See ch. 2.5 See also Scotland Act, 1998, Schedule 6.
[37] *The Federalist* no. LXVII and LXIX (Hamilton).
[38] *L'esprit des lois*, book XI, ch. 4 (ed. L'Intégrale, p. 586).

are not always able to resist the course of factual developments. The presidency has grown into a kind of office the founding fathers could never have imagined.

One of the main reasons is probably the gradual unification of the United States. In the late eighteenth century, it was still possible to consider the country chiefly as a group of thirteen (later sixteen) states 'united' by a common constitution. During the nineteenth century, the opening up of the West, the concomitant institution of new states, the construction of railways, the start of industrialization, the immigration movements and other social factors encouraged people to consider themselves primarily as Americans, rather than as citizens of their own state; in the Southern states, this process took rather longer. The process of 'Americanization' continued in the twentieth century: the wounds left by the Civil War were gradually healing; modern means of communication and mass production created a certain similarity in life style and culture; shared experiences like the two world wars strengthened the awareness of being more American than anything else.[39] And the most important political problems, such as urban poverty and racial integration, existed nearly everywhere on the territory of the USA.

A second reason for the evolution of the presidency is the development of economic and social legislation. It increased federal powers at the expense of state powers and enhanced the role of the executive, owing to its use of delegation of legislation and the growth of the administration and of administrative decision-making. Social security, welfare and health regulations provide eloquent examples. Franklin D. Roosevelt promised his voters a 'New Deal' in his 1932 presidential campaign; and he was seen as a leader who could fulfil that promise by putting pressure on Congress, or rather by orchestrating the necessary political processes. This example has been followed by other presidential candidates, most notably by Ronald Reagan; each tries to present himself to the voters as the man who will carry out a complete political program. Gradually, the President developed into the spider at the centre of the web of government.

A third reason is the tremendous growth in the importance of foreign relations. The USA has strategic and economic interests in the most remote corners of the planet. The President is the head of the diplomatic and military network created for the protection of those interests. Since the

---

[39] See Brogan, *Penguin History of the United States of America*, chs. 12-13.

collapse of the Soviet Union and the enfeeblement of Russia, the Americans have been alone in the entire world in having such a strong position. It may weaken over the coming years, but it is unlikely to break down very soon. The role of the President as head of a world power enhances his authority in the internal American constitutional framework.

A final element to be considered is the personal role of the President. The executive power is vested in the President, not in his ministers or a cabinet in the British sense of the word; and he alone is the Commander in Chief of the army and the navy.[40] Since the days of Franklin D. Roosevelt, Presidents have organized their own personal staff in the White House.[41] But although the President is at the summit of a large hierarchy of ministers, generals and admirals, diplomats, heads of department and civil servants, he can always bypass the entire bureaucracy by just consulting an old friend from his native state, or one of his personal assistants, or nobody at all. The decision will be his. In fact, the decision-making process often combines these different possibilities. The National Security Council, which prepares the most important military decisions, consists, for example, of some ministers and some of the military as well as of White House assistants.[42]

This evolution reached its apogee in the Kennedy years. The president seemed more able than Congress to show dynamic leadership and embody the consensus of the nation. Authors wrote about presidential leadership;[43] courtiers flocked to Washington to share in the splendour of the White House world; socialites and journalists circled around leading politicians. It could not last. The assassination of President Kennedy, the failure of his successor Lyndon B. Johnson to put an end to the Vietnam War, and the corruption of the presidential administration under Nixon heralded the end of an epoch in American political history.

These events enabled Congress to reassert its role. In 1973, when the country had already shown its dissatisfaction with the growing American involvement in the Vietnam War, both Houses of Congress passed a 'war powers resolution', intended to restrict the President's powers to introduce

---

[40] Art. II s.2(1) US Constitution.

[41] See Charles O. Jones, *The Presidency in a Separated System* (Washington, D.C., 1994), ch. 3; Matthew J. Dickinson, *Bitter Harvest: FDR, Presidential Power and the Growth of the Presidential Branch* (Cambridge, 1999), chs. 8 and 9.

[42] See Theodore M. Sorensen, *Decision Making in the White House* (New York and London, 1963), ch. 5; Jones, *The Presidency in a Separated System*, ch. 3.

[43] Examples: Arthur M. Schlesinger, *The Imperial Presidency* (Boston, 1973); Richard Neustadt, *Presidential Power and the Modern Presidents* (New York, 1990).

armed forces into hostilities. This power could be exercised, the resolution stated, only after a declaration of war or specific statutory authorization, or in case of a national emergency created by an attack on the USA or on its armed forces. President Nixon vetoed the resolution, but his veto was overruled by a two-thirds majority in both Houses.[44]

Gradually, Congress began to refuse presidential leadership in matters of legislation. The Republican Congress majority in the 1990s developed its own congressional program. It went further: it sometimes openly defied the authority of the President by adopting a budget that fixed congressional priorities in matters of government administration. This led to some bitter conflicts.

The courts have kept aloof from this evolution. However, they were required to examine the constitutionality of the appointment of 'independent counsel'. The Ethics in Government Act, 1978, had provided for the appointment, by the federal court of appeals for Washington on the application of the Attorney-General, of independent counsel to investigate certain high-ranking government officials for violation of federal criminal laws. The Supreme Court held that these provisions did not interfere with the President's exercise of his constitutional functions; neither did they violate the principle of separation of powers by 'unduly' interfering with the role of the executive branch.[45] However, Justice Scalia, dissenting, expressed the view that the task of an independent counsel could only be considered as the exercise of executive functions, so that, under the Constitution, the counsel could not be outside the President's supervision and control.

The President can be removed from office only by impeachment for treason, bribery or 'other high crimes and misdemeanors'.[46] Impeachment had its origin in English law, but it fell into disuse in Britain during the nineteenth century, when the evolution of the parliamentary regime had the effect of enabling Parliament to compel the Prime Minister, or any other member of the government, to resign. In American history, cabinet ministers and federal judges have sometimes been convicted on impeachment; but to date, no President has ever been convicted. In these cases, Congress acts in a semi-judicial capacity: the House of Representatives prosecutes;

---

[44] Art. 1 s.7(3) US Constitution. The war powers resolution was published as Public Law 93-148 (1973).
[45] *Morrison* v. *Olson*, 487 US 654 (1988).   [46] Art. 11 s.4 US Constitution.

the Senate, for this occasion chaired by the Chief Justice, renders judgment by a two-thirds majority.[47] President Clinton, faced with a hostile Congress, narrowly survived impeachment in 1999. Congress had asked an independent investigation into certain practices with regard to land transactions in Arkansas during Clinton's pre-presidential days; but since the independent counsel could find no evidence on this point, he turned his attention to some of the President's sexual peccadilloes. The resulting debates were ludicrous rather than enlightening; although occasionally funny, they did not shed any light on the interpretation of the concept of 'high crimes and misdemeanors'.[48]

So, if there was, at any time in the twentieth century, an 'imperial presidency' of the kind repelled by the founding fathers, it certainly shrunk again to more manageable proportions in the last part of that century.

The British Queen (or King) and the German President cannot be compared to the President of the USA, as they have no independent executive powers. French constitutional law presents some parallels, however.

Under the first President of the Fifth Republic, a kind of 'imperial presidency' seemed to develop: Charles de Gaulle enjoyed a prestige rivalled by no French statesman since Napoleon (with the possible exception of Clemenceau). He had a compliant National Assembly, with a 'Gaullist' majority, on his side; his ministers, prime ministers included, faithfully followed his wishes; the Constitutional Council had not yet developed into the important judicial body it was to become; and the country was happy that the Algerian war was ending and a peaceful future appeared assured.[49] It was only during the student revolt of 1968 that the paternalism of the ageing President was challenged. Later Presidents could not count on the same favourable conditions as had characterized the early years of the Fifth Republic: they had little or no charisma, the solid Gaullist bloc disintegrated, courts began to keep a keen watch on the exercise of government powers, and the population was more restless than before.[50] When 'cohabitation' between the President and a Prime Minister of different political colour became habitual, the road to further growth of presidential power appeared to be blocked.

---

[47] Art. 1 s.2(5) and s.3(6) US Constitution.

[48] See also *New York Review of Books*, 5 November 1998 (xlv no. 17, Lars-Erik Nelson) and 18 March 1999 (xlvi no. 5, Ronald Dworkin).

[49] See also Charles de Gaulle, *Mémoires d'espoir, le renouveau 1958–1962* (Paris, 1970), ch. 7.

[50] See René Rémond, *La politique n'est plus ce qu'elle était* (Paris, 1993), ch. iv.

The French Constitution provides for a particular form of impeachment. It stipulates that the President of the Republic is only answerable for acts accomplished in the exercise of his functions in case of 'high treason'. The two Houses of Parliament must accuse him; he will be judged by the 'High Court of Justice', composed of members of the Assembly and of the Senate in equal numbers. The Constitution adds that ministers can be prosecuted before the High Court of Justice for any act accomplished in the exercise of their functions, if that act could be considered as a crime at the moment it was performed.[51] One former Prime Minister, Laurent Fabius, had to appear before the High Court of Justice for his part in a scandal involving contaminated blood, which had shocked the country; but this prosecution seemed politically motivated, as there was not a shred of evidence to show the minister's involvement in the affair.

In the course of 2000, President Chirac was brought into disrepute by press reports about his involvement in improper practices during the years before his term of office, when he was the mayor of Paris. This incident raised the question whether the President could be prosecuted in the ordinary courts for activities preceding his presidency. That discussion was, quite surprisingly, brought to an end by an 'official communication' from the Constitutional Council, recalling that, according to earlier case law, the criminal liability of the head of State could be considered only by the High Court of Justice as provided for by the Constitution. This intervention by the Council in a current debate was severely criticized in the press, but no further action was taken.[52]

French and American experiences both show something about the political and moral authority of the presidency: it seems subject to ebb and flow. That movement is caused by different factors, none of which can be clearly identified as being the force of the law.

7.4. Cabinet government

The British system of cabinet government has a beguiling kind of simplicity. After the general elections, the leader of the winning party is invited to Buckingham Palace 'to kiss hands'; thus installed in the office of Prime Minister, he selects the senior politicians of his party for his cabinet.

---

[51] Arts. 67–8 Constitution 1958.
[52] See *Le Monde*, 21 October 2000 (Frédéric Thiriez). For the American parallel: *Clinton* v. *Jones*, 520 US 681 (1997): the President is not immune from liability actions.

Together, they are supposed to run the country until the next general election. The Prime Minister decides on the date of the next election, but a House of Commons cannot sit for a period longer than five years. The cabinet can be considered as a 'parliamentary executive': it is responsible to Parliament, the ministers remain members of Parliament, and the head of the executive is not the head of State.[53] This form of government is often referred to as the 'Westminster model'.

There have been coalition governments in Britain, for example the wartime cabinets under Winston Churchill, but they do not represent the normal pattern. Since 1945, Conservative and Labour governments have alternated. An electoral system based on the 'first-past-the-post' rule in constituencies (electoral districts) discourages voters from supporting third-party candidates. A bare majority suffices for the cabinet to govern; any minority in the Commons, however large it may be, is consigned to the opposition benches.

The system looks simple and unadorned, but its actual working presents a somewhat different picture. Parliament is supposed to 'control' the cabinet, as the Commons can vote a cabinet out of office; but in reality, the relationship is reversed. The cabinet consists of the leaders of the majority party in the House of Commons, with the result that it will normally be backed by the majority. As long as there is no leadership crisis, the cabinet can confidently count on staying in office and getting its policy approved and its legislative proposals adopted.[54] The cabinet, which can consider itself as a kind of executive committee of the parliamentary majority, will also organize the parliamentary timetable (after consulting the leader of the opposition) and feel responsible for the cohesion of its majority. Party discipline will help to enforce this cohesion. From a political point of view, the position of the cabinet is very solid.

At this point, a second problem emerges. Within the cabinet, the position of the Prime Minister has become exceptionally strong. The politician and journalist Richard Crossman was the first to contend that the period of cabinet government was over and that the British political system had become one of 'Prime Ministerial government'.[55] The Prime Minister, he argued in 1963, dominates the cabinet. He can in fact appoint and dismiss

---

[53] James, *British Cabinet Government*, ch. 1.   [54] See Lijphart, *Patterns of Democracy*, ch. 2.
[55] R. Crossman, Introduction to Fontana edition of Bagehot, *The English Constitution* (1963, reissue London, 1993). See also John Mackintosh, *The British Cabinet*, 3rd edn (London, 1977), ch. xx.

ministers or give them a different job in the government; he decides which problems will be discussed in the cabinet and which will be referred to cabinet committees; he chairs most of the important cabinet committees himself, and he fixes their composition; he decides on the most important appointments (life peerages, senior civil servants, bishops of the Church of England, chairmen of public bodies such as the Arts Council); and finally, the decision to dissolve Parliament and 'go to the country' for a general election is his alone. Some of these arguments are stronger than others, and political practice has not always been the same over the years. Some Prime Ministers have been disposed to bring important issues in the full cabinet, while others have tried to evade cabinet debates if they were not sure about the outcome.[56] Some Prime Ministers have been less willing than others to listen to the point of view of their colleagues before deciding. And strong personalities in the cabinet with important portfolios, like the Treasury or the Foreign Office, are often proud or stubborn enough to defy the Prime Minister's wishes. Commentators agree, however, that the choice of the day for the next general election is in the hands of the PM alone, and that this is one of his major trump-cards in dealings with his colleagues in the cabinet.[57] Besides, it is also possible to point to more recent developments that strengthen the PM's position: nowadays, media attention is more concentrated on the personality of political leaders than on the policy of the cabinet; and Prime Ministers now have their own personal advisers or independent experts in Downing Street (the 'kitchen cabinet'). Strong Prime Ministers like Harold Wilson and Margaret Thatcher could thus exercise a certain control over the most important government departments.

Mrs. Thatcher's career seems to confirm the Crossman thesis. She became the leader of the Conservative party when the party was in disarray, after the last Tory administration had shown a considerable lack of backbone when faced with large-scale social unrest. Margaret Thatcher had her own radical but simple opinions on social and economic matters, and she inspired trust to the Conservative rank and file. She was brought to power at the next general election, and when she had shown her cunning as political leader, she gradually removed the old Conservative barons from her government and started to fill jobs, in the government and in the party organization, with her

---

[56] Bernard Donoghue, *Prime Minister: The Conduct of Policy under Harold Wilson and James Callaghan* (London, 1987), chs. 1 and 9.

[57] Further materials in Marshall, *Constitutional Conventions*, ch. III.

political allies. In so doing she exploited all the resources she could mobilize as Prime Minister: ministers who had the courage to resist the strictness of her economic policy ('the wets', as they were called) might be offered a very unattractive government job (Northern Ireland, for example) at the next cabinet re-shuffle. Initially, she was certainly successful, in particular in curbing inflation, combating the influence of the trade unions and pushing through her European and foreign policy.[58] When Thatcher ultimately overplayed her hand, by imposing a very unpopular form of taxation, the so-called poll tax, first on her cabinet, then on the parliamentary majority, a vehement wave of popular resistance to it roused Conservative politicians from their torpor; her leadership was challenged and she finally resigned.[59] Her successor, John Major, was a completely different kind of person, whose actions seemed to belie any idea of Prime Ministerial government. He felt himself to be a victim rather than an orchestrator of cabinet intrigues.

It is clear, therefore, that the effectiveness of the PM depends very much on the character of the main political players. Crossman's theory is perhaps too general to be correct.[60] However, it initiated an important debate on the growth of the PM's powers. A side-line of this debate concerned the constitutional position of political leadership in general. If Parliament can make and unmake any law whatsoever, and if, in British practice, Parliament means the parliamentary majority, and if that majority is actually guided by the cabinet, in particular by its leadership, i.e. the Prime Minister, the system begins to look like an 'elective dictatorship'. That term has already been used by Lord Hailsham in a 1976 radio lecture. He insisted that the unlimited powers of Parliament, cherished by students of constitutional law, were being gradually transformed into unlimited powers of the cabinet or its leaders. There were hardly any checks and balances in the British system, he said.[61] That view may also be somewhat too general. We shall have a look at three types of checks and balances: political expediency, the House of Lords, and the courts.

Harold Wilson, an experienced politician who was twice Prime Minister, wrote after his periods of office that the British PM is much more dependent

---

[58] See Robert Blake, *The Conservative Party from Peel to Thatcher* (London, 1985), ch. XI.
[59] See David Butler, Andrew Adonis and Tony Travers, *Failure in British Government. The Politics of the Poll Tax* (Oxford, 1994), ch. 8.
[60] See also Geoffrey Marshall, 'The end of Prime Ministerial government?' *Public Law* (1991), 1.
[61] Lord Hailsham, 'Elective dictatorship, the Richard Dimbleby Lecture 1976', *The Listener* (1976), 496.

on the collaboration of others than is often assumed:[62] if he is to secure his party's re-election, his policy cannot be too far removed from public opinion; some groups in society or important organizations must remain inclined to favour the government (traditionally the City for the Conservatives, the trade unions for Labour); senior politicians from the PM's own party must have the opportunity to satisfy some of their political ambitions; adverse elements in that party will be less of a nuisance when they are in the government than when they are kept out. In Wilson's view, the PM's role in framing compromises is more important than his ability to impose his will. According to some observers, however, the Labour administration under Blair is more or less run on the basis of a 'command model', just as the Thatcher administration was.[63]

The House of Lords is often a formidable obstacle to a Labour government, because of its inbuilt Conservative majority. As the 1999 House of Lords reform left some of the nobility, as well as the representatives of the Church of England, in place, that majority continues to exist. The Crown's power to appoint 'life peers' cannot constitute an adequate counterbalance. The Lords can only delay, not finally reject, bills adopted by the Commons; but the government will usually be annoyed to find that one part of a 'package' of proposals has not been accepted by the Lords. Moreover, the House of Lords can amend a bill and thus compel the Commons to re-examine it; this may be time-consuming. After Labour's convincing electoral victory in 1945, the Conservative leader of the House of Lords, Lord Salisbury, announced that the Lords would not obstruct the will of the voters. Therefore, measures promised in Labour's electoral manifesto would not be blocked on political grounds (these measures included a huge nationalization programme); government proposals not corresponding to the manifesto would, however, be 'fair game for the peers'.[64] In later years, the Lords has seemed less inclined to exercise a similar kind of restraint, although the 'Salisbury doctrine' has never been publicly retracted.

The courts are much more critical of what the government does than they were thirty or forty years ago. They never openly criticize political leadership, but they sometimes show their concern with the way the government

---

[62] Harold Wilson, *The Governance of Britain* (London, 1976), ch. 2.
[63] See Peter Hennesy in *The Independent*, 20 May 2000.
[64] See Peter Cosgrave, *The Strange Death of Socialist Britain* (London, 1992), p. 26.

uses its powers. When, in 1977, a member of the public asked for an in-junction against striking post office workers, and was refused the Attorney-General's consent (required under the common law, because he was acting not in his own interest but in the general interest), the Court of Appeal nevertheless granted the injunction.[65] Lord Denning, Master of the Rolls, poured scorn on the political process: the Attorney-General's argument that he was answerable to Parliament, and to Parliament alone, was rebuffed in strong words. It was, Lord Denning said, 'a direct challenge to the rule of law'; and he continued: 'Suppose that he refused his consent for party political reasons, and not in the interest of the public at large. Is he then answerable to Parliament alone? Where he would, perchance, be supported by his own political party?' This piece of rhetoric failed, however, to impress the law lords: the judgment was reversed by the House of Lords.[66]

This irritation of the Court of Appeal at the way cabinet ministers exer-cise their powers was not an isolated incident. Nearly twenty years later, the same court examined the legality of regulations issued by the social security minister concerning the right of asylum seekers to welfare support.[67] In the future, such support would be available only to those asylum seekers who had asked for asylum immediately on arrival in the United Kingdom, but only after a decision on asylum had been taken; the regulation did not af-fect immigrants who did not ask for asylum. A Congolese woman who had made her request for support upon her arrival in a refugee centre attacked the legality of the refusal by way of judicial review. The Court of Appeal held that the regulations were *ultra vires* because they were 'uncompromis-ingly draconian' in their effect. As Lord Justice Brown put it: 'Parliament cannot have intended a significant number of genuine asylum seekers to be impaled on the horns of so intolerable a dilemma: the need either to abandon their claims to refugee status or alternatively to maintain them as best they can but in a state of utter destitution.' Such a 'sorry state of affairs', he thought, could only be achieved by statute, not by government measures.

Authors frequently complain that it is difficult to predict how cabinet government will develop in the next decade. It is clear, though, that the

[65] *Gouriet v. Union of Post Office Workers* [1977] QB 729.
[66] *Union of Post Office Workers v. Gouriet* [1978] AC 435. The strike had been organized for political reasons (anti-apartheid).
[67] *R v. Secretary of State for Social Security*, ex p *Joint Council for the Welfare of Immigrants* [1996] 4 All ER 385.

British system of government no longer shows the balance between the executive and the legislature which the Westminister model was once thought to embody.[68]

I should add that the position of the federal chancellor in Germany reveals some similarities to that of the British Prime Minister. He is not just the first among equals (*primus inter pares*) like the Belgian or Dutch prime ministers; he is elected by the Bundestag, other ministers are appointed by him, and the no-confidence vote must be directed against him. The Bundestag can only express its lack of confidence if it at the same time elects a new chancellor (the 'constructive' no-confidence vote).[69] The Basic Law explicitly provides that the federal chancellor can issue 'general guidelines of policy', which determine and limit the responsibility of other federal ministers.[70] The accountability of ministers to Parliament is restricted to the affairs of their department left to them by the 'guidelines'.

The legal character of these 'guidelines' has given rise to a persistent debate among constitutional scholars: do they relate only to general problems of policy, or also to specific issues of departmental responsibility? Can they affect any aspect of government administration, or only matters of principle? Practice on these points shows little uniformity. In a somewhat legalistic way, German authors assume that the chancellor's power to issue such guidelines implies that the federal government as a whole cannot issue directives to individual ministers. The constitutional court went a step further: it held that Parliament had no power to issue such guidelines, except when the Basic Law provided otherwise.[71]

For our purposes, it is important to emphasize the dissimilarities between the federal chancellor and the British Prime Minister. The PM's strength is based on the political circumstance that a majority of the Commons accepts him and his cabinet and will support him in time of trouble. The chancellor has his own tasks and responsibilities by virtue of the federal consitution, the Basic Law; and although he ultimately depends on the Bundestag's acceptance of his administration and his policy, his relationship with that body is governed by rules of law, not just by political practice.

---

[68] See Peter Richards, *Mackintosh's The Government and Politics of Britain*, 6th edn (London and Melbourne, 1985), pp. 142 and 245.

[69] Arts. 63–4 and Art. 67 Basic Law.   [70] Art. 65 Basic Law.

[71] BVerfGE 1 no. 43, *Deutsch–Französisches Wirtschaftsabkommen*, 1952.

7.5. Dualism in France

In France, the executive power is two-headed (*bicéphale*). The President of the Republic is directly elected by the voters, and he appoints the Prime Minister; but the Prime Minister can remain in office only as long as the National Assembly has not passed a no-confidence vote or expressed its disapproval of the government's policy programme.[72] The Prime Minister directs the operations of government, and the government 'determines and conducts' national policy; but the President chairs the Council of Ministers.[73] For most regulations or decisions, the President can only act on the advice, and with the counter-signature, of the Prime Minister; but he can exercise some important powers independently, without the consent of the government or the Prime Minister.

Most important among these independent presidential powers (apart from the power to appoint and dismiss the Prime Minister) are the dissolution of the National Assembly, the submission of certain bills to a referendum and the proclamation of a state of emergency.[74] The power to dissolve the Assembly empowers the President to choose the most opportune moment for getting the parliamentary majority he likes. He may, however, make miscalculations, as voters are sometimes more volatile than the political pundits have assumed. Submission of important measures to a referendum can be used in order to bring interminable political debates to a conclusion; but the President may also provoke a referendum for the sole purpose of strengthening his own position. President de Gaulle, whose aversion to political parties made him into a supporter of the referendum, was often accused of transforming it into a plebiscite: he asked the people for a vote of confidence rather than for an opinion on a piece of legislation. He always made it clear that he would resign if the voters did not accept his plans (and that is what he actually did in 1969). Later Presidents have been less eager to submit bills to a referendum. The referendum about the ratification of the Treaty on European Union (the Maastricht Treaty, which broadened the scope of the European integration process) took place in an atmosphere of nearly total indifference. The outcome, a narrow majority in favour, was considered as a political setback for President Mitterrand,

---

[72] Arts. 8 and 49–50 Constitution 1958.   [73] Arts. 21, 20 and 9 Constitution 1958.
[74] Arts. 12, 11 and 16 Constitution 1958.

whose wish to demonstrate that the country stood behind his European policy was snubbed by the electorate. It is important to realize that, in French political thinking, there is a direct link between the referendum and the sovereignty of the people, which is one of the basic tenets of the 1958 Constitution.[75]

The President's power to proclaim a state of emergency accords with the principal task of the President as described by the Constitution: he guarantees the proper working of institutions and the continuity of the State. He must fulfill this task 'par son arbitrage',[76] a concept that, in legal French, is far from clear. The usual meaning of the term is the settling a dispute between two or more parties by a third person; but in the context of the Constitution, it may also refer to an authoritative decision (something like 'arbitrament' in English).[77] French authors regard the term as ambiguous, but they tend to think that it is intended to mean that the President is not a participant in the political power game but an outsider, who can sort things out in times of crisis.[78] There is no case law or political practice to clarify matters. The only time the continuity of the State and its institutions may have been threatened was in 1961, when the generals in Algiers revolted; then the President proclaimed a state of emergency, and the Conseil d'Etat held that it could not examine the compatibility of that proclamation with the Constitution.[79]

The basic idea behind the presidential responsibility for the continuity of the State and its institutions is probably the concern to prevent the kind of disorder that characterized the final days of the Fourth Republic. If things are in danger of going wrong, one institution, unshaken by events, should symbolize the continuity of the Republic. De Gaulle felt that he had represented that continuity after the collapse of the French army in 1940 and again in the turbulent days of May 1958. If the need should arise again, his successors should do the same. It is also possible to argue, however, that on this point the 1958 Constitution confirmed an earlier practice, which already existed under the Third Republic. In 1918, the Conseil d'Etat recalled

---

[75] Art. 3 Constitution 1958.   [76] Art. 5 Constitution 1958.

[77] This is the translation used in Bell, p. 246.

[78] Maurice Duverger, *Institutions politiques et droit constitutionnel*, vol. 2, *Le système politique français*, 15th edn (Paris, 1980), p. 241; Georges Burdeaux, *Droit constitutionnel et institutions politiques*, 19th edn (Paris, 1980), pp. 501–3.

[79] CE 2-3-1962, *Rubin de Servens*, *Rec.* 143, *Les grands arrêts* no. 96; see also ch. 5.1.

that, under the constitutional laws of 1875, the President of the Republic was the head of the administration, with the power to execute the laws; 'therefore', the court said ('dès lors'), it was his task to ensure that the public service established by the laws and regulations always functioned properly and that particular difficulties such as a situation of war would not paralyse its working.[80]

The extent of the powers and responsibilities of the President is influenced not only by constitutional and legal provisions, but also by earlier government experience in France. Ever since 1789 the country has been prone to political unrest, occasionally to fits of violence. The continuity of the public service, so often emphasized in the case law of the Conseil d'Etat, can be interpreted as a principle of law intended to act as a counterbalance to occasional irregularities. The courts recognise that, in times of war or civil commotion, police powers must have a wider scope than in times of peace, as national security will require a different type of measure. A decree restricting the freedom of movement of 'filles galantes' (courtesans) in an important naval base during the First World War might, according to the Conseil d'Etat, have been invalid in ordinary times, but it should be upheld in times of danger to the nation.[81] Here again it would seem that the continuance of the Republic prevails over other considerations. One could argue that the 1958 Constitution reflects a similar concern in its description of the President's responsibilities.

The exact boundary line between presidential and governmental powers is difficult to trace. That difficulty has been increased by the President's tendency to claim an important say in matters of foreign relations and defence. De Gaulle considered this area more or less as his 'domaine réservé': the 'grandeur' of France in the world was, after all, one of his main political doctrines. However, since government ministers accepted or tolerated this practice, it seemed to become part of the constitutional framework. De Gaulle's successors continued to behave as if the Constitution had allocated responsibility for foreign affairs to the President. When the first cohabitation government was formed in 1986, after the defeat of the left-wing parties in the parliamentary elections, President Mitterrand insisted that he had to approve personally the appointment of the Minister of Foreign Affairs, who

---

[80] CE 28-6-1918, *Heyriès*, *Rec.* 651, *Les grands arrêts* no. 35.
[81] CE 28-2-1919, *Dames Dol et Laurent*, *Rec.* 208, *Les grands arrêts* no. 37.

ought to have opinions on European and international issues close to his own.[82] Later cohabitation governments have shown the same pattern. We could perhaps use Justice Frankfurter's metaphor here and maintain that 'life' has written a 'gloss' on the wording of the Constitution.[83]

As a result of all this, the Prime Minister is often in an unenviable position. He is very much the President's man if the parliamentary majority has the political colour of the President. Nevertheless, he can be summarily dismissed when the President is dissatisfied, or just feels that a different Prime Minister might do better.[84] In case of cohabitation, the Prime Minister's position is in one way stronger, as it is backed by recent parliamentary elections, but in another way more difficult, as he will have to find the necessary compromises between the often diverging views of the parliamentary majority and the President. In other words, whatever the political situation, the Prime Minister will always be walking on eggs.

One way of interpreting the dualist character of the French executive is to consider it as a form of 'orléanisme'. This expression refers to the system of government under King Louis-Philippe, who came to power in 1830 after a brief popular uprising.[85] During his reign, ministers were answerable both to him and to the Houses of Parliament. The King was thought to represent the element of continuity in the nation, as opposed to the fluctuating opinions of the voters as expressed in the representative bodies. It is quite possible that the drafters of the 1958 Constitution had such a construction in mind; but that model does not explain the actual working of the constitutional system. On some points, there is not only a dual responsibility of the government, but also a division of tasks between the President and the government, and that fits badly with the *orléaniste* conception.

The most suitable characterization is perhaps that of a 'dyarchy', an expression used in India when it was under British rule. Under the Government of India Act, 1919, some powers (such as law and order) were held by the colonial governor, others (such as education and health) by provincial legislative councils. At the same time, regional rulers were

---

[82] See Pierre Avril, *La Vme République. Histoire politique et constitutionnelle* (Paris, 1987), nos. 239 and 242.

[83] See ch. 1.1 and ch. 7.1.

[84] See René Charrière, *La Vme quelle République?* (Paris, 1983), pp. 65–71.

[85] Louis-Philippe was a descendant of Philippe, Duke of Orléans, Regent of France after the death of King Louis XIV. .

responsible to the governor as well as to the provincial legislative council. The 'dyarchy' did not work very well, and the 1919 Act was replaced by new legislation in 1937.[86]

A French kind of dualism was adopted in Portugal when the country returned to democracy in 1976. The government can remain in power only so long as it enjoys the confidence of the President, who is directly elected, as well as of the parliamentary majority. Besides, the President can exercise some powers independently, without ministerial counter-signature (dissolution of Parliament, submission of bills to a referendum, appointment and dismissal of the Prime Minister). As in France, the President's main responsibility is to ensure the continuity of the nation and the proper working of the institutions. Thus the Constitution has an unmistakable French look. Political practice is, however, not entirely the same as in France. Since 1982 the government's link with the President has been gradually loosened.[87] One possible explanation is that Mario Soarez, who was then elected to the presidency, was himself a supporter of parliamentary supremacy; he was inclined to consider his role as President in this light. It appears that he thus set a pattern for his successors. For France, such a development has been predicted, but has not materialized so far. France has not only a weak parliamentary tradition, but it also still feels that the misadventures of the Fourth Republic were at least partly caused by this defect. Seen in that light, the 1958 Constitution has instituted a new political balance between a strong President and a government supported by Parliament, and that balance has worked without major upheavals for more than forty years.

---

[86] See Joshi, Pinto and Da Silva, *The Indian Constitution and its Working*, 3rd edn (Bombay, 1986), ch. I under II-B; Michael Edwardes, *A History of India*, revised edn London, 1967), part VI ch. 2.

[87] See Jorge Miranda, 'Le chef du gouvernement au Portugal', in *Droit, institutions et systèmes politiques: Mélanges en hommage à Maurice Duverger* (Paris, 1987), p. 153.

Courts and individual rights

8.1. Freedom of expression

The American Bill of Rights starts, in the First Amendment, with the protection of 'the freedom of speech, and of the press', as well as the freedom of religion and of peaceful assembly. Freedom of expression is indeed traditionally considered as an element of democratic decision-making, and also as one of the most important bulwarks against undemocratic tendencies in government.

One of the charms of American case law is that the US Supreme Court often identifies the rationale of constitutional provisions before trying to define their meaning. Decisions on the First Amendment are frequently based on a philosophy of freedom, which is explicitly expounded in some of the Court's judgments. A famous example can be found in the concurring opinion of Justice Brandeis in a 1927 case concerning the constitutionality of a state statute banning communist trade unions.[1] The opinion sets out to explain 'why a state is, ordinarily, denied the power to prohibit dissemination of social, economic and political doctrine which a vast majority of its citizens believe to be false and fraught with evil consequence'. The men who won American independence, Justice Brandeis states, believed 'that freedom to think as you will and to speak as you think are means indispensable to the discovery and spread of political truth; that without free speech and assembly discussion would be futile; that with them, discussion affords adequate protection against the dissemination of noxious doctrine'. These men knew, he continues, 'that order cannot be secured merely through fear of punishment for its infraction; that it is hazardous to discourage thought, hope and imagination; that fear breeds repression; that repression breeds hate; that hate menaces stable government; [...]and that the fitting remedy for evil counsels is good ones'. And he concludes: 'Believing in the power of

---

[1] *Whitney v. California*, 274 US 357 (1927).

reason as applied through public discussion, they eschewed silence coerced by law – the argument of force in its worst form.'

There may be some old-fashioned Enlightenment optimism in this prose, which most of the present generation of lawyers will not share; but it is impressive in its succinct rendering of an important theory, which has continued to inspire the Court's case law. In 1964, Justice Brennan, speaking for the Court, referred to 'a profound national commitment to the principle that debate on public issues should be uninhibited, robust and wide-open, and that it may well include vehement, caustic and sometimes unpleasantly sharp attacks on government and on public officials'.[2]

Considerations like these brought the Court to the conclusion that freedom of speech has a 'preferred position' in the scale of values of the American Constitution. The expression was coined by Justice Stone in the 1940s, and rapidly embraced by the Court.[3] It would certainly be going too far to suggest that the 'preferred position' doctrine implies a presumption of invalidity affecting any statute relating to communication; but there is no doubt that, in case of conflict between freedom of speech and one of the other civil liberties, such as the privacy of individuals, the former will normally prevail. Moreover, the Court is usually very suspicious of any measure liable to limit the freedom of expression, even if there are good grounds for such a measure. Many statutory provisions have been struck down by the Court for being 'overbroad': although legislative measures may make certain inroads into the freedom of speech in order to ensure the protection of an overriding public interest, such as national security, these restrictions should not go beyond the limits of absolute necessity. A statutory provision barring members of communist organizations from jobs 'in any defense facility' was overbroad, and therefore unconstitutional, because it failed to take into account that there are also non-sensitive jobs in defence facilities.[4] The Court referred to 'the fatal defect of overbreadth', on the ground that the statute contained an interdiction that sometimes could and sometimes could not be justified in terms of First Amendment rights. Recent case law does not refer very frequently to the 'preferred position' of these rights, but the doctrine has not been abandoned by the Court, as many judgments show.

---

[2] *New York Times* v. *Sullivan*, 376 US 254 (1964).
[3] *Jones* v. *Opelika*, 316 US 584 (1942) and 319 US 103 (1943).
[4] *United States* v. *Robel*, 389 US 258 (1967).

As the Court's rationale is based on the protection of public speech and
political discussion, it is consistent with the Court's approach that political
protest in non-verbal forms is also protected under the First Amendment.
Burning the American flag as a political protest could not be prohibited by
legislation, as it benefited from First Amendment protection: it expressed
a viewpoint the legislature was not allowed to suppress.[5] However, forms
of speech without any political connotation are also covered by freedom
of speech. After some initial hesitation, the Court held that 'commercial
speech' was also protected. A state statute forbidding pharmacists to ad-
vertise prescription drug prices was invalid:[6] speech which did no more
than propose a commercial transaction was still speech deserving the protection of the First Amendment. Thus the link between the scope of the
Amendment and the Court's justification of it was loosened. That made it
more difficult to determine the exact boundary of demonstrations covered
by the freedom of expression.

In 1991, for example, the Court held that nude dancing, forbidden by
an Indiana statute, was a form of 'expressive conduct', which fell within the
'outer perimeters' of the First Amendment.[7] The majority thought that the
prohibition could nevertheless be upheld, because of the state's overriding
interest in protection of public morals. Four dissenting judges refused to
accept this balancing of interests: the prohibition aimed at suppressing a
form of free expression, and was consequently unconstitutional. Justice
Scalia, though concurring in the result, rejected the idea that nude dancing
could be protected on the basis of the First Amendment: the Indiana statute
was a law regulating conduct, not speech, he said.

The limits of the First Amendment were further explored in a 1998
case concerning the funding of the arts.[8] Members of Congress had been
shocked to discover that highly provocative exhibitions, including homo-
erotic photographs, had been funded by federal money through the National
Endowment for the Arts. After a debate in Congress, the enabling statute
was amended to provide that the Endowment, in judging the artistic merits of grant applications, should take into consideration 'general standards
of decency and respect for the diverse beliefs and values of the American
public'. Some performing artists challenged this provision, arguing that it

---

[5] *Texas* v. *Johnson*, 491 US 397 (1989).
[6] *Virginia State Board of Pharmacy* v. *Virginia Consumer Council*, 425 US 748 (1976).
[7] *Barnes* v. *Glenn Theater Inc.*, 501 US 560 (1991).
[8] *National Endowment for the Arts* v. *Finley*, 524 US 569 (1998).

was void owing to its vagueness and impermissibly viewpoint based. The majority of the Court held that the provision was merely 'hortatory' and could not be considered as a restriction on artistic expression; but Justice Souter, quoting earlier case law, thought the complaint was justified. He pointed in particular to the 'chilling effect' on free expression that could result from provisions of this kind. Justice Scalia, consistent with his earlier opinions, said that the system of funding the arts has nothing to do with the liberties protected by the First Amendment.

From a comparative point of view, it is interesting to note that the US Supreme Court's decisions are normally devoid of any kind of deference towards the political institutions. When the federal government asked, in 1971, for an injunction against publication of 'very secret' military documents concerning the run-up to the Vietnam War, the Court refused to grant it. Although the papers had been stolen from the Pentagon, the interest of unimpeded public access to information concerning events of great political importance had to prevail, the Court held; and it invoked the First Amendment when coming to this conclusion.[9] This 'Pentagon papers' case was the occasion for some well-constructed judicial reflections on the importance of the free flow of information; but some of the concurring opinions also show the Justices' distaste for the Vietnam War. This is, for example, what Justice Black said: 'Only a free and unrestrained press can effectively expose deception in government. And paramount among the responsibilities of a free press is the duty to prevent any part of the government from deceiving the people and sending them off to foreign lands to die of foreign fevers and foreign shot and shell.' The US government may have been annoyed by judgments on symbolic speech such as flag burning; but it must have been extremely irritated by the Court's protection of – what the government primarily saw as – theft of secret documents from the Ministry of Defense. There is little doubt that in most other countries the government's interest in keeping war information secret would have prevailed.

An English case that raised comparable issues concerned publication by the press of confidential information about the actions of the counter-espionage branch of the British Security Service.[10] A former employee had gone to live in retirement in Tasmania; there he wrote a book on the working

---

[9] *New York Times* v. *United States*, 403 US 713 (1971).
[10] *AG* v. *Guardian Newspapers Ltd.* [1990] 1 AC 109.

of the service, which contained allegations of irregularities and unlawful activities carried out by some of its members. The book (*Spycatcher*) was published in Australia. The British government tried to prevent publication, but the Australian courts refused to grant relief, on the grounds that they had no jurisdiction to enforce an obligation of confidence owed to a foreign government. When the book was also published in the United States, English newspapers started to serialize it. The Attorney-General, acting for the Crown, tried to prevent further publication and sought damages in tort; but he was only successful in the second claim. The House of Lords held that the Crown would have been entitled to an injunction restraining the author if his book had been first published in Britain. However, such an injunction could only be granted when it could be shown that publication was harmful to the public interest; the circumstances of the case included, however, the world-wide dissemination of the book's contents. Nevertheless the newspapers were in breach of an obligation of confidentiality, the court held, when they started serialization; they had therefore enriched themselves and were liable for damages. Lord Goff's speech (the five law lords each gave an individual opinion) observed that he saw no inconsistency between English law on this point and Article 10 of the European Convention on Human Rights, protecting the freedom of expression. 'This is scarcely surprising', he said, 'since we may pride ourselves on the fact that freedom of speech has existed in this country perhaps as long as, if not longer than, it has existed in any other country in the world.'[11]

This expression of pride (and perhaps of some prejudice) does not alter the fact that the American Supreme Court gives greater scope to the freedom of expression than the English courts traditionally do. When the Crown sought an injunction to restrain publication of the political diaries of Richard Crossman (relating juicy details about cabinet meetings), it was unsuccessful on the ground that more than ten years had elapsed since the recorded events took place.[12] Therefore, publication of the diaries, though in breach of confidentiality, could do no harm to the public interest. This judgment was given five years after the 'Pentagon papers' judgment in the USA.

In a similar way, there is no parallel in English law to the particular protection of 'public speech' in American case law, which resulted in the rule that public figures cannot bring a libel action for statements relating to

---

[11] Art. 10 European Convention did not have any direct effect in English law at the time.
[12] *AG v. Jonathan Cape Ltd* [1976] QB 752.

their official conduct, except in case of actual malice.[13] The House of Lords accepted that public bodies such as institutions of local or central government could not bring an action for damages against newspapers reporting their activities.[14] Such an action would, their lordships declared, amount to an undesirable fetter on the freedom to express that uninhibited criticism of government activities that is the hallmark of a democratic society. Therefore a county council could not sue for libel. However, the judgment made it perfectly clear that individual councillors themselves could bring an action for libel if their individual reputation was wrongly impaired by the same publication.

In a 1999 case concerning libellous press statements about a former Irish Prime Minister, the House of Lords expressly refused to consider a generic defence protecting political discourse.[15] Although some of the law lords made eloquent remarks on the importance of the freedom to disseminate and receive information on political matters, they seem to have given a relatively narrow scope to that freedom. Some of the speeches (the law lords were not unanimous) were to the effect that that the courts should primarily examine whether it would be 'in the public interest' for the material to be published, a concept which seems a far cry from the rationale formulated by Justice Brandeis in 1927.

The frank and libertarian, but also very individualistic, tone of the US Supreme Court on these matters has a kind of uniqueness which makes it difficult to find parallels in Europe. It is true that the European Court of Human Rights sometimes uses a terminology it seems to have borrowed from American case law. For example, it has repeatedly used expressions to the effect that the freedom of information encompasses dissemination of ideas 'that shock, offend or disturb', and that it should enable everyone to 'participate in the free political debate which is at the very core of the concept of democratic society'.[16] But, as far as I am aware, these expressions have not yet found their way into the case law of national supreme courts; these courts are, of course, often inspired by quite different traditions.

The German constitutional court refuses, for example, to give privileged status to the freedom of the press. In a case concerning an action for damages by a former Iranian princess, on account of the publication

---

[13] *New York Times* v. *Sullivan*, 376 US 254 (1964). See ch. 3.3.
[14] *Derbyshire County Council* v. *Times Newspapers* [1993] AC 534.
[15] *Reynolds* v. *Times Newspapers* [1999] 3 WLR 1010.
[16] Example: ECHR 23-4-1992, *Castells*, Series A no. 236.

of a backbiting interview that had in fact never taken place, the Court rather emphasized the importance of the *Persönlichkeitsrecht* ('right of the personality') based on the constitutional protection of human dignity and of everyone's right to the free development of his or her personality.[17] It recognised that the freedom of the press might, in individual cases, have a restrictive effect on the protection offered to these personality rights, but it was these rights, rather than the freedom of the press, which should have preference in such a situation. In the case of the unfortunate princess, the Court went out of its way to strike the balance between the different rights and interests on the basis of the facts of the individual case. More generally, the Bundesverfassungsgericht tends to interpret human rights in such a way that they are in harmony with each other and with the 'constitutional order' the Basic Law is thought to establish.[18] That leaves no place for the rugged individualistic tone frequently adopted by the American Supreme Court.

Similar remarks could be made with regard to the orientation chosen by the French Constitutional Council. Bills examined by the Council which raise issues of press freedom normally concern the limits of legislative activity in economic, social or cultural matters, in other words the question of where French *dirigisme* must give way to the requirements imposed by the freedom of the press. Thus the Constitutional Council examined the constitutionality of a bill instituting a separate competition regime for corporations engaged in press publications, and of measures reorganizing the national system of television broadcasting.[19] The first of these two decisions made some interesting observations on the freedom of the press as first and foremost a right of the readers, who are the 'main beneficiaries' of that freedom; but this view may be a reaction to the old French press law of 1881, which has many provisions on the rights of authors, publishers and printers, but seems to forget the rights of readers. And the television case tried to strike a balance between the freedom of information, on the one hand, and technical requirements and constitutional objects such as the protection of public order, respect for the liberty of others and the preservation of the pluralist character of the media, on the other. It recalls the classical case law of the Conseil d'Etat on the obligation of the public

---

[17] BVerfGE 34 no. 25, *Princess Soraya*, 1973.   [18] See ch. 4.1.
[19] CC 11-10-1984, *Entreprises de presse, Rec.* 73, *Les grandes décisions* no. 38; CC 17-1-1989, *Conseil Supérieur de l'Audiovisuel, Les grandes décisions* no. 44.

authorities to reconcile the exercise of their tasks, for example those relating to public order, with the freedom of expression.[20]

This clearly is a non-American approach. The American courts would probably think that 'reconciling' things is a matter for politicians, not for the courts.

8.2. Protection against police powers

Police powers have a close link with the exercise of individual rights. The police can be an instrument of oppression, in particular when they are biased against certain groups of the population, and more in particular when their activities are backed by the courts. An extreme example was the position of blacks in the American South in the post-reconstruction years: they were denied full participation in political and social life by a silent conspiracy between the police and leading groups of the white population, with the help of the courts. That situation lasted well into the twentieth century.

An illustration can be found in a 1960 case, where the US Supreme Court annulled a conviction for 'loitering and disorderly conduct' by the police court of Louisville, Kentucky.[21] It was a strange case, probably one of the strangest in the annals of the Supreme Court. The suspect had been denied due process of law, the Court held, because he had been convicted without any evidence of guilt. The man, a black, had a past of habitual drunkenness, and he had often been detained in custody on grounds of protection of public order. When he stopped drinking, the police continued to pick him up as soon as they saw his face, bringing fake charges or sometimes just detaining him for a couple of hours. The courts in the South would do nothing, at the time, to oppose such forms of harassment of blacks.

One of the reactions of the Supreme Court has been the gradual strengthening of the procedural guarantees mentioned in the Bill of Rights. The ban on 'unreasonable searches and seizures' under the Fifth Amendment was strictly upheld, and it was made applicable to state measures on the basis of the due process clause of the Fourteenth Amendment ('incorporation').[22] Initially, searches and seizures without a specific search warrant were always considered as unreasonable, although there were some narrowly defined exceptions to the warrant requirement. Later case law accepted, however, that

---

[20] See ch. 6.2.   [21] *Thompson* v. *Louisville*, 362 US 199 (1960).   [22] See ch. 3.3.

searches and seizures could be reasonable in the absence of individualized suspicion. The trial judge should assess this reasonableness by undertaking a 'context-specific inquiry', said the Supreme Court in 1997.[23] Thus a sharp rise in drug use by student athletes could justify random drug testing without individualized suspicion. It is not yet clear how far this weakening of Fifth Amendment requirements will ultimately go. The anti-drugs policy, pursued by federal and state authorities alike, seems to be strengthening police powers once again. In the city of Charleston, South Carolina, pregnant women were urine-tested in state hospitals for medical purposes, but when it turned out that many of them tested positive for cocaine use, the results were turned over to the police without any search warrant. After their babies were born the mothers were arrested.[24] It is not yet clear whether this practice will be recognised as lawful, but it seems indicative of a change of opinion on the relationship between police powers and individual rights.

Perhaps there is a cyclic movement in the attitude towards police powers. The libertarian ideas characterizing the intellectual and cultural climate of the 1970s put the emphasis on the restriction of police powers. In the USA the civil rights activists of the 1960s, and the protest movements against the Vietnam War, had considered the police more or less as enemies who used all the powers they had to suppress dissent. However, the climate of the 1990s was different: experience with terrorism, the growth of organized crime and the increased use of narcotics shifted the emphasis to the effective use of police potential rather than its limitation. Shifts in public opinion influence politics, but they also seem to influence judicial attitudes. There has been a swing of the pendulum, not only in the USA but also in Europe.

An interesting instance of the swing occurred in Germany. The inviolability of the home had always been considered as a very important fundamental right, expressing the idea of the rule of law. Initially, the Basic Law provided that the home was inviolable and that searches were permitted only in case of acute danger or after judicial authorization.[25] In 1998, the Basic Law was amended in order to permit 'acoustic surveillance' of private houses. If specific facts justify the suspicion that a person has committed a particularly serious crime, the amendment provides that 'technical means of acoustic

---

[23] *Chandler* v. *Miller*, 520 US 305 (1997).

[24] *Ferguson* v. *City of Charleston*, case 97-2512, US Court of Appeals for the Fourth Circuit, 13-7-1999. I took the case from the Court's home page: www.law.emory.edu/pub.

[25] Art. 13 Basic Law, now ss. (1), (2) and (7).

surveillance of any house where the suspect is supposedly staying may be employed'.[26] There is no time limit in the text of the provision itself, but it requires judicial authorization, which can only be granted for a limited period of time. Some procedural guarantees for a moderate use of this new possibility have been added. Nevertheless, the constitutional change did not meet with universal approval. The new rules had an unsympathetic look: there is, in a way, a treacherous element in acoustic surveillance, as the victim will normally not be aware of it – he can only remonstrate when it is too late. According to some authors, the amendment cunningly changed a fundamental freedom from state interference into a sophisticated system of legitimate restrictions to that freedom.[27] However that may be, the constitutional amendment illustrates the shift in ideas concerning the risks and benefits of extended police powers.

In France, the discussions have more a political than a legal character. It started in 1980, when the government proposed legislation to 'strengthen the security and protect the liberty of individuals'. The left-wing parties, then in opposition, vehemently attacked the bill, in particular the obligation of 'everybody' to show identity papers to the police in certain situations, for example in case of threats to public order. The bill was passed after an acrimonious debate full of complaints that 'liberty' should not be sacrificed to 'security', or the other way round. When the bill had been submitted to the Constitutional Council by the opposition parties, however, the Council upheld the provisions on identity checks. It held that the protection of public order was necessary to safeguard the security of persons and goods and could therefore be considered as implementing principles and rights of constitutional value.[28] The Council softened this uncompromising view somewhat by recalling that the bill would not increase the power of the police to keep people in custody: those who refused to reveal their identity could only be brought to a police station for further identity checks and for no longer than six hours. Some other provisions of the bill were, however, considered incompatible with the Constitution. Thus, the power attributed to the presidents of civil or criminal courts to ban advocates from the hearings for a maximum of two days if they had troubled 'la sérénité des débats' (something like 'the quiet atmosphere of the court room') was struck

---

[26] Art. 13 s.(3) Basic Law.
[27] See Sabine Michalowski and Lorna Woods, *German Constitutional Law. The Protection of Civil Liberties* (Aldershot, 1999), ch. 19.
[28] CC 20-1-1981, *Sécurité et liberté, Rec.* 15, *Les grandes décisions* no. 32.

down: it violated, said the Council, the rights of the defence resulting from the fundamental principles recognised by the laws of the Republic.[29] The decision did not put an end to the conflict of views. When the left won the parliamentary elections of 1981, it issued new legislation to modify the statute, albeit not as profoundly as it had promised its electors. When, some years later, laws were passed to facilitate the prevention of tax evasion, the Constitutional Council ruled that searches of private homes always required a judicial warrant, even in cases not covered by criminal law or criminal procedure.[30] The debate between the 'libertaires' and the 'sécuritaires' is not yet ended.

In Great Britain the debate took a different turn. The English have always been proud of their police. For a long time there was a generally held conviction that the lack of a centralized police authority and the independence of the local police forces constituted an important guarantee against misuse of police powers. As Lord Denning said in 1968 about the Metropolitan Police Commissioner in London:

> He is not subject to the orders of the Secretary of State, save that under the Police Act, 1964, the Secretary of State can call upon him to give a report, or to retire in the interest of efficiency. I hold it to be the duty of the Commissioner of the Police of the Metropolis, as it is of every chief constable, to enforce the law of the land. He must take steps so to post his men that crimes may be detected and that honest citizens may go about their affairs in peace. [...] The responsibility for law enforcement lies on him. He is answerable to the law and to the law alone.[31]

The traditional trust in the police forces began to decline in the 1980s, after the first large-scale race riots in the London area, which appeared to have been triggered off by unnecessarily violent police behaviour in Brixton, South London. When, somewhat later, prisoners convicted of terrorist attacks were set free because the evidence had been concocted by the police, political pressure led to an investigation and to new legislation. The independence of the metropolitan police and of the regional police

---

[29] See on this concept Jean Rivero, *Le Conseil Constitutionnel et les Libertés*, 2nd edn (Paris, 1987), II-3.

[30] See L. Favoreu, 'La constitutionnalisation du droit pénal et de la procédure pénale', in *Droit pénal contemporain: Mélanges en l'honneur d'André Vitu* (Paris, 1989), p. 167.

[31] *R v. Metropolitan Police Commissioner* ex p *Blackburn* [1968] 2 QB 118. The Secretary of State mentioned in the judgment is the Home Secretary.

forces was maintained. The Police Act, 1997, instituted complaints procedures. However, the same statute and later legislation also created new
police powers with regard to entry to property for the detection of serious crime, and established new police measures for preventing 'anti-social'
behaviour.[32]

In 1998 the European Court of Human Rights held that the United
Kingdom had failed to respect Article 6 of the Convention (on access to
justice and fair trial) by not providing judicial relief when complaints about
police behaviour had led nowhere.[33] The case concerned the interesting
question whether the police have a duty of care with regard to persons feeling
threatened by criminal acts; but the answer of the court to that question
is too case-oriented to allow any general conclusion. English courts do not
accept such a duty of care towards potential victims of crime; but German
courts do.[34]

It is difficult to find any precise statements in legislation, judgments or
the literature on the exact limits of police powers. The courts do not seem
to have progressed much further in trying to delimit these powers than the
Conseil d'Etat did in 1933, when it introduced a line of case law it still adheres
to: the *maire*, as head of the local police, is responsible for the observance of
public order in his territory, and he therefore has power to prohibit public
meetings, the distribution of press publications and the public showing of
films, if such meetings, publications or films are liable to provoke serious
trouble; but he is obliged to reconcile this power with respect for civil
liberties such as the freedom of the press and of peaceful assembly.[35] Such
a rule leaves much unresolved: it is a perfectly clear standard if there is
no justification for police action at all, or if no reasonable person could
possibly have doubted the necessity of such action. For the rest, it is a
matter of balancing competing interests, and that is, of course, a job that
can very well be left to the courts. The difficulty, however, is this: it is also a
job police officers often have to perform on the scene of action, with only a
limited knowledge of the exact situation and in difficult or even dangerous
circumstances. It is then, perhaps, too easy for the courts to censure police

[32] See part III, Police Act 1997; ch. II, Crime and Disorder Act 1998.
[33] ECHR 28-10-1998, *Osman* v. *United Kingdom*, ECHR Reports 1998-VIII (p. 3124).
[34] See B. S. Markesinis, 'Judicial style and judicial reasoning in England and Germany', *CLJ* 2000,
    294 (no. 59–2).
[35] CE 19-5-1933, *Benjamin*, *Rec.* 541, *Les grands arrêts* no. 27; see ch. 6.2. See also CE 18-12-1959,
    Les films Lutétia, *Rec.* 693, *Les grands arrêts* no. 93.

action because they know better by hindsight what should have been done. This is probably why the courts generally leave wide discretion to the police in their operational decisions.[36] The courts act at the margin: by requiring respect for procedural guarantees, by imposing complaints procedures, by interfering in case of misuse of police powers, and by accepting liability for dangerous police behaviour.[37] Nevertheless, the principal assessments are to be made by the police themselves, in the light of the circumstances of the case.

Two and a half centuries ago, Montesquieu expressed the view that the courts constituted a power terrible among men ('terrible parmi les hommes') if they were not embedded in a balanced constitutional structure.[38] Under present conditions, such a remark might very well apply to the police.

8.3. Church and State

In England there has been an established church since the days of Henry VIII, and the British King or Queen is still the nominal head of the Church of England. At present, the most important practical effect is that the Anglican bishops are appointed by the Queen, on the advice of the Prime Minister. Sixteen bishops have seats in the House of Lords in their own right. And the Prince of Wales, as heir apparent to the throne, is supposed not to marry a Roman Catholic (a 'papist'). Scotland has its own established church, which is Presbyterian, not Anglican. Generally speaking, however, discrimination against Catholics, dissenters and Jews vanished from British public life in the course of the nineteenth century (but not from Ireland when still under British rule).

As a reaction to the unequal treatment of different denominations under British colonial rule, the newly independent United States soon adopted the principle that an established church is contrary to the American concept of the freedom of religion. The First Amendment to the US Constitution bars any law 'respecting an establishment of religion, or prohibiting the free exercise thereof'. We should probably bear in mind that, from the very start, the inhabitants of the USA formed a less homogeneous group than

---

[36] See Wade and Forsyth, *Administrative Law*, pp. 361–3.
[37] See also CE 24-6-1949, *Consorts Leconte*, *Rec.* 307, *Les grands arrêts* no. 72.
[38] *L'esprit des lois*, book xi, ch. 6 (edn L'Intégrale, p. 587).

the English or Scottish peoples, religiously as well as ethnically, and that the heterogeneous composition of the American population increased considerably, particularly in the North and the West, when the great migration movements from Europe started in the early nineteenth century.

The 'establishment clause' of the First Amendment (as opposed to its 'free exercise clause') has been given a wide interpretation. This is how Justice Black, speaking for the Court, saw its implications in 1947:[39]

> Neither a state nor the federal government can set up a church. Neither can pass laws which aid one religion, aid all religions, or prefer one religion over another. Neither can force or influence a person to go to or to remain away from church against his will or force him to profess a belief or disbelief in any religion. No person can be punished for entertaining or professing religious beliefs or disbeliefs, for church attendance or non-attendance. No tax in any amount, large or small, can be levied to support any religious activities or institutions, whatever they may be called, or whatever form they may adopt to teach or practice religion. Neither a state nor the federal government can, openly or secretly, participate in the affairs of any religious organizations or groups and *vice versa*.

And Justice Black referred to the words of Thomas Jefferson that the establishment clause was intended to erect 'a wall of separation between church and state'. He added that this wall 'must be kept high and impregnable'.

These high-minded considerations have not always provided a clear guideline for dealing with the manifold expressions of religious feelings. School prayers and bible reading at the opening of the school day in public schools were banned by the Court: they constituted an 'endorsement' of religion that was contrary to the First Amendment. There is endorsement, said the Court, when the school conveys a message that religion is to be favoured, preferred or promoted over other beliefs [40] But when a school district followed a policy of allowing high school principals to invite a religious official to give a non-sectarian, non-proselytizing invocation and benediction on graduation day, the Court considered that it was nevertheless a school-sponsored religious activity, which might have a 'coercive effect' on students.[41] The same test was applied when students were allowed to say prayers at the start of school basketball games. It is not always easy to

---

[39] *Everson v. Board of Education of New Jersey*, 330 US 1 (1947).
[40] *County of Allegheny v. American Civil Liberties Union*, 492 US 573 (1989).
[41] *Lee v. Weisman*, 505 US 577 (1992).

determine, it would seem, what kind of psychological pressure amounts to coercion. The lawfulness of the prayers or benediction depends, then, on the specific circumstances of the case; thus the test leaves some leeway to the trial courts.

A third test used by the Court is 'entanglement'. The Court banned the use of public funds to aid the construction of church-related schools on the ground that the government was not allowed to promote 'sectarian education', and that it could not undertake the surveillance necessary to check whether the money was only used for neutral purposes, because it would then get 'entangled' in parochial affairs.[42] Tax exemptions for churches were subjected to the same test. Chief Justice Burger recognised, in one of these cases, that it was impossible to envisage a total separation between church and state activities, in particular as far as schools and buildings were concerned. Fire inspections, building and zoning regulations and state requirements under compulsory school-attendance laws necessarily implied contacts and collaboration. Perhaps, the Chief Justice thought, the line of separation, far from being a 'wall', was rather a variable barrier, depending on all the circumstances of the particular relationship. The 'entanglement' standard is, however, not very clear: the Court leaves the states free to provide church-related schools with neutral services or facilities, such as transportation, school lunches or health services. It is difficult to understand, in that light, why subsidies for building activities might lead to more 'entanglement'. The argument that any building may later be converted into a chapel, or otherwise used to promote religious interests, looks somewhat slight: a bus can also be used for religious purposes.[43]

In spite of the strict line the Court traditionally pursues, it is rarely unanimous. In a 1989 case (a 6–3 decision), which concerned tax exemptions for religious publications, Justice Scalia, dissenting, opined that the interpretation of the establishment clause should be reconciled with the free exercise clause: states should feel free to favour the free exercise of religion in a non-sectarian way.[44] The judges of the majority were, however, not impressed. But when in 1961 Jewish shopkeepers alleged that Sunday closing laws endorsed Christian beliefs and so amounted to an establishment of religion, the Court refused to accept it: 'Sunday is a day apart from all others. The cause is irrelevant; the fact exists.' That is hardly a convincing

---

[42] *Lemon* v. *Kurtzman*, 403 US 602 (1971).·   [43] See also *Agostini* v. *Felton*, 521 US 203 (1997).
[44] *Texas Monthly Inc.* v. *Bullock*, 489 US 1 (1989).

argument for non-Christians. It may suggest, though, that in some cases the free exercise clause is more important than the establishment clause: the Court found that the petitioners did not allege 'any infringement of their own religious freedoms due to Sunday closing'.[45] An argument based on free exercise failed, however, to convince the Court (again in a 6–3 decision) when two members of the Native American Church had used a forbidden drug for sacramental purposes during a service. An Oregon statute prohibited the use of the drug in question, peyote, and made no exception for the sacramental use of it. The two petitioners had been denied unemployment benefits because they had been dismissed for work-related misconduct. Part of the Court's majority relied on precedents holding that the First Amendment was not offended when obstacles to the exercise of religion were merely the 'incidental effect' of a generally applicable legal provision. A second part of the majority could accept this reasoning only if the particular criminal interest of the state authorities asserted by the Oregon government presented a 'compelling interest' of the state; but they thought that Oregon did have such a compelling interest in the specific circumstances of the case. The minority rejected this assessment; they held that Oregon's interest in refusing to make an exception for the religious use of peyote was not sufficiently compelling to outweigh the petitioners' right to the free exercise of their religion.[46]

Consequently, it would seem that the metaphor of the 'wall of separation' rests on an oversimplification. To make matters even more paradoxical, unchallenged federal statutes provide that the US motto, 'In God we trust', must be put on American coins and banknotes; prayer in Congress is permitted; and every hearing of the US Supreme Court itself is opened by a 'crier' shouting: 'God save the United States and this honorable Court!' But when certain states adopted a religious motto in recent times (such as: 'With God all things are possible' in Ohio), the federal courts were inclined to consider this as an unconstitutional reference to Christianity. The endorsement test, it appears, does not necessarily ban the word 'God', but the Ohio motto was a direct quotation from the New Testament.[47]

Some of the Court's more severe judgments, for example on nonsectarian school prayers, have been criticized for being anti-religious, in

---

[45] *McGowan v. Maryland*, 366 US 420 (1961).

[46] *Employment Division of Oregon v. Smith*, 494 US 872 (1990).

[47] See Matthew 19:26 ('With men this is impossible; but with God, all things are possible').

particular by born-again Christians and Republican politicians; but it is fair to say that the principle itself of separation between church and state is generally accepted in the USA. There is no political debate of any significance. Such a debate is slowly starting in Great Britain. As the country gradually turns into a nation of many faiths, the position of the Church of England is being more and more considered as an oddity which can only be explained by historical reasons. Nevertheless, it has led to a more or less accepted social and cultural pattern that could hardly be imagined elsewhere. The opening of the English legal year, for example, takes place in Westminster Abbey, where the Lord Chancellor mounts the pulpit to read the Scripture to his judges; and that doesn't seem to disturb his or their consciences very much. Times, however, may be changing. Nowadays it is difficult to see why the monarch should be the 'defender of the faith' as professed by the 'C of E' and forget about the millions of Catholics, Muslims, Methodists, Buddhists and others living on British soil. So, unobtrusively, a debate on a possible disestablishment is beginning in academic and journalistic circles.[48] As there is no clearly perceptible popular pressure for achieving such a mini-revolution, politicians have kept aloof so far.

Historically speaking, France occupies an intermediate situation between the two extreme positions represented by Britain and the US. Under the *ancien régime*, the French kingdom was considered as the most loyal partner of the Roman Catholic Church ('fille aînée de l'Eglise' or eldest daughter of the Church).[49] The kings were supposed to rule France by virtue of the *droit divin*: they were sacred kings, whose authority had a divine origin. The State prosecuted Protestant heretics, or tried to come to terms with them; monastic orders and other Catholic organizations ran the educational system and the hospitals; there was often a merging of religious and secular functions. The vehemence of the Revolution was also directed against the Church: monasteries were destroyed, priests were dismissed or killed, possessions of the Church and the monastic orders were sold, and for a short time, a new State religion was introduced based on 'Reason' ('la déesse Raison'). After the Napoleonic interlude, the Restoration tried to re-establish the *status quo ante*, and part of the conflicts that made nineteenth-century French history into such an agitated period concerned the role of the Church. It was

---

[48] See *The Independent*, 18 April 2000 ('Disestablishmentarianism is no longer a dirty word').
[49] See Alain Peyrefitte, *Le mal français* (Paris, 1976), p. 176.

only in the Third Republic, after 1875, that the separation between Church and State was ultimately achieved. An 1882 statute solemnly proclaimed the lay character ('la laïcité') of the Republic.[50] Education was secularized. The preamble to the 1946 Constitution, to which the 1958 preamble refers, explicitly provides that free and secular public education ('enseignement public gratuit et laïque') will be provided by the State.[51] The Church is free to establish its own schools, but that does not mean that they can be subsidized from public funds.

A law of 1905 brought the finishing touch to the separation. It abolished the concordat Napoleon had concluded with the Pope in 1801; it cut all remaining administrative links with the Church; it prohibited any form of subsidy to any religion or religious organization or group; it even stated that the Republic did not recognise any form of worship (*culte*).[52] I have it from reliable sources that after the entry into force of the 1905 statute the last Madonna sculptures were removed from the Paris Palais de Justice; but the statue of St Louis remained in one of the corridors (he had, after all, been King of France), and the medieval Sainte Chapelle was left as it had always been, at the heart of the court buildings ('the pearl in the oyster'). The full rigour of the rule has been moderated since 1905: it was not introduced in Alsace when the region was reunited with France in 1919, and in 1959 a new statute allowed the subsidizing of Catholic education.

Sometimes the secular character of the State schools gives rise to new problems. When Muslim girls insisted on wearing their headscarves in class, on the ground that Islamic teaching told them to do so, the initial reaction of head teachers was to send them home, as religious symbols could not be tolerated on the school premises. This led to a public debate, which revealed profound disagreement among the participating journalists, academics and politicians. After the Conseil d'Etat had given advice which was far from clear, the government decided to leave it to head teachers to determine whether the girls' headscarves could be considered as religious symbols important enough to constitute a threat to the *laïcité* of the school. This lukewarm defence of the *école laïque* led to some criticism from Catholic authors who were wondering why, after this decision,

---

[50] See Jean Rivero, 'La notion juridique de laïcité', *Recueil Dalloz* (1949), Chr. 137.

[51] Preamble, Constitution 1946, s.13.

[52] See Valdrini, Vernay, Durand and Echappé, *Droit canonique*, 'Précis Dalloz' (Paris, 1989) nos. 780–99.

crucifixes and other cross-like symbols were still banned. Case law has not yet shown the way to a clear solution.[53]

Earlier in this book we saw that the German federal constitutional court has held that the obligation imposed by Bavarian *Land* legislation to put crucifixes on class walls of public schools is contrary to the Basic Law.[54] For our present purposes, it is interesting to note that the Bundesverfassungsgericht interprets religious freedom in such a way as to guarantee the right of individuals not to get involved in acts of worship of a religion which they do not share. The cross, says the Court solemnly, is the specific symbol of Christianity. Putting that symbol in classrooms does not have a coercive effect, in the sense that pupils would feel compelled to identify with the Christian message; but it has the effect of appealing to the pupils to follow its moral lessons. Cautiously, the Court adds that it is impossible to disregard the contribution of Christian religion to present-day forms of thought and of behaviour, and that public education should reflect that influence. The obligation of Bavarian schools to put crucifixes in every classroom goes, however, beyond these limits.[55] The reasoning of the Court recalls, therefore, that of the American Supreme Court, but it is more subtle.

Obviously, the concept of separation of Church and State is less unambiguous than the term would suggest. In constitutional law, simplicity is often a virtue; but, one would be tempted to say, only up to a point.

8.4. Methods of protection

Individual rights are not always protected in the same way and according to the same methods. To begin with, the concept of 'rights' itself is not unambiguous: it is applied to dissimilar claims and interests, and that dissimilarity may concern the very nature of the rights in question. Freedom of expression and the right to social assistance do not belong to the same category of rights. Some citizens' rights can be protected by the courts because they merely prevent public authorities from doing something, for example, imposing censorship of books or newspapers. Other rights, on the contrary, can only be exerted by administrative action or by political decisions: the right to a suitable education cannot be effectively exercised unless the public authorities have been able to create an appropriate school system. Second

[53] See Claude Durand-Prinborgne, 'Le port de signes extérieurs à l'école', *RFDA* 13(1) (1997), 151.
[54] See ch. 4.1.   [55] BVerfGE 93 no. 1 *Kruzifix*, 1998, under c–ii.

complication: there are several 'layers' of human rights protection. In the USA, state constitutions often have their own bills of rights, with the result that there is, at least in theory, a double system of protection. In Western Europe, citizens can usually rely on rights established by national constitutional law as well as on those guaranteed by the European Convention on Human Rights. So different distinctions must be made.

We shall first turn to the second problem. It presents itself most clearly in the American situation. The initial thirteen states were established before they formed the Union. The Virginia Declaration of Rights, considered as the oldest of the state bills of rights, was adopted in 1776, fifteen years before the Bill of Rights was added to the federal Constitution. The Ninth Amendment to the US Constitution explicitly provides that the enumeration of 'certain rights' in the Constitution cannot be interpreted in such a way as to deny or disparage 'others retained by the people'. In a similar vein, the Tenth Amendment adds that powers not attributed to the federal institutions are reserved to the states 'or to the people', respectively.

In the second half of the twentieth century, the wide interpretation of the rights protected under the federal Bill of Rights by the US Supreme Court had the effect of overshadowing state constitutions.[56] The Supreme Court's case law on equal protection, for example, was entirely based on the federal Constitution; moreover, in its early years it had to be enforced on the unwilling, or at least uncooperative, authorities of the Southern states. Legal literature focused on the protection of individual rights as laid down in the federal Bill of Rights and the Fourteenth Amendment. This was part of the centralizing tendencies that characterized the 1960s and 1970s.

Gradually, however, the Supreme Court began to rediscover the Tenth Amendment. In 1941, Justice Stone, speaking for the Court, could still emphasize that the Amendment 'states but a truism that all is retained which has not been surrendered'.[57] In later years, this expression was sometimes quoted in individual opinions; but the evolution took a different turn. It is well worth taking a rapid look at the history of this 'truism' in the hands of the Supreme Court. The Tenth Amendment resurfaced in 1976, when the Court invoked it when deciding that congressional legislation authorized by the commerce clause could not compel a state to do things it was not allowed to do under its own state constitution.[58] The effect of this ruling has never

---

[56] See ch. 7.2.   [57] *United States v. Darby*, 312 US 100 (1941).
[58] *National League of Cities v. Usury*, 426 US 833 (1976).

been entirely clear. Later case law tried to water it down, in particular by holding that the Tenth Amendment only shields states from the application of federal laws addressing matters that are 'indisputably' attributes of their state sovereignty. On this ground, the Court ruled, for example, that the Amendment did not immunize states against the extension of the federal Age Discrimination Act to state and local governments. The fixing of the limits between what is, and what is not, indisputably within the scope of the autonomy of the different states can, of course, give rise to extensive legal debate.[59]

In 1985, the Court frankly overruled its earlier judgments (in a 5-4 decision), by holding that neither the Tenth Amendment nor the structure of the federal system justified restrictions on the power of Congress to apply otherwise valid commercial regulations to state or local governments.[60] Justice Blackmun, speaking for the Court, referred to the difficulties the lower courts had experienced when trying to implement the earlier rulings; but he also stressed that the political processes established by the Constitution were the primary safeguard against congressional legislation impairing the position of state governments. The implication seemed to be that the ball was back in the field of the political institutions, particularly Congress. However, shortly afterwards the Court resurrected the Tenth Amendment again. In a case on environmental law, it held that Congress was free to regulate the disposal of radioactive waste, but that it could not compel state legislatures to adopt statutes on this point.[61] The Court said it did not 'revisit' its earlier case law, but it is difficult to see how it could strike down a federal statute for violation of the Tenth Amendment on the basis of its own precedents. Anyway, the new line of thinking has been welcomed by authors who favour the use of federalism as a serious constraint on the powers of Congress.[62]

Is the Ninth Amendment also a 'truism'? Generally speaking, there is an increasing tendency in the Supreme Court's case law to pay respect to state constitutions, and to the way they are interpreted by the states' highest courts. The US Supreme Court has, for example, authority to decide issues of state law underlying federal claims; but in order to promote what it sometimes calls 'a cooperative judicial federalism', it will often refer the

---

[59] Further materials in Laurence H. Tribe, *Constitutional Choices* (Cambridge, Mass., 1985), ch. 9.
[60] *Garcia* v. *San Antonio Metropolitan Transit Authority*, 469 US 528 (1985).
[61] *New York* v. *United States*, 505 US 144 (1992).
[62] See also Erwin Chemerinsky, *Constitutional Law* (New York, 1997), ch. 3.

state law question to the state supreme court, under a procedure called 'certification', so as to have a proper basis for its ruling on the federal issue. A federal *habeas corpus* action will, for example, often raise questions of criminal procedure that are within the province of the states. The Supreme Court now recognises that state courts may be better equipped to interpret and understand state criminal legislation or practice.[63] Thus, there is now a certain reluctance to 'federalize' matters, even when touching individual rights.

This new policy has, however, not been associated with the Ninth Amendment. In earlier individual opinions, the Amendment had been advanced as a justification for recognising rights not explicitly mentioned in the Constitution, for example the right to privacy;[64] but the Court ultimately decided to found such rights exclusively on the due process clause of the Fourteenth Amendment. And anyway, unlike the Tenth Amendment, the Ninth Amendment has never been considered as a protection of state constitutions against usurpation of federal power.[65]

There are also layers of protection in Europe, but from a legal point of view they have a different character. Protection of individual rights is afforded by national constitutions as well as by international treaties, in particular the European Convention on Human Rights. In the latter case, the operation of the system of protection depends on the relationship between national and international law. In some constitutional systems, for example that of the Netherlands, national courts simply apply the provisions of the European Convention, and the interpretation given to these provisions by the European Court of Human Rights. British judges, on the other hand, traditionally refused to apply the Convention directly, until an Act of Parliament, the Human Rights Act 1998, authorized and obliged them to do so.[66]

A curious intermediate position is occupied by France. The 1958 Constitution provides, as does the Dutch Constitution, that treaties duly ratified and published shall have priority over national legislation; but it adds that this is subject to reciprocity, i.e. to the condition that the treaty in question is also implemented in this way by the other party or parties to it.[67] The

---

[63] See *Fiore* v. *White*, 528 US 23 (1999).
[64] Example: concurring opinion of Justice Goldberg in *Griswold* v. *Connecticut*, 381 US 479 (1965).
[65] See also Nagel, *Constitutional Cultures*, ch. 4.
[66] See, respectively, ch. 4.3 and ch. 2.5. [67] Art. 55 Constitution 1958.

Convention does not play the same important role in France as it does in the Netherlands, for reasons which appear to have more links with differences in the psychology of lawyers than in constitutional provisions. In the case of Germany, the low profile of the European Convention in legal practice can be explained by the wide protection of individual rights courts can offer on the foundation of the Basic Law and its elaborate catalogue of human rights; for France, however, such an argument does not apply.

There is one other striking difference between the attitudes of French and Dutch courts. It concerns the interpretation of the Convention provisions. The Dutch courts apply these provisions as interpreted in the case law of the European Court; in France, courts take account only of European judgments that have been rendered in cases against the French Republic.[68] It is not easy to find a justification for that restriction. However, the proper working of the European Convention is not put at risk by differences of this kind. Whereas European Union law often has the purpose of unifying or harmonizing provisions of national law, the European Convention on Human Rights merely aims at setting minimum standards.[69]

I come now to the other problem of plurality: the dissimilarity of 'rights'. As constitutionalism developed, from the eighteenth century onwards, the emphasis was put on what we would nowadays call 'negative' freedoms, or rights which have a protective character (*Abwehrrechte* or rights of defence in German). These rights and freedoms debar public authorities from doing certain things, such as imposing censorship, arbitrarily searching homes or persecuting people for their opinions. These 'civil liberties' traditionally constitute the hard core of human rights protection. However, even the oldest declarations and bills of rights also refer to rights of a quite different nature. The French *Déclaration des droits de l'homme* of 1789 referred, for example, to the right of 'society' to require a rendering of accounts from any public official.[70] Modern examples abound. According to the Dutch Constitution, Dutch citizens residing in the country are entitled to social assistance from public funds if they have insufficient means of existence.[71]

---

[68] See Régis de Gouttes, 'La Convention européenne des droits de l'homme et le juge français', *RIDC* 51 (1999), 7.

[69] See Art. 53 European Convention on Human Rights.

[70] Art. 15 *Déclaration des droits de l'homme et du citoyen*, 1789.

[71] Art. 19 s. 3 Constitution of the Netherlands. See also Art. 11 s. 1 UN Covenant on Economic, Social and Cultural Rights.

German literature distinguishes between three categories of rights: the traditional 'negative' freedoms such as the freedom of expression; 'social' rights requiring the public authorities to do something, for example the right of citizens to a clean environment, sometimes mentioned in modern constitutional documents;[72] and *Leistungsrechte* or rights to some financial performance by the public authorities, such as the right to social assistance. The difficulty with the construction of such categories is that it is impossible to draw neat boundary lines between them. Under German law, the freedom of association embodies trade union freedom, which would be incomplete without the right of unions to participate in collective bargaining agreements; and under German law, such a right can only be effectively exercised if there is an appropriate legislative basis. Similarly, French constitutional lawyers take the view that freedom of expression implies the necessity of a pluralistic press; but that may require government action rather than abstention.[73] Although it is clear, therefore, that the exercising of some rights depends primarily on the courts, that of others primarily on political or administrative action, it is not possible to say exactly which types of rights belong to the first, and which to the second group.

A word should be added on equality. From a legal point of view, it is founded on a 'right' to equal protection. It is very difficult, however, to characterize that right: it is certainly not a mere freedom, or a right that can be fully implemented by the courts. Nor does it fit in the categories of social rights or rights to a performance. The main difficulty may be that, though couched in terms of individual rights, equality is something more. It requires a comparison between groups in the population (blacks and whites, women and men, Catholics and Protestants etc.) rather than of individuals, and the concept of rights is ill adapted to that situation. Civil litigation, for example, is not always the appropriate tool for arriving at a balanced view of the relationship between groups. Individuals may claim that they are entitled to equal treatment with other individuals; but a full enforcement of rights of that kind concerns the organization of society as a whole rather than the position of specific individuals. This may be one of the reasons why courts encounter so many obstacles when trying to implement equality principles without a solid legislative backing. The

---

[72] Example: Art. 37 EU Charter of Rights.
[73] See also CC 17-1-1989, *Conseil Supérieur de l'Audiovisuel, Les grandes décisions* no. 44.

history of American case law has shown that, ultimately, courts are unable to impose, for example, a system of education entirely free from racial and ethnic distinctions.[74] Such a situation can only be achieved, if at all, by legislative and administrative action. But American experience also shows that this action can be prepared, or even unleashed, by the courts.

8.5. The institutional framework

In most countries, the judiciary is considered as the principal institutional device for protecting citizens against violation of their rights and liberties. That is particularly noticeable in countries where a constitutional court, such as the German Bundesverfassungsgericht, acts as a watchdog against legislative encroachment upon constitutional rights. It is also true for countries where administrative courts, such as the French Conseil d'Etat, supervise administrative practice with an eye to shielding citizens from any illegal behaviour which might concern their rights and interests. The individual whose rights are affected will turn to the courts for redress.

Traditionally, this vision has been less popular in Great Britain. Parliament is seen as the main protector of the citizens' rights. In Dicey's view, the concept of 'human rights' did not apply in English law: freedoms existed because the rule of law prevailed in England, not because of any declaration or bill of rights or other written document. There was freedom of the press, or of religion, he thought, because everybody was free to do whatever Parliament had not forbidden, and there was little chance that Parliament would disregard these freedoms since it had been elected by the citizens for the very purpose of protecting their rights and liberties[75]. In this rosy view, the English are a pre-eminently liberty-loving people; therefore, a parliamentary majority that did anything to impair individual liberties would risk a resounding defeat at the polls. That concept was one of the main pillars supporting the theory of the sovereignty of Parliament.[76]

A more realistic perception has been gaining ground these last years. In present circumstances, a parliamentary majority might very well enact rules, for example on the prevention of terrorism, which could involve considerable risks to human rights protection. In situations of danger to public security, political institutions are often inclined to yield to

[74] See ch. 3.4.   [75] Dicey, *Introduction to the Study of the Law of the Constitution*, ch. iv.
[76] See ch. 2.1 and 2.5.

popular pressure and adopt strict rules that might have the effect of curtailing the rights of innocent individuals. Judicial protection would then be more effective than reliance on the wisdom of Parliament.[77] But official attitudes are not changing very rapidly. That is illustrated by the Human Rights Act 1998, which incorporates the provisions of the European Convention on Human Rights into English law without, however, accepting the priority of these provisions over British statutes. According to the Act, statutes are to be 'interpreted' in a way which is compatible with Convention rights. Should a court come to the conclusion that such an interpretation is not possible – still an unlikely event, in English eyes – it will adopt a 'declaration of incompatibility', which has no effect on the parties to the litigation, but may serve as an admonition to Parliament to pass the necessary measures.[78]

A second caveat concerns the role of the courts with regard to the implementation of social, economic and cultural rights figuring in modern constitutions and international treaties. We have already seen that this implementation depends on the activities of the political institutions, rather than on the courts.[79] Normally, provisions on these rights use a loose terminology which leaves a wide discretion to the legislative or administrative bodies. Apparently the wording indicates that the tasks of the courts are minimal. The right to 'appropriate facilities for vocational training' or the right to 'social security' are mentioned but not really defined in the European Social Charter. This treaty has been adopted as the social rights equivalent to the European Convention on Human Rights, but the Convention is much more precise in delimiting the scope of the civil and political rights it guarantees and in outlining the restrictions on the exercise of these rights it admits.[80] These differences in drafting reflect differences in the nature of the rights and in the art and manner of their implementation. The creation of 'a system of social security' and the endeavour 'to raise progressively' that system to a higher level cannot be achieved by the courts. Provisions of this kind impose duties and responsibilities on the legislative bodies. In extreme cases, it might be possible for a constitutional court to rule that the social security legislation of the country can, on proper examination, be considered as having failed to establish 'a system of social security' in

---

[77] See Sir Leslie Scarman, *English Law: the New Dimension*, 26th Hamlyn lecture (London, 1974), ch. II–a. See also Brazier, *Constitutional Reform*, ch. 8.

[78] Human Rights Act 1998, ss. 3–4.   [79] See ch. 8.4.

[80] See Arts. 10 and 12 ESC; Art. 11 ss. 1 and 2 European Convention.

the true sense. That, however, seems a somewhat remote hypothesis, and I have not been able to find case law illustrating any such judicial audacity.

Additional institutional devices have been framed to improve the protection of citizens' rights. In cases where these rights have been disregarded by factual behaviour, rather than by decisions or regulations, neither the courts nor the political institutions can easily provide a direct remedy. Obvious examples are complaints about needlessly rude police attitudes, about waiting lists in public hospitals or mental homes, or about the lack of reaction to letters written to tax authorities. Tort actions against the public body concerned may sometimes be possible, but they are costly and cumbersome, and their outcome is uncertain, because of problems of evidence or for other reasons. In such cases, an ombudsman can investigate matters, try to mediate between the applicants and the institution they complain about, and issue a public report if mediation fails. He can counteract maladministration by providing a quick, inexpensive and informal means of settling complaints. He is easily accessible and, as an English judge once put it, he can deliver 'rapid, unlegalistic justice, without cutting too many legal corners'.[81]

The ombudsman institution originated in Sweden in the early years of the nineteenth century. Swedish constitutional developments had led to a strict distinction between 'political' decisions, embodying the policy options of the government, and 'administrative' decisions, concerning the day-to-day running of the administration. Most administrative decisions were not taken by the government, or in its name, but by more or less autonomous official bodies. In the course of a long evolution, which had started as far back as the sixteenth century, decentralized 'boards' or 'offices' had been responsible for tasks like running the public education system, carrying out public building programmes, issuing conservation measures in rural areas, exercising surveillance over the state monopolies on wines and spirits, levying taxes, monitoring housing subsidies, supervising unemployment schemes, etc.[82] With the growth of the powers of Parliament, in the late eighteenth century, Swedish evolution could not take the same turn as British constitutional law: there could be no comprehensive accountability of ministers to Parliament because there was no comprehensive responsibility of ministers

---

[81] *Westminster CC* v. *Haywood* [1998] Ch. 377.
[82] See Art. 11 s. 7 *Regeringsform* (Instrument of Government). For the history, see Neil Elder, *Government in Sweden, The Executive at Work* (Oxford and New York, 1970), ch. 3.

for acts of administration. Instead, Parliament appointed an 'ombudsman' (literally 'trustee') to keep an eye on the country's administration. He could prosecute civil servants for neglect of official duty, acting on complaints from citizens or on his own initiative. In actual fact, however, his most important method of influencing administrative behaviour was the annual publication of his report to Parliament, in which he explained what had gone wrong and what could be done to prevent the same things happening in future. Gradually, the findings of the ombudsman came to be considered by the civil service itself as a standard for administrative behaviour.

This development made the ombudsman institution attractive to countries that had followed the British practice of accepting comprehensive ministerial accountability to Parliament. The growth of the administration and the diversity of its tasks and powers made it difficult for the political institutions to oversee completely what happened at the administrative level. The combination of citizens' complaints and public reports by the ombudsman could give an indication to Parliament of the areas and subjects to be discussed with the government. Thus, the ombudsman institution could be reconciled with the system of ministerial accountability. Denmark introduced a national ombudsman in 1954; other countries followed suit, including the Netherlands in 1981. Danish and Dutch practice show how the ombudsman can help to foster the protection of civil liberties, by setting standards for administrative behaviour or by provoking public debate on administrative failures. This is particularly important in areas where judicial or political supervision cannot always be effective. A famous Danish case concerned management of public hospitals: the ombudsman's report on a shocking case of mismanagement, and the government's refusal to follow its recommendations, gave rise to an extensive public debate.[83] The Dutch National Ombudsman was able to correct police misbehaviour by gradually developing standards through a long series of decisions, characterized by a profound investigation into the facts in each case. The use of violence, the seizure of stolen goods, the way of arresting suspects, and many other police activities, were thus subjected to informal requirements of decent behaviour.[84] In this way, the ombudsman seems to be developing into a semi-judicial institution in countries like Denmark and the Netherlands.

[83] *Milfeldt* case, 1965 (Folketingets Ombudsmand Beretning 1965 no. 44).
[84] Examples: NO 5-12-1995, Adm. Besl. 1996, 43; NO 7-2-1996, Adm. Besl. 1996, 133.

That is, however, not true of Great Britain. The Westminster Parliament considered that the ombudsman institution could not be introduced in its traditional form. Citizens' complaints about administrative behaviour were and are usually addressed to the Member of Parliament (MP) of the constituency, who can then put parliamentary questions to the minister concerned during the daily 'question time' in the House of Commons. This particular form of parliamentary control should not be jeopardized by new institutional provisions. It was therefore decided that a 'parliamentary commissioner' would be established, who would act only on complaints referred to him by an MP. He would then investigate the facts of the case and report to the House, which would consider the appropriate action.[85] The Parliamentary Commissioner lacks the autonomy of the ombudsman in the Scandinavian countries and the Netherlands; the British Parliament was jealous of its powers and responsibilities and created only a form of assistance to its own examination of citizens' complaints ('ombudsmouse', as the press put it at the time). Intermediate forms (between 'mice' and 'men') exist in other European countries. There is no equivalent in the USA, at any rate not at the federal level.[86]

Britain found, however, other ways of strengthening the position of citizens by institutional provisions. An illustrative example is the Equal Opportunities Commission, established with the aim of contributing to the full realization of equal protection.[87] It is an independent institution, which can investigate complaints about discriminatory practices in employment relations. The Commission tries to mediate between the applicant and the enterprise or body concerned; it issues public reports on its findings; if mediation efforts fail, it can also bring an action before the courts on behalf of the applicant. The latter possibility has turned out to be extremely important: not only for its preventive effect, but also because it actually helped the courts to develop their case law on the true meaning of equality and discrimination. It was on the insistence of the Equal Opportunities Commission that the concept of indirect (or 'hidden') discrimination was developed by the courts, for example in cases where part-time workers received lower hourly wages than full-time workers in the textile industry

---

[85] See Parliamentary Commissioner Act 1967, as amended by the Parliamentary and Health Service Commissioners Act 1987, s. 5(1) and s. 10. For the history: David W. Williams, *Maladministration* (London, 1976), ch. 4.

[86] Some mid-Western states have an ombudsman.

[87] There was an earlier body with similar tasks: the Commission for Racial Equality.

(where the female workforce is mostly part-time).[88] Other countries have followed the British example, but normally without the possibility of bringing lawsuits on behalf of the applicant.[89]

It is important to emphasize that in this area the European institutions tend to reinforce the national institutional framework. That is obvious in the case of the European Court of Human Rights, to which complaints on violation of Convention rights can be addressed when the national remedies have been exhausted.[90] It is also true, however, of European Union institutions such as the EU Commission and the Court of Justice. The elimination of obstacles to free trade in the Union implies, for example, a ban on discrimination founded on nationality. This ban has been given a wide interpretation by the Court of Justice. The Court has held that unequal treatment of citizens on the basis of their residence must be considered as an indirect discrimination founded on nationality, unless the unequality can be justified by reasons of public policy.[91]

The predominant impression is that the main distinction is the one between the European countries and the USA. On the one hand, the strong position of the American judiciary and the opportunity for private associations and public bodies to act as *amicus curiae* in litigation[92] have the effect of bringing any debate on the violation of individual rights before the courts. On the other hand, the extension of the public sector in Europe, and the entanglement of public bodies and private organizations in the field of economics and welfare, have no true equivalent in the USA. New forms of government organization have been developed in countries like France, Italy and Britain, where decisions are often taken in the opaque surroundings of dialogues between different bodies and organizations, public or private.[93] Nationalized industries are often managed by independent boards, but the minister or the government will usually have the power to issue general guidelines. In consequence, important decisions are normally prepared in close collaboration between the managers of the industry and the civil servants of the ministerial department; organizations of consumers or trade unions may join the consultations. Ultimately, it is not always very

---

[88] Case 96/80, *Jenkins* v. *Kingsgate Clothing Productions* [1981] ECR 911.
[89] Compare the Dutch example (*Commissie Gelijke Behandeling*).
[90] Art. 35 s. 1 European Convention on Human Rights.
[91] See case 152/73, *Sotgiù* v. *Deutsche Bundespost* [1974] ECR 153.   [92] See ch. 4.5.
[93] For the history of this phenomenon, see Keith Middlemas, *Politics in the Industrial Society* (London, 1979), chs. 11–13.

clear by whom the decision was actually taken. Proceedings of this kind may be quite satisfactory from a political point of view, but they are embarrassing for lawyers, who like to be sure about the final responsibility for the result of the negotiation process. In England, the expression 'government by moonlight' has been coined.[94]

The privatization policies of the 1980s and 1990s ought to have put an end to these shadowy forms of decision-making, but bad habits die hard. In case of complaints, the difficulty is still in deciding where to locate responsibility. That is why judicial remedies are not always very helpful; an independent investigation, for example by an ombudsman-like institution, may be more effective.

[94] In a book by P. Birkinstead and others, reviewed in *Public Law* (1997), 141.

9

Techniques of judicial protection

9.1. Filling the gaps

Constitutional provisions, in particular those on human rights, tend to use lapidary expressions. Their actual wording is not always very helpful to those who wish to understand their meaning, as a German author once put it.[1] Some provisions will at the least have a hard core that leaves no room for ambiguities: 'freedom of the press', although uncertain in its exact scope, is a term that admits no censorship of the press by the government. Other constitutional provisions, however, use a terminology where the words themselves can contribute only a little to the definition of the meaning. Expressions like 'human dignity' or 'due process of law' do not convey a definite legal meaning by themselves.[2] Problems of interpretation therefore have a great importance in constitutional law.

Some authors try to deny or to minimize that importance. According to Justice Scalia, in his efforts to combat activist attitudes with regard to the US Constitution, it would be contrary to democracy for unelected judges to decide what the law ought to mean, as its meaning should quite simply be founded on the text of the relevant provisions. In case of a venerable constitutional document like the US Constitution, it might be necessary to give old words and phrases a broad rather than a narrow meaning, but 'not an interpretation that the language will not bear'.[3] This sounds like good advice, but it is not very helpful in difficult cases. Most lawyers would agree that an old constitutional provision on freedom of the press, such as the First Amendment to the US Constitution, might be interpreted as protecting not only written words, but also anti-government speeches broadcast by radio or television or disseminated by e-mail; but it can never be interpreted in such a way as to protect, for example, the freedom to build

---

[1] E. W. Böckenförde, 'Grundrechtstheorie und Grundrechtsinterpretation', *NJW* 27 (1974), 1529.
[2] See Art. 1 (German) Basic Law; Fifth and Fourteenth Amendment US Constitution.
[3] Scalia, *A Matter of Interpretation*, pp. 22–3, 37.

a house wherever one thinks fit. That is not the real problem, however: the real problem is to make sense of words that, in themselves, are devoid of any precise meaning. We cannot understand what the 'social state' is, or the 'protection' of mothers, or the 'free development' of the human person,[4] unless we look not at the words alone, but at the legal traditions these words are intended to reflect and at the reasons for their inclusion in the constitutional document. The reference to 'Indians not taxed' in the US Constitution can only be understood against its historical background; the same applies to the abolition of slavery in one of the post-Civil War Amendments.[5] In other words, the problem of interpretation cannot be conjured away.

Filling gaps is one of the most obvious forms of judicial interpretation. No statute, no code, no constitution can be so complete and detailed that it renders the interpretive work of the judge superfluous. Great legislators have been aware of this. When the draft for the original French Civil Code, the *Code Napoléon*, was presented, one of the drafters, Portalis, made an introductory speech which included the warning that legislation is necessarily incomplete:

> Un code, quelque complet qu'il puisse paraître, n'est pas plus tôt achevé que mille questions inattendues viennent s'offrir au magistrat. Car les lois, une fois rédigées, demeurent telles qu'elles ont été écrites. Les hommes, au contraire, ne se reposent jamais.
>
> (A code may look very complete, but a thousand unexpected questions present themselves to the judges as soon as it is finished: for laws, once drafted, remain as they have been written down, but people never rest.)

For that reason, the judicial task consists, he said, 'à saisir le vrai sens des lois, à les appliquer avec discernement et à les suppléer dans les cas qu'elles n'ont pas réglés' (to grasp the true meaning of the laws, to apply them with understanding, and to supplement them in cases they have not provided for).[6]

Such a view is not only accepted in France. The American judge Benjamin Cardozo, in his well-known lectures on 'the nature of the judicial process',

---

[4] Respectively Art. 20 s. (1), Art. 6 s. (4) and art. 2 s. (1) Basic Law.

[5] Respectively Art. 1 s. 2 and Thirteenth Amendment s. 1 US Constitution.

[6] Portalis, *Discours préliminaire*. The text can be found in P. A. Fenet, *Recueil complet des travaux préparatoires du Code civil*, vol. VI (Paris, 1827).

used exactly the same arguments when discussing the task of the judge: 'There are gaps to be filled. There are doubts and ambiguities to be cleared. There are wrongs and hardships to be mitigated if not avoided.'[7] In performing these tasks, judges remain faithful to the legal texts they are applying. The words of such a text are only clear when their sense has been determined. That is true for a constitution as it is for a civil code, or for a statute on carriage of goods by sea.

The protection of privacy provides an example in most constitutional systems. It was not part of the rights and liberties proclaimed in such early constitutional documents as the American Bill of Rights or the French Declaration of 1789. There seemed to be no need to include a right to privacy in these documents, as the need to protect private life was not acutely felt in the rural and still slightly feudal world of the late eighteenth century. With the progressive growth of urbanization, of mass industrial employment and of communication, especially during the twentieth century, more and more potential ways appeared to interfere with a man's, or a woman's, private life. Employers wanted to know about the home life of their workers; the press began to discover the public's interest in salacious tales about the private life of political leaders and sport or movie stars; the police became aware that following somebody's movements might help to disclose his participation in criminal plots; sophisticated electrical equipment could be used for eavesdropping on neighbours, friends or enemies. Correspondingly, the need to protect private life increased, and it was raised to the rank of a constitutional right because of its elevated place in the scale of values. But the prevailing impression was that this right, though dormant over a long period of time, had always existed. Justice Douglas thought that it was a right 'older than our political parties, older than our school system'.[8]

The US Supreme Court filled the gap by interpreting the Fourth and Fifth Amendments as a protection against all government invasions 'of the sanctity of a man's home and the privacies of life'; by considering its case law on the right to educate one's children as one chooses in the light of the right to privacy; and by emphasizing the high moral value of such a right. The leading case concerned the validity of a provision in a Connecticut statute on birth control which made it a criminal offence to 'use' contraceptives.

---

[7] Benjamin N. Cardozo, *The Nature of the Judicial Process* (1921), lecture I. I used the 37th edition (New Haven, Ct., and London, 1976), pp. 14–15.

[8] In *Griswold* v. *Connecticut*, 381 US 479 (1965).

That brought Justice Douglas, never shy of dramatizing things, to the exclamation: 'Would we allow the police to search the sacred precincts of marital bedrooms for telltale signs of the use of contraceptives? The very idea is repulsive to the notions of privacy surrounding the marital relationship.'[9] The right of privacy was implied, if not mentioned, in the Constitution.

Even a modern constitution like the German Basic Law has no general clause on the right to privacy. It protects the privacy of correspondence, post and telecommunications; it has a provision on the inviolability of the home; and it guarantees the 'special protection of the State' to marriage and the family.[10] It is silent, however, on privacy rights that could shield individuals from intrusions into their private lives by the mass media. The Bundesverfassungsgericht filled the gap by considering that the combination of the two opening provisions of the Basic Law, on human dignity and on the free development of the human person, implied a more general protection of a 'personality right'. That right, said the court, included the protection of an autonomous area where each man was allowed to give shape to his private life and could develop and promote his own individuality.[11] That right had to be balanced against the freedom of expression in a case where German television planned to broadcast a documentary film on the history of a heinous crime at the very moment one of the accomplices in it was released from prison. The court tried to define the various rights and obligations very carefully; but like the American court, it founded its reasoning on a privacy right that was implied rather than mentioned by the constitution.

There are, of course, more spectacular instances of courts filling gaps in the constitution: for example, the French Constitutional Council started to examine the compatibility of legislation with human rights protection not mentioned in the 1958 Constitution but referred to in its preamble.[12] Eventually, it managed to construct an important body of case law with regard to human rights on the basis of the assumption that, if these rights were not specifically dealt with in the 1958 Constitution, its drafters must have considered that their protection was already sufficiently guaranteed by earlier constitutional developments. The references in the 1958 preamble served to confirm that assumption. As the Constitutional Council put it in 1982, the referendums of 1946 and 1958 approving the two respective constitutions had thereby approved texts conferring constitutional value

---

[9] In *Griswold*; see note 8.   [10] See Art. 10 s. (1); Art. 13 s. (1); and Art. 6 s. (1) Basic Law.
[11] BVerfGE 35 no. 16, *Soldatenmord von Lebach*, 1973.   [12] See ch. 4.2.

on the principles and rights proclaimed in 1789; and though some of these rights had undergone an evolution, for example with regard to their scope, they retained their full constitutional value, founded as they were on the republican tradition.[13]

A comparable development occurred in the European Union. The initial EEC treaty was silent on the protection of human rights and fundamental freedoms, probably because it was drafted at a time when the political leaders of the six original Member States were considering the prospect of concluding a 'political' community after the entry into force of the 'economic' community represented by the EEC. It was hard to imagine, though, that the EC-institutions, in exercising their far-reaching powers and competences, would not be obliged to respect human rights. The Court of Justice held that protection of these rights formed part of the general principles of law to be observed by the EC institutions and to be upheld by the courts. Initially, it founded this case law on 'the constitutional traditions which are common to the Member States' and on 'the international obligations these States have subscribed to'.[14] In later judgments, the Court referred in particular to the European Convention on Human Rights. Finally, it accepted that the human rights to be observed by the EC institutions were those enumerated in the European Convention.[15] That idea was laid down in the Treaty on European Union, when the European Communities were brought together into a 'Union' by one of the treaty revisions.[16] Here the political institutions followed the lead given by the Court of Justice.

One additional observation should be made. In filling gaps, judges may not be founding their decisions on a specific constitutional provision, but they remain faithful to the constitutional system as they find it. For such purposes, it is not necessary to evoke the 'spirit' of the constitution or the 'mind' of its framers. The constitution, or the constitutional traditions it reflects, will suggest parallels, with the result that solutions to be devised by the courts will be as close as possible to those explicitly envisaged by the written texts. A constitution cannot be regarded as a collection of isolated provisions; in order to be applied in practice, it must be considered as a coherent body of rules and principles. If courts have difficulty in finding any cohesion at all, they should make an additional effort: they will find it by

---

[13] CC 16-1-1982, *Loi de nationalisation*, *Rec.* 18, *Les grandes décisions* no. 33.
[14] Example: case 374/79, *Hauer* [1979] ECR 3727.
[15] See case 374/87, *Orkem* [1989] ECR 3283.
[16] See Art. 6 ss. 1–2 Treaty on European Union (Amsterdam version).

examining the constitutional rules in their relations to each other and to the professed aims of the constitutional document in question. This cohesion will usually suggest solutions for cases that are not explicitly covered by any constitutional provision.[17]

9.2. General principles of law

The tools of the judge's trade include, albeit in different forms, reliance on general principles of law. These principles are usually not laid down in written provisions, and they cannot always be found by interpreting these provisions. They are rather the outcome of ancient legal traditions; or perhaps one should say that each of them embodies the form such a legal tradition at present assumes. In France, where the concept of general principles of law was first developed, these principles served principally as standards for judicial review of administrative action. Decisions disregarding these principles were annulled; the courts went one step further by founding an important part of the law of State liability on legal principles, in particular the principle of equality ('égalité devant les charges publiques')[18].

Legal principles never have the same degree of accuracy as statutory provisions, if well drafted, may show. The principle of non-retroactivity is one of the general principles of law applied by the French administrative courts. As a general guideline, non-retroactivity is clear enough; but in actual practice, it cannot always settle the details. According to the Conseil d'Etat, the principle implies that newly introduced taxes cannot be applied to corporations with regard to a financial year for which the accounts have already been closed.[19] Such a ruling leaves many questions open, however: for example concerning companies whose financial year is different from the fiscal year, or companies that have been unable to close the accounts for the last financial year for purely administrative reasons. A well-drafted provision in the tax legislation could have avoided such problems. Similarly, the rule embodied in the European Convention on Human Rights that, in case of criminal charges, everybody is entitled to 'a fair and public hearing within a reasonable time' (Article 6 s. 1) led to the principle that no 'undue

---

[17] See also T. Koopmans, 'The theory of interpretation and the Court of Justice', in David O'Keeffe (ed.), *Judicial Review in European Union law*, Liber amicorum Lord Slynn of Hadley vol. I (The Hague and London, 2000), ch. 4.

[18] See ch. 6.2-6.3.   [19] CE 16-3-1956, *Garrigou, Rec.* 121.

delay' should occur in the prosecution and trial of suspects. Under the case law of the European Court of Human Rights, the reasonableness of the delay depends, among other things, on the complexity of the case and the behaviour of the suspect himself.[20] There is little doubt that statutory provisions on the limitation of actions have a sharpness, for example with regard to the beginning and the length of the delay, which is lacking in expressions like 'reasonable' and 'undue'. As a result, general principles leave the courts more freedom to decide according to the circumstances of the case.

Thus, reliance on general principles of law presents two characteristics that concern the position of the courts in the constitutional system. First, these principles have been introduced into the law by the courts, though often on the basis of time-honoured legal traditions, without any mandate having been given by the legislature, the government or other political institution. Secondly, the practical operation of these principles usually leaves far greater discretion to the judge than statutory provisions do; there is a larger sphere of autonomous action for the courts. Consequently, general principles of law are often at the centre of debates concerning the limits of judicial interference with government decisions.

From this point of view, the legal literature tends to make a distinction between procedural principles and those which concern the substance of the administrative decisions. Under the first heading we could include the right to a hearing, the rule against bias, non-retroactivity, the care to be exercised in determining the relevant facts, *ne bis in idem* and so on. The main example of a substantive principle is the principle of proportionality: in gauging whether the advantages pursued by the decision are or are not fully outweighed by the problems and difficulties it creates, the judge has to look at the merits. That is probably the reason why English courts are extremely reluctant to accept the principle of proportionality: in their view, questions of form, competence and procedure are typically within the area of judicial scrutiny, but assessment of the merits should be left to political institutions, in particular to the representative bodies.[21]

English authors are not always happy with this distinction. Their first argument is that the proportionality test must certainly be applied to decisions

---

[20] See R. A. Lawson and H. E. Schermers, *Leading Cases of the European Court of Human Rights* (Nijmegen and Antwerp, 1997), pp. 450–1.

[21] See *R* v. *Secretary of State for the Home Department*, ex p *Brind* [1991] 1 AC 696.

covered by European Community law, as it is part of the standards developed by the EC Court of Justice.[22] Secondly, they argue that English courts do not entirely refrain from examining the merits of administrative decisions: under the *Wednesbury* rule,[23] they refuse to accept the validity of a decision that is so manifestly unreasonable that no reasonably acting administrative body could have come to it. This '*Wednesbury* unreasonableness', so runs the argument, may represent a lighter form of judicial review than proportionality, but it is also less well defined: under it, the courts are not obliged to specify the reasons why the decision is to be considered as manifestly unreasonable, whereas under the proportionality test courts have to explain which interest or argument outbalances which other interest or argument.[24] These considerations occasionally find an echo in judgments of the House of Lords, but they have not, or not yet, been conducive to a clear change in case law.[25]

From a comparative point of view, one of the problems is the emergence of general principles of law that are not so called in some constitutional systems. Under the US Constitution, 'due process of law' to be observed by the public authorities implies compliance with certain standards this expression is thought to embody, standards European lawyers would almost certainly call general principles of law. American lawyers agree that procedural standards are covered by the concept of due process. When police officers have been overzealous in tracking down culprits (for example 'stomach-pumping' in a drugs case), the conviction may be overturned for violation of due process. State law enforcement, said Justice Frankfurter for the Court, must respect certain decencies of civilized conduct; standards of this kind are 'deeply rooted in reason and in the compelling traditions of the legal profession'.[26] This approach of the Court has been largely accepted in the American legal world. However, there was always debate and argument when the Court developed, as it sometimes did, non-procedural standards on the basis of due process ('substantive due process').

---

[22] See ch. 4.4.

[23] See ch. 5.3. The case in question is *Associated Provincial Picture Houses* v. *Wednesbury* [1948] 1 *KB* 233.

[24] See Jeffrey Jowell and Dawn Oliver, 'Beyond Wednesbury: substantive principles of administrative law', *Public Law* (1987), 368.

[25] Example: *R* v. *Chief Constable of Sussex*, ex p *International Trader's Ferry Ltd* [1999] 1 All ER 129.

[26] *Rochin* v. *California*, 342 US 165 (1952).

There have indeed been different periods in the Court's interpretation of due process. In the first half of the twentieth century, due process was interpreted as protecting the freedom of contract. For that reason, state legislation on maximum working hours in industry was held unconstitutional in a long series of decisions.[27] When the Court had abandoned this view, after its conflicts with President Franklin D. Roosevelt, the due process clause seemed to retain only its procedural meaning. Gradually, however, substantive elements crept back into the case law of the Court, not in matters of economic or social legislation but in the interpretation of the protection of civil liberties. Due process was considered to mean that the rights guaranteed by the federal Bill of Rights could be exercised not only vis-à-vis federal institutions, as the text of these provisions suggests, but also against state authorities ('incorporation'). Subsequently, due process was taken to comprise constitutional protection of fundamental rights not expressly mentioned in the Constitution, for example privacy rights. Both interpretations occurred in the period when the Court (the 'progressive' or 'liberal' Court of the 1960s and 1970s) particularly emphasized the protection of fundamental rights and freedoms. However, the legal techniques it used to arrive at this wide protection were not dissimilar to those the 'conservative' Court had relied on in its hopeless battle against social legislation half a century earlier. Substantive due process, chased away through the front door, re-entered quietly through the back door; and there are no signs yet that it will soon go out again.[28]

Comparable developments have taken place in German constitutional law. General principles of law are not expressly recognised as a separate source of law. However, the wide concepts used by the Basic Law are sometimes considered as embodying legal principles. Although these principles find their legal basis in a constitutional provision, legal traditions contribute a lot more to their interpretation than the wording of the Basic Law. The notion of *Rechtsstaat*, one of the key concepts of the Basic law, implies protection of legal certainty, according to the Bundesverfassungsgericht. Legal certainty, in its turn, includes non-retroactivity as well as the protection of legitimate expectations.[29] Some non-procedural requirements are part of

[27] See ch. 3.5.
[28] See Robert G. McCloskey, *The American Supreme Court*, 3rd edn revised by Stanford Levinson (Chicago and London, 2000), ch. 8.
[29] See ch. 4.1.

the standards developed by the courts on the basis of the general notions referred to in the the the Basic Law.

It is interesting to speculate about the reasons for the growing importance of general principles of law. In Europe, the influence of European Union law and of the European Convention on Human Rights has had a great significance; it popularized the general principles and it showed how these principles could be developed. A second element is probably the growing importance of judicial review of administrative, and in most countries also legislative, action. If the State itself is subject to control of legality, it should not be the State alone which should fix the standards to be applied by the supervising courts. According to some authors, the law is going through an emancipation process which will free it from the restraints imposed by the State.[30] That may be an overstatement, since under present conditions courts owe their jurisdiction, as well as the efficacy of their decisions, to the State, its powers and its institutions; but the idea is nevertheless indicative of a change in intellectual climate, whereby the emphasis is shifting from the rules fixed by the State to other sources of legal evolution. The autonomy of the courts, in finding and developing the standards to be applied to the activities of public authorities, has grown considerably. Reliance on general principles of law fits perfectly in this picture.

There may be a further factor of influence, which is slowly becoming perceptible in various parts of the Western world. It is the rapidity with which new problems of society emerge, as compared to the slow reaction, or the lack of reaction, of governments and representative bodies. Developments in the field of bio-medical science, communication technology and mobility of persons and goods, as well as air and water pollution, urbanization of the countryside, the emergence of new types of animal diseases and of mass calamities occasioned by technical failures have led to new challenges to which statutory rules and judicial precedents provide no answer. Politicians are not always interested in these new societal problems. In some periods, the political debate centres around traditional political questions: balancing the budget, the level of taxation, the extent of the public sector, the future development of urban planning or of road and railway networks. In other instances, political bodies prefer to wait until developments are completely settled: legislation may be useful, they seem to think, but it can

---

[30] E.g. Laurent Cohen-Tanugy, *La métamorphose de la démocratie* (Paris, 1989), ch. v. See also, by the same author, *Le droit sans l'Etat* (Paris, 1985), in particular chs. iv–v.

only be effective when more is known about the subject. Courts, however, cannot just wait: they have to decide the cases submitted to them, in one way or another. Since the French Revolution, 'déni de justice' by a judge has been a punishable offence under French law. In England, Magna Carta proclaimed in 1215 that justice would not be denied to anybody (or sold or delayed, the document adds).[31] In other words: faced with completely new problems, not yet dealt with by any form of legislative or government regulation, judges must find their own way. Their professionalism will induce them to look for objective standards. General principles of law qualify for that purpose.

One or two words should be added on the particular situation in the United States. The European countries share, to varying degrees, in the evolution I have tried to outline above; but the case law of the US Supreme Court shows a somewhat different picture. The degree of judicial freedom the Court thought it had found in the words and principles of the American Constitution in the 1960s and the 1970s was inevitably followed by a slow reversion to earlier attitudes, in particular when popular dissatisfaction with the Court's innovative decisions became manifest.[32] Republican Presidents appointed conservative judges with the avowed aim of putting a brake on the Court's 'liberalism'. Irrespective of new appointments, however, the Court seems to have pursued a quieter line after the heyday of its activist period. In a certain sense, there was a swing of the pendulum when the Court abandoned its banishment of the death penalty and had to admit the difficulties attending on the affirmative action programs it had approved. Nevertheless, substantive due process is still a kind of magician's hat from which judges can extract a surprising number of standards to be applied in difficult cases.

9.3. Access to justice

Access to justice is a preliminary to the judicial protection of the rights of citizens. Procedural guarantees for the protection of these rights would be of little use if access to the courts were denied. As the European Court of Human Rights once said, in response to the argument that the European Convention does not mention access to justice among the procedural guarantees it

---

[31] 'Nulli vendemus, nulli negabimus, aut differemus, rectum aut iustitiam' (cl. 40).
[32] See ch. 3.4-3.5.

of fraud, or of violent or arbitrary conduct. Moreover, criminal appeals necessarily have a different effect in different penal systems; in English law, for example, 'leave to appeal' will be required, usually to be given by the appeal court itself – a construct which is unknown on the European continent. Besides, in England and in some other countries operating a jury system in criminal cases, facts determined by the jury cannot always be challenged in appeal, so that the debate before the appeal court focuses on procedural irregularities rather than on the conviction itself. After some serious miscarriages of justice, the English system has been made more flexible in recent years.[41] There are, however, still considerable differences among the European states as to the implications of a right to appeal in criminal cases.

Third question: does access to justice imply a right of the citizen to defend his own case in court, without any legal assistance? And if not, should public funds be available to those who have a serious case but cannot afford to pay for legal assistance? On the first part of the question I have been unable to find any materials. In some legal systems, for example in English and Irish law, parties in judicial proceedings are entitled to defend their own cases. In practice, this possibility is not very important: it is often unwise to do without legal assistance, in particular in civil cases; legal technicalities may be considerably more important than most citizens realize. On the second point, the right to legal assistance, there is some case law. The European Court of Human Rights has ruled that Article 6 of the European Convention imposes on the Member States the obligation 'to secure an effective right of access to the courts'. In an Irish case on family law (a separation case), it would therefore be unacceptable if access to the courts were to be obstructed by lack of financial means. Under the Convention, the state was not obliged to institute a general system of free legal aid, said the Court; but it was compelled to provide for the assistance of a lawyer if such assistance was indispensable for an effective access to the courts. The argument of the Irish government that the woman in question was free to go before the court without the assistance of a lawyer was set aside as irrelevant, since she would probably not be able to present her case 'properly and satisfactorily'.[42] The European Court emphasized the particular importance, for the woman, of

---

[41] See Michael Zander, *Cases and Materials on the English Legal System*, 7th edn (London and Dublin, 1996), ch. 7.
[42] ECHR 9-10-1979, *Airey* v. *Ireland*, Series A no. 32.

the separation proceedings; but it did not indicate to what extent its ruling extended to other types of litigation. The US Supreme Court followed a largely similar line of reasoning in a case where welfare recipients were unable to pay the court fees and the costs of service of process in a divorce action. The state had refused to waive payment, but the Court held that this financial barrier restricted access to the courts in a manner which was incompatible with the Constitution.[43] Justice Harlan (the second Justice Harlan), speaking for the Court, identified access to the courts as an element of due process; some individual opinions would have preferred to find a basis in the equal protection clause. In the Supreme Court's view, the necessity of financial assistance seems to depend on the nature of the case. In a later decision it held, for example, that the interest of an indigent bankrupt in his discharge did not 'rise to the same constitutional level' as the fundamental interest involved in marital relationships. The assessment of this 'level' of interest appears to be a matter of judicial discretion.[44]

The fourth question is whether access to justice implies that the court or tribunal should have jurisdiction for a full review. The answer seems to be in the negative. In France, the *recours en annulation* cannot, in spite of its general character, be called a 'full' review: it can only be based on certain grounds, and it can lead only to annulment of an illegal decision, not to its substitution by a correct decision.[45] Comparable observations could be made regarding remedies against administrative decisions in other legal systems. This situation has not, however, been challenged as a breach of the principle of access to justice. The German literature sometimes suggests that the principle necessarily implies that the court has power to strike down unconstitutional legislation, as it would not be possible to have an 'effective' legal protection without such a power. That statement, though not generally accepted by German authors, may be true for German law, but it cannot have general validity. It would indeed be hard to imagine that the concept of access to justice alone could oblige countries like the United Kingdom or the Netherlands to bring about an important constitutional change by introducing judicial review of legislation.

Fifth and final question: can access to justice be restricted by reason of the immunity of States? On this point, it is necessary to make a distinction between actions against foreign States and those involving the home State.

---

[43] *Boddie* v. *Connecticut*, 401 US 371 (1971).
[44] See McCloskey and Levinson, *The American Supreme Court*, p. 197.   [45] See ch. 6.1-6.2.

There is a generally recognised rule of public international law on the immunity of foreign States, which, simply put, means that the courts of State A cannot have jurisdiction over State B. It is true that the scope of this rule has slowly been limited to litigation involving the foreign State in its capacity as a State (*iure imperii*), excluding cases in which the State is engaged in purely commercial transactions; for the first category of cases, the immunity rule is still widely respected as part of unwritten international law. In Great Britain and the United States, legislation codifying the rule has been adopted.[46] The American Constitution also includes the opposite rule: foreign citizens are not allowed to sue one of the United States before an American court.[47] Against its own citizens, however, a State cannot invoke its own immunity. It was different in Great Britain before the Crown Proceedings Act, 1947;[48] but since then the British position has been gradually brought into harmony with that in most other legal systems.

Towards the end of the twentieth century State liability became one of the most important subjects of litigation. That is not only true for countries like France and Germany, where government decisions can always be challenged and give rise to liability; it also applies to common law countries. As Lord Hoffman said in a 1996 House of Lords judgment:[49]

> a public body is in principle liable for torts in the same way as a private person. But its statutory powers or duties may restrict its liability. For example, it may be authorized to do something which necessarily involves committing what would otherwise be a tort. In such case, it will not be liable. [...] Or it may have discretionary powers which enable it to do things to achieve a statutory purpose notwithstanding a foreseeable risk of damage to others. In such a case, a *bona fide* exercise of the discretion will not attract liability.

That statement must be considered as summarizing the present state of English law on this subject.

I should add that the evolution of the European integration process increases the risk that national regulations or decisions will be found to violate or to disregard European Community rules. This situation tends to enlarge the area of State liability.[50] Occasionally that is a matter of regret

---

[46] For Britain: State Immunity Act 1978. See in particular s. 3 (3).
[47] Amendment xi to the US Constitution.
[48] See ch. 6.5.   [49] *Stovin* v. *Wise* [1996] 1 AC 923.
[50] See Walter van Gerven, *Tort Law, Scope of Protection. A Casebook* (Oxford, 1998), ch. 9.5. See also cases c-6 and 9/90, *Francovich and Bonifaci* [1991] ECR i-5357.

for politicians who have invented schemes that are subsequently quashed by the courts.

9.4. Higher law

'Higher law' is an emotionally charged expression. It can only mean that there is law which is higher than 'ordinary' law, in particular higher than the law established by the legislature in the form of codes, statutes or Acts of Parliament. The expression imparts the message that the law is not determined, or at least not completely determined, by the political institutions of the State: somewhere, higher norms can be found, which must prevail over the rules established by the competent authorities. In that sense, the expression itself denotes a certain political philosophy.

It is not difficult to associate this vision with Chief Justice Marshall's reasoning in *Marbury* v. *Madison*. The written constitution is the 'fundamental and paramount law of the nation', he said, and acts of the legislature are therefore void when they are repugnant to it.[51] In American practice, this conception has made the US Supreme Court into a kind of arbitrator with jurisdiction to fix the limits between higher law and ordinary law. That has given the Court a particularly strong position in American government. And because the Court enjoyed this position, the judges were able to use it to strengthen it still further. The Court interpreted *Marbury*, for example, to mean that the federal judiciary in the US 'is supreme in the exposition of the law of the Constitution'.[52] The Court said this in a case where it was trying to bring one of the southern states into line with its case law on racial desegregation (Arkansas was refusing to comply at the time); but its appropriation of the final say in matters of constitutional interpretation is not entirely consistent with the careful balance the US Constitution tries to strike between the three 'powers' or 'departments of government'. However that may be, the result is that Congress and state legislatures are not only bound by the provisions of the US Constitution, but also by standards the Supreme Court discovers as part of constitutional expressions such as due process of law.

The potential conflict between rule-givers and justice was not something the *Marbury* judgment introduced into legal history. On the contrary, that conflict appeared regularly during the period when the European

---

[51] See ch. 3.1.   [52] *Cooper* v. *Aaron*, 358 US 1 (1958).

nation-states were being formed. In the Middle Ages, the influence of the Roman Catholic Church and the acceptance of doctrines of natural law often acted as counterweights to the unrestricted rule of the kings and their feudal vassals; but mutual accommodation was not attained without a struggle. The rediscovery of Aristotle's works and the reception of Roman law had given added weight to the natural law tradition.[53] Nevertheless, there is no unbroken historical line leading from these medieval conflicts and skirmishes to the debates provoked by *Marbury* and its aftermath. In their earlier discussions with the King, judges and clerics could say, using a maxim attributed to Bracton, that the King was not under any man, but was under God and the law.[54] When the rule of kings was replaced by that of elected bodies representing the citizens, that argument became inoperative. Did the victory of parliaments, or of popular uprisings, over absolutism not signify that the law would henceforth correspond to the will of the people? By subjecting the result of democratic processes to higher law, *Marbury* may have opened a new chapter in the ongoing story of the relationship between courts and politics.

When *Marbury* was decided, the concept of higher law was at a low ebb in Europe. In Britain, the political leadership had slowly been shifting from the King to the political leaders in Parliament, and the doctrine of the supremacy of Parliament was beginning to take hold. In continental Europe, the most important States, such as France, Prussia and Austria, were in the process of putting an end to legal uncertainty and legal pluralism, sometimes of feudal origin, by codifying civil law, commercial law, criminal law and procedural law into systematically organized collections of statutes. The famous *Code Napoléon* was the most illustrious though not the earliest example.[55] Legislation was considered to govern the law and its evolution. In France and the countries influenced by it, such as Belgium and the Netherlands, the interpretation of Code provisions on problems of contract or property was assimilated to disclosure of the intention of the legislature, which could only be found by close inspection of the history of the legislative process. There seemed to be no place for the natural law tradition or for any other variety of higher law.

---

[53] See Walter Ullmann, *A History of Political Thought: the Middle Ages*, 2nd edn (Harmondsworth, 1970), chs. 6 and 8.

[54] See Pound, *The Spirit of the Common Law*, ch. III.

[55] See Stein, *Roman Law in European History*, ch. 5.

The revival of these concepts took place in the twentieth century, particularly during the second half of it. Two developments contributed to this revival. The first was the decline of the faith in the wisdom of democratic decisions that had characterized political thinking in more optimistic periods of European history. The second was the growing importance, for the evolution of civil, commercial, criminal and administrative law, of the influence of European and international law.

On the first point, the experience of the 1920s and 1930s was particularly telling. Newly established democratic republics in Germany, Spain and Austria proved unable to cope with street violence, inflation and economic and political crisis; at the same time, it became obvious that the communist revolution in Russia, though unchained in order to bring the working classes to power, had led to a full-fledged totalitarian state. In Germany, the Nazi regime started in 1933 when the Nazi leader Adolf Hitler was appointed as prime minister (Reichskanzler) by the President of the Republic in accordance with the rules of the Weimar Constitution. It was only after this appointment that the abolition of democratic institutions began: the prohibition of the other political parties, the imprisonment of communist and social-democrat leaders and journalists, the bringing into line (*Gleichschaltung*) of the trade unions and the press, growing discrimination and violence against Jews, the organization of semi-military Nazi gangs, the abolition of decentralized government, and so on. And that was only the beginning: it all ended in what a German author has rightly called 'an inferno of violence and destruction'.[56]

When Germany arose from its ashes, after the end of the Second World War, it opted for a form of government which would avoid the difficulties that the Weimar Republic had proved unable to overcome. The new constitution made it perfectly clear that the legislative bodies, the government and the head of State were to observe the rules and principles it laid down (in particular on federalism, representative government and human rights protection), and that a constitutional court was to settle conflicts of interpretation and be the ultimate arbiter. Higher law, in the same sense as it had been advanced by Chief Justice Marshall in 1803, was explicitly recognised in the German Basic Law. But there was more to it: by its provision on the

---

[56] Karl Dieter Bracher, *Die Auflösung der Weimarer Republik. Eine Studie zum Problem des Machtverfalls in der Demokratie*, part II ch. XI. I used the 5th edn (Villingen, 1971), pp. 632–8.

immutability of some of the main constitutional rules, and by its reliance on moral notions such as human dignity, the Basic Law also seemed to recognise that there was a higher law than that established by man-made institutions.[57] This return to natural law concepts also found its expression in German legal theory. A famous legal philosopher, Gustav Radbruch, was so much impressed by the experience of criminal behaviour by the State itself that he abandoned his more or less relativist views in favour of a natural law philosophy. The State, and the rules issued by it, have no claim to obedience, he said, when the violation of justice reaches so intolerable a degree that the rules amount to 'lawless law'.[58] The German experience is only one example of the change of outlook that occurred in many parts of continental Europe. The collapse of communist domination in Eastern and Central Europe gave it a new impetus in the 1990s. So natural law is back on the legal agenda.

A second, and parallel, evolution was the growing impact of international law. This growth started right after the end of the Second World War, when international courts (though consisting only of appointees from the victorious States) in Nuremberg and Tokyo developed the concepts of 'war crimes' and 'crimes against humanity': this can, with hindsight, be described as a first example of the administration of international criminal justice by international courts. In 1948, the General Assembly of the United Nations proclaimed the 'Universal Declaration of Human Rights', which may have been a first step towards the internationalization of human rights protection.[59] It is a non-binding instrument, but it has great authority and constitutes an encouragement and a guideline for international treaties in this area. The European Convention on Human Rights states explicitly, in its preamble, that its aim is to secure the recognition and observance of the rights set out in the Universal Declaration.

Technically speaking, the recognition of international law as higher law was realized in two different ways. First, national legal orders were more and more opened to its influence. That was particularly apparent in constitutional systems like that of the Netherlands, where treaty provisions are directly applied by the courts and overrule national provisions in case of incompatibility.[60] Secondly, a new type of international organization was established: they had their own rule-giving, administrative and sometimes

---

[57] See ch. 4.1.   [58] See Wolfgang Friedmann, *Legal Theory*, 5th edn (New York, 1967), ch. 28.
[59] See also Louis Henkin, *The Age of Rights* (New York, 1990), chs. 1-3.   [60] See ch. 4.3.

judicial institutions. The European Communities constituted the chief example. Courts of the EC Member States have to accept that Community law is higher law as compared to national law and that the specific structure of the EC obliges them to apply Community rules and principles as interpreted by the EC Court of Justice. The two avenues to recognition of international rules as part of higher law work jointly towards a growing awareness of the role of European and international law among the judiciary of the European States.

In England this evolution has been somewhat slower than on the European continent. British participation in the European integration process came late, and was half-hearted when it came. Besides, direct application of (non-EC) international rules was contrary to British traditions and to the doctrine of parliamentary sovereignty. Consequently, the courts did not begin to discover the European dimension to many legal problems until a relatively late stage. They had to wait for the entry into force of the Human Rights Act 1998 before they were allowed to acknowledge the rights enumerated by the European Convention on Human Rights.

There is, however, a second difference from the evolution on the European continent: natural law concepts have never been popular among English authors (Scotland may be in a slightly different position), and it would be very difficult to find traces of such concepts in modern English case law. It is true that the courts still adhere to 'principles of natural justice' as developed in the early years of the common law. These principles were largely forgotten in the nineteenth century, but they have made a kind of come-back in more recent times. However, under the English rule of precedent, they can only have the meaning attributed to them in earlier case law. As a result, these principles have a technical character and a limited scope, because they include only the right to a hearing and the rule against bias. Though having a well-defined meaning, natural justice is, however, an important instrument in the hands of the courts. The principles are considered as standards to be respected in administrative decision-making; but they are also used as canons of statutory interpretation. More and more, courts are tending to assume that Parliament intends to act in accordance with them. In this view, Parliament is at liberty to set aside principles of natural justice if it wishes, but when it makes no express provision to that effect, the statute is assumed to respect these principles.[61] This line of interpretation had the

---

[61] See Lord Browne-Wilkinson in *R* v. *Home Secretary* ex p *Pierson* [1998] AC 539, at 550.

effect of revivifying the importance of natural justice. Perhaps there is some truth in the old French proverb that it is no use to chase away what is natural as it will very quickly rebound.[62]

The USA shares some of the British traditions in this field. American judges will not refer to natural law concepts in their judgments. Nevertheless, some interpretations given to the Constitution reveal the influence of such concepts in the minds of the judges. When the notion of due process of law is taken to mean that police investigations have to respect standards of common decency, or that fundamental rights should be protected when not explicitly mentioned in the Constitution,[63] one has the impression that the judges have looked not only at the text of the provisions but also at the requirements of 'natural' justice. The main difference from developments in Europe is the undisguised refusal of the American courts to give direct application, let alone priority, to rules of international law. In a criminal case where the suspect was a Mexican citizen who had been seized in Mexico and forcibly abducted to Texas, and pleaded lack of jurisdiction of the US courts, the Supreme Court said squarely that it had no business examining the influence of international law on the American rules concerning the competence of American courts. In fact, the Court went somewhat further by also refusing to interpret these American rules in the light of international law.[64]

From an academic point of view, it is certainly worth considering the concept of higher law as a judicial strategy for strengthening the position of the courts vis-à-vis the political institutions. That is not to say that judges have consciously acted with this purpose in mind; but the effect of what they did can be understood in those terms. If we put ourselves momentarily in this position, it seems clear enough that the courts have won the battle, not just in one constitutional system but in a more general way. If we limit our inquiry to the USA, Britain, France and Germany, we see that the traditions are different, and that diverging legal techniques are being used, but that a similar phenomenon can be found in each of these systems. That phenomenon liberates the judiciary from strict subservience to the legislative institutions of the State; but at the same time, it makes them dependent on legal traditions and on rules or principles of international origin.

---

[62] 'Chassez le naturel, il revient au galop.' Cf. Horace, *Epistles* I, 10, 24: 'Naturam expellas furca, tamen usque recurret.'
[63] See ch. 9.2.   [64] *United States* v. *Alvarez-Machain*, 504 US 655 (1992). It was a 6-3 decision.

The political institutions readily accept reliance on norms of higher law when these are applied to matters of form or procedure. No politician worries when the courts rule that police officers are subjected to standards of common decency, even when doing their job under difficult circumstances, or that civil servants cannot be dismissed without having an opportunity of putting their own point of view before the authority in question. Politicians begin to get worried when the courts hold that substantive rules validly issued by the competent authorities must be set aside on the basis of higher law. American politicians had no great difficulty in accepting that privacy rights, though not included in the Bill of Rights, were protected under the due process clause of the Fourteenth Amendment; but a virulent debate flared up, even accompanied by occasional violence, when the Supreme Court also found that these privacy rights encompassed a woman's right to terminate her pregnancy, and that the abortion legislation of most states was therefore invalid.[65] The legal road from due process to freedom of abortion was indeed a long one; it gave the adversaries of the Court's ruling – quite apart from the merits of their case – sound legal arguments. The acceptance of the concept of higher law was, however, not at issue. It was rather the vagueness of the higher rule, as compared to the specific nature of the problem to be solved, which worried many observers. A court is, perhaps, not always on firm ground when it proceeds to considerations which the national parliament, or, in the American case, fifty state legislatures, consider as their proper field of activity. The more indefinite the higher rule, the greater the temptations of politicians to allege political involvement of the judiciary when they don't like the result.

9.5. Modern constitutionalism

In its simplest form, constitutionalism means that the powers of the state are not exercised arbitrarily, reflecting the mere will of the political leaders of the day, but in accordance with the law, which creates or recognises permanent institutions and organizes the powers to be exercised by them. The Constitution of the United States was thought to embody this idea from its inception: by instituting federalism, as well as a system of separation of powers at Union level, it aimed at averting concentration of power in the hands of one person or group of persons. At the time, constitutionalism in the

---

[65] *Roe* v. *Wade*; see ch. 3.4.

American sense of the term was felt to be in opposition to the monarchy, or to 'hereditary systems of government', as Thomas Paine put it in his defence of the French Revolution against its English detractors. Hereditary government, he thought, was 'in its nature tyranny', and could not be considered as having a constitution properly so called.[66]

Paine's thesis was, however, disproved by the evolution of the British monarchy during the very period his books were written. The increase of the powers of Parliament gave rise to a constitutional system which was to dominate the nineteenth and early twentieth century in Britain. That system was characterized by an organization of powers based on two concepts: the sovereignty of Parliament and the rule of law. Analytically speaking, these two concepts are not fully compatible. However, as long as the respective spheres of political and legal action were different, the two notions went together very well.[67] The question which of the two was to prevail in case of conflict did not arise until relatively late in the twentieth century.

Developments over the last fifty years have not left the basic tenets of the concept of constitutionalism untouched. It is still possible to operate a constitutional system on the basis of separation of powers: it happens in the USA. It is also feasible to make a conceptual distinction between legislative functions on the one hand, government and the administration of the country on the other. Nevertheless, constitutional practice in most countries shows that these neat distinctions and classifications are gradually being overshadowed by one all-embracing contrast: that between the world of politics and the world of law. The distinction between the proper spheres of legislative and executive institutions is vanishing. Nowadays, most of the rules binding the citizens are fixed not by the legislature but by statutory instruments, or by administrative bodies. In Britain, the separation between legislative and executive functions has always been part of a theory that had little to do with actual political experience: many formal and informal links unite the parliamentary majority and the government. The same is true, albeit to varying degrees, of other parliamentary regimes, for example in Germany, Sweden and the Netherlands. However, the two functions are also slowly merging in the USA. Since Franklin D. Roosevelt's days, Presidents have come to power with a legislative program which they try to persuade

---

[66] Thomas Paine, *The Rights of Man*, part II (1792), chs. III–IV. I used Bonner edn (2nd edn, London, 1954), pp. 144 and 166.

[67] See T. R. S. Allan, *Law, Liberty and Justice. The Legal Foundations of British Constitutionalism* (Oxford, 1993), chs. 1-2.

Congress to implement. By sending messages to Congress, by cajoling or bullying individual Senators or members of the House of Representatives, by creating favourable conditions for their legislative plans, Presidents and their ministers and White House assistants give guidance to the legislative process. Strong Presidents are thought to embody the political leadership of the country as a whole. The Senate and the House, from their side, try to influence the government of the country in whatever way they can: by using their budgetary powers, by making official inquiries into political scandals or administrative failures, by exercising the advice and consent power of the Senate, by drafting their legislation in such a way as to have a say in its implementation, and so on. The legal difficulties with respect to the legislative veto have illustrated this tendency.[68] But the judiciary is not involved in this merger of powers.

There are, therefore, good arguments for the thesis that the idea of separation of powers is in practice being replaced by a 'bipolar' distinction, that between the judiciary on the one side, the legislative and executive bodies on the other. The French literature refers, as Pierre Pescatore phrased it, to the 'bipolarité' of modern constitutional systems.[69] That way of thinking finds its confirmation in a sociological observation: just as lawyers have long made up a separate class of the population, with its own idiosyncrasies, for example from a point of view of language, philosophy of life, circle of acquaintances, outward appearance and so on, politicians are now rapidly developing into a kind of exclusive social class, with shared values, agreed conduct and a common sense of vocation. In many political systems, the main dividing lines are no longer between political parties, but between the politicians and the non-politicians. There is a 'political class', characterized by its own outlook on the problems of society. Those who are elected to political functions become rapidly absorbed into it.

The professionalization of politics creates the danger of a growing distance between the opinions held by the population and those of the political class. Free elections cannot always cure that difficulty, because candidatures are largely monopolized by the political parties. That phenomenon explains the development of the concept of 'civil society' in recent years. In democratic countries, the citizens are bent on finding their own methods of opposition if the political channels are closed to them or unfit for achieving

---

[68] See ch. 7.1.
[69] See Pierre Pescatore, 'La légitimité du juge en régime démocratique', *Commentaire* 90 (2000), p. 339.

their aims. They will ask for referendums, set up single-issue movements (pacifist, or pro-environment, or anti-abortion, or pro animal rights); and, if nothing else works, they will turn to the courts. The courts are indeed, in the view of many, the only official institutions not entirely manned by the political class.[70] For the citizens, the judiciary has become, to quote Mr Pescatore once again, 'the only independent interlocutor'.[71]

From a sociological point of view, therefore, the main actors in the political field belong to one of three categories: the political class and the government bureaucracy under its control; the judiciary and the close-knit world of lawyers surrounding it; and the manifold forms in which civil society manifests its divergent claims. In a certain sense, one could still speak of three 'powers'. Civil society can, however, hardly be called a true power; it is rather, as a Canadian sociologist has called it, a house with 'varied voices'.[72] For purposes of comparative public law, the concept of bipolarity seems a more workable hypothesis.

In the bipolar model, the interplay of forces does not always have the same effect in different constitutional systems. However, one permanent development has been perceptible in each of the four systems we have tried to examine. Human rights protection has tended to reinforce the position of the judiciary. It has enabled the courts to interfere in matters that previously were very often left in the hands of the political institutions. It has also changed the judges' perception of their own task, as they tend to assume the role of pre-eminent protectors of the citizens. This has not always been clearly perceptible in the USA, where the courts' power to strike down statutes for violation of the Bill of Rights started at an early stage and developed very slowly. There was no awareness of a 'mighty problem of judicial review' – to quote a contemporary author on comparative law[73] – since important judicial powers appeared as always having been part of the American constitutional framework. Elsewhere, the situation may have been different. That was plainly demonstrated by the Canadian Supreme Court when it was faced with its first case on the compatibility of a statute with the Canadian Charter of Rights and Freedoms.[74] Before the entry into force of the 1982 Constitution, of which the Charter is now a part, the Court had exercised powers of judicial review when umpiring the Canadian federal

---

[70] See also Bradley and Ewing, *Constitutional and Administrative Law*, ch. 5.
[71] See note 69.   [72] David Lyon, *Postmodernity*, 2nd edn (Buckingham, 1999), p. 76.
[73] Cappelletti, *The Judicial Process in Comparative Perspective* (Oxford, 1989), pp. 150–3.
[74] *Law Society of Upper Canada* v. *Skapinker* (1984) 9 DLR (4th) 161.

system. However, it had no power at that time to strike down statutes for human rights violation. The change must have seemed momentous to the judges: the Supreme Court goes out of its way to explain the legitimacy of its powers of judicial review. Quoting *Marbury* v. *Madison* and the American literature, it rejects the argument that constitutional adjudication under the Charter would turn the Court into a 'super-legislature'. The task of the judiciary in a system of judicial review is not to allow the judge to question the wisdom of legislation, said the Court, but to measure it against the guarantees of the Constitution.

That statement is certainly correct, but it does not solve the problem of legitimacy. Human rights protection adds a new dimension to judicial review. First, problems of human rights can, unlike (for example) problems of federalism, be raised with regard to almost any kind of statute. Secondly, human rights provisions are often couched in broad and vague terms, sometimes based on ethical concepts rather than legal preoccupations. It is occasionally difficult to make a strict distinction between political and legal elements in the interpretation of these provisions. And thirdly, some expressions reflect moral ideas and social traditions which may be susceptible to change: the question is then whether an elected body is not in a better position than a court of justice to assess the present phase of that evolution. A judicial decision on the recognition of transsexuality may, for example, be founded on concepts of marriage and the family that do not necessarily correspond to majority feelings in the population.[75] For the courts, the problem seems to disappear once settled case law has come into existence, and judges are then not always aware that their role perception has changed meanwhile.

The bipolar model also leaves room for the opposite development, i.e. the possibility that other subjects than human rights protection may become more and more attracted to the political pole. The evolution in the USA illustrates this. The US Supreme Court abandoned its use of the due process clause for reviewing economic legislation in 1937, and since then, it has been extremely reluctant to examine choices of economic policy made by Congress. In Germany, the Bundesverfassungsgericht has explicitly ruled that the Basic Law takes no sides in matters of economic policy: it is 'wirtschaftpolitisch neutral'.[76] Decisions concerning nationalization of

[75] See Judge Martens, dissenting, in ECHR 27-9-1990, *Cossey*, Series A no. 184.
[76] BVerfGE 12 no. 34, *Volkswagenwerkprivatisierung* (1961).

means of production, or privatization of public enterprises, are left to the political institutions. The latest trends, however, indicate that the dividing line between economic policy and human rights protection is not as clear-cut as it used to be. In Europe, economic measures such as fishing quotas, restrictions on pig farming and bans on sugar or banana imports have given rise to claims based on violation of property rights or the right to the free choice of an occupation or profession.[77] Further developments may follow: have citizens a 'right' to quiet nights even if they live close to an airport? And will courts uphold State liability in case of violation of such rights? New boundaries to judicial interference must probably be defined by the courts; but it is too early to predict the outcome of this new search for manageable standards.

In the bipolar model, the chief characteristic distinguishing the courts from the political institutions is judicial independence: independence from government and from political leadership, independence from political parties and the latest political fashion, independence from popular feelings. Judicial independence is at the heart of the bipolar model; it makes bipolarity work. Modern constitutionalism cannot exist without it. It is, therefore, remarkable that the literature on constitutional law is mostly silent on judicial independence. Perhaps authors just take it for granted. That is probably the case in England, where the independence of the courts is firmly rooted in society on the basis of a tradition handed down from medieval times. In France and Germany, the independence of the courts is entrenched in the constitution.[78]

New risks for judicial independence have emerged after members of the political class in different countries have become the target of criminal investigations. Cases involving bribery, illicit campaign financing, favouritism and sometimes perjury have occurred in Italy, Germany and France as well as in Britain. In France, examining magistrates (*juges d'instruction*) may still incur the wrath of political leaders when they come close to disagreeable realities. Persons like the President of the Republic and the Prime Minister still see themselves as the embodiment of the will of the sovereign people; they should not be hindered in their grand designs by 'un petit juge' ('a petty judge': the expression was once used by M. Chirac). This resistance

---

[77] See Art. 1 Protocol 1 to the European Convention on Human Rights; Art. 14 and Art. 12 Basic Law.

[78] Respectively: Art. 64 Constitution 1958; Art. 97 s. (1) Basic Law.

to the general application of criminal procedure has, however, been slowly breaking down since a series of scandals involving all major political parties was uncovered in 2000. It had its funny moments, for example when the presence of 'des emplois fictifs' (non-existent but well-paid jobs) in the Paris Town Hall was revealed.[79] In Britain, there is more willingness to accept the application of criminal law to acts committed by important political or administrative functionaries. In 1994, the House of Commons instituted a committee on 'standards to be respected in public life', the idea being that politics itself should develop a code of conduct for politicians, and not leave this to the courts. However, it is also accepted that courts are the only effective remedy when political mechanisms are found to be wanting.[80]

We could perhaps put our findings in terms of political philosophy by stating that modern constitutionalism is founded on two currents, or movements, which have each their own rhythm and direction. One of these currents links the administration to the government and to the parliamentary majority supporting it, and thereby to the feelings of the electorate. The other links judicial decisions to the constitutional system, and is finally based on legal traditions rather than personal opinions. In the first current, choices are to be made; in the second, limits are to be observed.[81] Of course, reality may be somewhat more complicated.

Perhaps bipolarity should be considered as the new constitutional paradigm, that will slowly take the place which the separation of powers has, in one form or another, enjoyed for so long.

---

[79] See *Le Monde*, 17 and 18–19 June 2000.

[80] See A.W. Bradley, 'The courts in conflict with Parliament?', *Public Law* (1999), 384.

[81] Further literature: Konrad Hesse, 'Funktionelle Grenzen der Verfassungsgerichtsbarkeit', in *Recht als Prozess und Gefüge, Festschrift Huber* (Bern, 1981), p. 261; Helmut Steinberger, 'Modèles de juridiction constitutionnelle', Report for the Commission Européenne pour la Démocratie par le Droit of the Council of Europe (Strasbourg, 1992).

10

A glance at the future

10.1. The emergence of new problems

The main charm of the future is probably that we know so little about it. Consequently, we can speculate more freely than about the past and the present, without being hindered by inconvenient data that don't fit with our preconceived ideas. However, we shall also be treading on slippery ground: there are no accepted methods or techniques for drafting the world of the future. Extrapolating existing trends and developments is the most obvious way of arriving at some kind of certainty; but it is a poor method, as experience has taught us that one or more of these trends and developments will certainly be disrupted, or change their course, with the result that the ensuing image of a future situation may be completely mistaken. Predicting where changes will occur is more difficult still, as hundreds if not thousands of elements may influence future developments, some of which will be more stable than others. Winston Churchill must have been right when he said, in answer to a parliamentary question: 'It is always wise to look ahead, but difficult to look further than you can see.'[1]

However, since our research has shown us that the relationships between courts and political institutions are at present in a state of flux, it is tempting not to put a full stop to our inquiry at this point; it may be preferable to express the continuous movement of constitutional developments by a rapid glance at the near future. I shall start my attempt to look ahead by explaining why some of the present trends will probably continue and others will not; moreover, I shall indulge in some speculations about entirely new developments. This chapter, unlike the previous chapters, is therefore based on personal impressions rather than on empirical materials. My aim is, however, not to impose a certain view on my readers but to give them arguments for reflection and discussion.

---

[1] In 1952, when he was again Prime Minister. See Colin R. Coote (ed.), *Sir Winston Churchill, A Self-Portrait* (London, 1954), p. 278.

The legal literature is not a great help. Lawyers are perhaps too professional to speculate about the future. The true lawyer is more worried about liability for soil pollution, or the effects of bankruptcy in foreign jurisdictions, than about the future development of constitutional systems. Political science literature is a more reliable source for our conjectures. It gives some indications on the coming evolution of the political systems, the economic order and the cultural environment; I shall use these findings for most of my speculations.

An interesting, and sometimes disquieting, political phenomenon of recent years has been the decrease in political participation. In Europe, the membership of political parties has lessened considerably these last years. There is a poor turnout at elections, in the USA as well as in Europe. At the 2000 presidential elections in the USA, just over 50% of the electorate turned out; and as it was a close race, a mere 25% constituted the triumphant majority. Besides, the middle classes are much better represented among voters than the poor. There is, therefore, a problem of representativeness. Reading newspapers or looking at TV, one also gets the impression that many people are more interested in football, opera or gardening than politics, and that their number is on the increase. The great rallying cries that could once mobilize the millions (like 'disarmament!' or 'socialism now!' or 'women ahead!') seem to be on the wane. There is, in a way, a diminishing sense of belonging to a political community. However, that is counterbalanced by a growing sense of individual autonomy.[2] People like to do their own thing, more than ever before, and they don't want to be disturbed by, or receive lessons from, the burgomaster, the tax authorities or the bishops. There may be a growing conformity in leisure activities, cultural tastes, lifestyles and so on, but citizens feel it is not imposed on them by the authorities: it is their own choice.

This trend is likely to continue in the near future. It is reinforced by the emergence of new, and sometimes ephemeral, social movements which are in no way linked to existing political parties, churches, trade unions or other established organizations. We came across this phenomenon when examining the role of 'civil society' and its varied manifestations, such as the 'single issue movements', in the political system. It looks like becoming a permanent feature of Western politics.[3]

---

[2] See, in particular, David Held, *Models of Democracy*, 2nd edn (Cambridge, 1998), ch. 9.
[3] See ch. 9.5. See also S. N. Eisenstadt, *Paradoxes of Democracy* (Washington, D.C., 1999), ch. 7.

The political scientist Robert Dahl, in one of his latest books, assumes that the future will probably be characterized by two main developments: the continuing dominance of an economic order based on market capitalism, and an increase in cultural diversity.[4] This growing diversity is occasioned, he thinks, by two influences. First, organizations initially aiming at non-discrimination or at the emancipation of certain groups, such as blacks, women, gays and linguistic or ethnic minorities, have developed into movements of cultural identity. Having secured equality of treatment, they are now asking society to recognise their particular position. The feminist movements of the 1980s and the 1990s have undergone this shift of ideas.[5] Secondly, cultural diversity has been magnified by the increasing number of immigrants, usually marked by ethnic, linguistic, religious and cultural differences that make them distinguishable from the dominant groups in the population. In the USA this evolution started earlier than in Europe, but it seems an irreversible process in the entire Western world.[6] There is little doubt that it is giving rise to new difficulties and questions, and will continue to do so in the near future. To give only one example: can Moslem or Hindu children be compelled to undergo state education which is, expressly or implicitly, founded on Christian traditions and conceptions? Experience so far, for example in France, shows the reluctance of the political institutions to take a clear stand in debates of this kind;[7] the odds are that courts will have to find their own way in case of conflict.

Thus old problems may continue to make their influence felt. They will, however, be accompanied by new problems that are slowly emerging. Technological and economic developments are raising new issues of what we might call controllability. A first example is the general availability of the computer and the concomitant expansion of communication technology. State authorities lack the physical means to impose rules on trans-boundary messages; they have also great difficulty in enforcing the prohibition on certain messages, the obvious example being the trade in child pornography. At the same time, the sending and receiving of messages give rise to problems of copyright and, more generally, intellectual property; but it is not always clear which national legal system applies. The legal infrastructure of the flows of information ('infostructure' in the language

---

[4] Dahl, *On Democracy*, ch. 15.

[5] In particular since C. Gilligan, *In a Different Voice* (Cambridge, Mass., and London, 1982); see ch. 2.

[6] Dahl, *On Democracy*, p. 183.   [7] See ch. 8.3.

of the experts) is still in the process of being shaped.[8] The courts will have to solve the problems until international rules have been established or, if established, are made to work.

According to some authors, the problem is much more dramatic. The possibility of world-wide communication has the effect, they argue, of making the concept of 'territory' slowly lose its substance, with the result that the authority of the state will ultimately disintegrate. The difficulty is then that, at present, the state embodies the only institutional framework in which the democratic processes can take place. In this view, we need national constitutional systems to organize elections and protect citizens' rights; but the solidity of these systems is threatened by the internationalization of communication.[9]

Situations are even more insecure when we look at the flow of capital. The concentration of tremendous amounts of money in the hands of a small group of people and companies, combined with electronic communication technology, can result in rapid movements of capital around the globe. There is, in practice, no way to control or influence such movements. In case of concerted action, national currencies can be wrecked by the sudden departure of foreign capital. Politics is powerless; the markets are merciless; and lawyers, used as they are to respecting, in principle, the freedom of commercial transactions, see no way of challenging these movements. To control the 'infostructure', certain measures can be envisaged, for example European Union rules on intellectual property; but to control transnational investment flows, we lack even the beginnings of forms of organization that could meet the challenge.

There is, consequently, a clear problem of controllability. Some developments, particularly in the technical and economic fields, pursue their own course, with its own rhythm, as if they had been cut loose from the existing legal and political systems. As a result, forms of authority that once had an aura of omnipotence seem to be vanishing. A striking example is contraception. It was for a long time outlawed by the churches and by criminal legislation, and perhaps also by the prevailing opinion. Opposition to these interdictions by libertarian groups had only a limited effect. However, once cheap, simple and effective contraceptives had been developed and brought on the market by the pharmaceutical industry, the

---

[8] See Anne Wells Brainscomb, *Who Owns Information?* (New York, 1994), Introduction.
[9] See in particular Jean-Marie Guéhenno, *La fin de la démocratie* (Paris, 1993), ch. 1-2.

existing prohibitions melted away like snow in the summer sun. The hostility of the Vatican looks more or less like a rearguard action without any perceptible effect.

Problems of controllability also occur when prohibitions or other measures are quite possible in theory, but have no effect in practice. Governments and members of representative bodies are fully aware that they could reduce the emission of harmful gases by restricting the use of motor cars, fridges and other equipment; but in the present situation, damage to the environment is seen as a long-term problem, which cannot convince the electorate, let alone the pressure groups, that draconian measures are required. The 'Great Globe itself' may be menaced, but the motor car is closer to people's hearts. The history of Prohibition – the prohibition on 'intoxicating liquors' in the USA between 1919 and 1933[10] – shows that even in a fairly law-abiding society governments are not always able to impose legal rules on an unwilling or indifferent population. In France, problems of this kind are part of a political tradition. Sometimes, the main social conflict is, as one author put it, 'le pays contre l'Etat' (the country against the State). Even the French Republic cannot always win such a case. That was illustrated in 1982, when the left-wing government, supported by the newly elected President of the Republic and by a strong parliamentary majority, proved unable to execute its plans for incorporating Catholic primary education into the public school system; the political price to be paid for breaking the resistance was too high.[11]

For our purposes, the main question is whether these speculations about the future shape of society tell us something about future relationships between the courts and the political institutions. In that perspective, three specific developments stand out. First, there is a growing incapacity of the State and its authorities to impose the solutions that result from the national political process. If the 'sovereignty' of the State means that its authorities have not only the legal power but also the effective force to make their will respected by the citizens, modern States are rapidly losing it. Secondly, many political problems are outgrowing the national context and can only be dealt with at an international level. Sometimes these matters can be put into the care of international institutions, for example those of the European Union or the United Nations; but not infrequently no institutional framework

---

[10] Amendments XVIII and XXI to the US Constitution.
[11] See Alain Touraine, *L'après-socialisme* (Paris, 1983), pp. 136–41.

is available. Thirdly, the growing incapacity of political institutions will increase pressure on the courts to provide legal solutions to new social problems; but there is not always a legal basis for judicial intervention, particularly in case of international entanglements.

I should like to emphasize that, for our purposes, the ongoing process of bureaucratization seems less important. Its influence concerns all the different actors on our stage: bureaucratization touches the White House, Downing Street and the Palais de l'Elysée as well as Congress, Parliament and the Bundestag; it will characterize the entire administration, independent agencies included; and it will not leave the courts untouched. The mutual relationship between these bodies will, however, probably not significantly change as a result.[12]

In order to get a clearer picture, I shall add some observations concerning the changing character of politics, the changing position of national authorities and the changing role of the law and the lawyers. After these further explorations, we should be able to come to some tentative conclusions about our main theme.

10.2. The end of ideologies

The title of this section alludes to the study written by the American sociologist Daniel Bell in the sixties, *The End of Ideology*, which concerned 'the exhaustion of political ideas in the fifties'. Bell discussed a certain number of social issues of the time, such as the existence, or non-existence, of power elites in the USA, social mobility in New York City, the American cult of efficiency, trade unionism and the workers, and the failure of socialism in the USA. By way of epilogue, he added some thoughts on 'the end of ideology in the West'[13].

Bell referred in particular to those political creeds that could be characterized as secular pseudo-religions: communism, national socialism, fascism, and to a certain degree also social democracy. They simplified ideas, Bell states, established a claim to truth and, in a union of the two, demanded a commitment to action. Mass action was to transform society into a new type of community where certain ideals would be realized: a classless

---

[12] See, for a different view, Paul Edward Gottfried, *After Liberalism: Mass Democracy in the Managerial State* (Princeton, N.J., 1999), ch. 3.

[13] Daniel Bell, *The End of Ideology: On the Exhaustion of Political Ideas in the Fifties* (1961, revised edn New York and London, 1965), pp. 393–407.

society, purity of race, the cult of physical force, or equality among human beings. However, things went completely wrong, according to Bell: many of the 'chiliastic hopes' resulted in totalitarianism, oppression, violence and war. The great ideological movements lost their truth and their power to persuade.[14] Although Bell's conclusions were contested, and even ridiculed, in the late 1960s and the early 1970s when revolutionary fervour seemed to be returning to the USA and Western Europe, there is little doubt nowadays that his vision was basically correct, in the sense that it has been justified by subsequent events. Towards the end of the twentieth century, even soft ideologies such as market liberalism and welfare state socialism shed their ideological feathers; pragmatism became the prevailing political slogan. Political debates between doctrines which once seemed irreconcilable, like belief in the market as opposed to belief in public measures or community action, were reduced to squabbles over somewhat more or somewhat less of the one or the other. Grand designs, idealism, mass enthusiasm, all appeared to fade away.

This evolution raises two important problems with regard to the relationship between the courts and the political institutions. The first concerns ways of financing political parties: once they have lost their character as mass movements, they can no longer rely on the enthusiasm of their rank and file. As a result, they will be tempted to look for large financial contributions from wealthy persons or companies, who will be more willing to come forward if they have an economic interest in the electoral victory of the beneficiaries. This kind of commercialization of politics might slowly modify the role of the political institutions. The second problem is a growing lack of trust in political parties, and perhaps in politics in general, among the population. The question is then whether this lack of confidence affects the problem-solving potential of the political institutions and increases pressure on the courts.

On the first point, legislative bodies were alerted at an early stage. There was a fear that large financial contributions to candidates for election could raise suspicions of influence peddling, which might ultimately destroy the citizens' confidence in the integrity of government. In the USA, state and federal statutes imposed limits on the amounts of money that could be contributed at any election. In 1976, the US Supreme Court was required to assess the compatibility of such a statute with the Constitution.[15] A

---

[14] Ibid., p. 402.   [15] *Buckley* v. *Valeo*, 424 US 1 (1976).

Missouri statute was attacked for violating the First Amendment: it would impair the freedom of communication, because it would affect the contributor's ability to engage in a free political debate; and the statute would also disregard the freedom of association, as it prevented the contributor from assisting personally in the efforts of the association of his choice to get its candidate elected. The Court rejected both arguments: limiting contributions leaves communication significantly unimpaired, the Court said, and it leaves alternative channels of association open. Later case law has tended to follow this precedent. The Court emphasized the dangers presented by large campaign contributions: to the extent that they were given to secure a political quid pro quo from current and potential office holders, one of the pillars of representative government might be undermined. Apart from that, the Court added, there would also be an 'appearance of corruption', stemming from public awareness of the opportunities for abuse inherent in a regime of large individual financial contributions.[16]

Campaign financing is not only an American problem. In Germany, the former federal chancellor Helmut Kohl was accused of having collected millions for the 'secret funds' of his political party, the Christian Democrats; he probably made things worse by stubbornly refusing to reveal the identity of the generous contributors. He fell into disgrace, although he had formerly been hailed as the architect of German reunification in 1989–90. In Britain, one of the Labour politicians who was close to Prime Minister Blair had to resign twice for what the newspapers called 'undue intimacy with the very rich'.[17] The relation between politics and big money has developed into a major political issue. Transparency of party finances is often regarded as a necessary condition for establishing, or re-establishing, the image of an incorruptible political system; and legislation to that effect has been adopted in a number of countries. It is not always effective, however, since accounting can be done in such an artistic way that it does not always reflect the real flow of money. Codes of conduct for politicians may be elaborated, but they can only work fairly if there is a mechanism of enforcement. The true question is, it would seem, whether the political institutions can be trusted to regulate fairly the conduct of political parties. On the one hand, the freedom of the political parties to organize their own activities as they think fit is an

---

[16] *Colorado Republican Federal Campaign Commission v. Federal Election Commission*, 518 US 604 (1996).

[17] Mr Peter Mandelson. See *The Independent* 10 March 2001 (first leader).

important asset in a democracy; on the other hand, recent developments show that complete freedom in the field of campaign financing can rapidly lead to allegations of semi-corrupt practices.

Sometimes, legislative bodies try to avoid problems of this kind by instituting a system of State aids for certain expenses of political parties, such as campaign expenses or the costs of study-groups or courses. It is not sure that such a system will attain its intended goals. More money is always welcome. Moreover, the grant of subsidies will inevitably raise new legal problems. In Germany, the Bundesverfassungsgericht has ruled that distribution of grants must be on the basis of objective standards. Standards based on the existing political divisions in the Bundestag were, however, incompatible with the principle of equality, as they failed to take account of parties not yet represented. Conditions imposed on the grant of subsidies will sometimes lead to complicated legal questions; and these complications may, in their turn, facilitate certain forms of abuse.[18]

The second problem, that of decreasing confidence in politics, is less easy to measure. Besides, there may be greater differences between countries or even between regions. Politics is more discredited in Italy than, say, in Britain; and in rural America, there are still close-knit communities with a degree of political participation that would be unthinkable in Los Angeles or Chicago. Nevertheless there is one common feature: the end of the ideological debate means that 'official' politics is becoming rather dull, and that often, new political ideas are not developed within the usual political channels, but outside. Environmentalist groups, anti-nuclear movements, women's action groups, squatters, homosexuals, animal rights groups, peace movements and religious organizations have tabled many of the new items for the political agenda over the last twenty or thirty years. They are much more inclined than the traditional political parties to try judicial remedies when persuasiveness does not work. They may also use action methods that incite others to bring them before the courts: civil disobedience, for example, or physical prevention of nuclear transports, or causing material damage to military equipment or to laboratories where animal tests are performed.

Thus, issues that fail to penetrate into the parliamentary debate are brought before the courts. Litigation is then often conducted in clouds

---

[18] See BVerfGE 85 no. 24, *Parteienfinanzierung*, 1991. An earlier judgment on this point was BVerfGE 20 no. 10, 1966.

of misapprehension. The action groups want their political views to be discussed; the judges usually consider that the courtroom is not the appropriate place for such a discussion. An English case, decided in 1985, is very typical. It concerned a group of women that was occupying Greenham Common, not far from London, as a form of protest against nuclear armament, and against nuclear energy in general. The legal question was whether they could vote in the borough where they had – literally – pitched their tents. The Court of Appeal gave an affirmative answer, but Sir John Donaldson, Master of the Rolls, began his opinion by observing that the women 'all made a point of telling us that each is committed to the anti-nuclear cause' and that one of them 'made it very clear that she has strong views about the position of men in society'. And the learned judge continued: 'We record these facts because we feel sure that the ladies would wish them to be recorded, but we disregard them for all purposes.'[19]

It is in keeping with this evolution that action groups and peace movements tend to attack political decisions before the courts. In Germany, practically every decision on the expansion of airports, on military installations or on nuclear power plants is submitted to the judgment of the administrative courts by the – extremely well organized – environmentalist movement. The elaborate, and constitutionally protected, German system of remedies facilitates access to the courts, even on matters of this kind. Sometimes the action groups manage to transfer the political debate to the courtroom: it may, for example, be impossible to assess the legality of a government decision to accept the installation of American missiles on German soil without examining the policy considerations that have led to this decision.[20] Similar developments have taken place in the Netherlands and Denmark.

Boundary lines between the political and the legal arguments, once considered as necessarily clear and distinct, are getting blurred as a result. This tendency is being strengthened by a growing awareness among the citizens of their rights and interests. Nowadays people will no longer swallow things they used to put up with half a century ago. They don't feel it affects them when political parties come to a compromise on a difficult issue. Often the debate will not stop after the decision has been taken, but continue before the courts. When financial necessities compel governments to propose

---

[19] *Hipperson v. Newbury District Electoral Registration Officer* [1985] QB 1060.
[20] See e.g. BVerfGE 68 no. 1, *Pershing II*, 1984.

cuts in social benefits, trade unions and *ad hoc* organizations will turn to the courts for redress, alleging that the measures violate legal certainty, or equal protection, or the right of property, or standards fixed in ILO labour conventions.[21] The increasing feelings of autonomy of individuals in American and European society also imply independence from political institutions. In Germany, for example, the 1983 census led to an avalanche of constitutional complaints, although censuses have been carried out at least since the days of King Herod. More recently, changes to legislation on the admission asylum seekers had a comparable effect.[22] Litigation is becoming a form of protest against political decisions. It is perhaps, as one author put it, developing into a 'side-scene of politics and wailing-wall for citizens'.[23]

Can the trend I have tried to describe be extrapolated? It seems unlikely that confidence in political parties, and in political representation, will return quickly in the coming years. It is more than likely, however, that confidence in the courts will diminish. Some of the popular feeling of estrangement from the political system may also turn against the judicial system in the long run. If many citizens want society changed, or nuclear energy abolished, or animal rights enforced, the judiciary can help them as little as the political institutions, possibly less so. It is, from this point of view, instructive to recall how the US Supreme Court tried to impose a racially integrated school system on the USA in the 1960s and 1970s, but the observer feels bound to admit that it ultimately failed.[24]

If confidence in the courts were to melt away, the consequence might be that many people would feel estranged from the institutions of society in general. Some experience points in that direction. One might think of feelings in large immigrant communities, for example in the *grande ban-lieue* (outskirts) of cities like Paris and Marseilles, where unemployed young people, though born in France, feel entirely disconnected from French cultural, social and political life. Such an evolution would, of course, be extremely dangerous for the political future of Western Europe and the USA: it might finally shatter society completely. Overcoming risks and dangers of this kind may well require some new thinking on the relationship between

---

[21] This happened in the Netherlands. See *Nederlands Juristenblad* (1991), pp. 1167 and 1537; (1992), p. 1462.

[22] See Erhard Blankenburg, 'Die Verfassungsbeschwerde, Nebenbühne der Politik und Klagemauer von Bürgern', *Kritische Justiz* (1998/2), p. 203.

[23] Ibid., see note 22.   [24] See ch. 3.3–3.4.

the street and the State.[25] After all, democracy does have a delicate constitution: generalized indifference is bad for its health.

10.3. Globalization and regionalization

According to some observers, particularly in England and France, the authority of the nation-state is gradually being nibbled away by two contradictory movements. On the one hand, some problems are becoming internationalized to such a degree that the State is no longer able to provide solutions: European Union institutions have a growing say in many matters, economic situations are part of a rapidly developing world market, and the military potential of Western Europe seems inextricably tied up with that of the USA. On the other hand, there is also a growing increase in the powers of regional subdivisions of the State, at the expense of the authority of national institutions. Federalization in Belgium, regionalization in Spain and Italy, devolution in Britain, all seem to fit into a certain pattern.[26] Even France tried its hand at regionalization in the early years of the Mitterrand era.

Decentralization doesn't come naturally to the French authorities. Since Napoleon's day the territory had been divided into about 100 *départements*, each of which used to be run by a *préfet* appointed by the central government and subject to its instructions. The names and boundaries of the departments were drawn up in such a way as to avoid any association with the traditional regions of the old French Kingdom. One of the departments situated in the ancient country of Burgundy is, for example, still called the 'département de Saône-et-Loire', after two neighbouring rivers. Local government was organized on a representative basis, but it had only limited powers in purely local matters, and the prefect of the department could annul local decisions and regulations if he considered them contrary to the law or to the general interest.[27] That system survived the Third and Fourth Republics, and it was still basically unchanged when regional government was instituted in 1982. One of the oddities of the reform was that the regional structure was superimposed on the departmental organization. A new layer was added to the administration of the country. The new regions assumed the names and boundaries of the old traditional regions

---

[25] See also Eisenstadt, *Paradoxes of Democracy*, ch. 9.
[26] See Barendt, *An Introduction to Constitutional Law*, ch. 3-4.
[27] For the history, see Brian Chapman, *The Prefect and Provincial France* (London, 1955), ch. 1.

(Normandie, Bourgogne, Poitou etc.), and they are governed on a representative basis: a *conseil régional* is directly elected and appoints its own *président*. But Paris has been somewhat mean as far as the attribution of powers is concerned, and the prefects retain most of their traditional competences.

Thus, regional government in France is squeezed between the ambitions of the national government and the settled practice of the *corps préfectoral*. In Spain, Italy and Britain, important powers with regard to language, culture, or urban planning can be exercised by regions like Catalonia, Lombardy or Scotland, but there is no parallel in France. All French regions have the same powers and the same institutions, just as the departments used to have. There is, however, one exception, because one of the regions is in a particular position: Alsace. It was part of the German Empire when the Third Republic was established, and it was allowed to retain some of its peculiarities when it was reunited to France in 1918. As a result, the strict rules on the separation of Church and State do not apply to Alsace, the French language is not imposed as the sole language in the schools and in the courts, and there are also some minor differences in taxation and social security. The government of Lionel Jospin has been trying to use the Alsatian precedent to create a separate administrative position for Corsica, but these plans have run into difficulties.[28]

The main obstacle to reform is probably that in France, centralization is not just a method of administrative organization: it is part of a way of life. Non-governmental activities are as highly centralized as the administration of the country. Paris is the centre not only of government, but also of art and business life; political parties, trade unions, large corporations, private associations, they all have their headquarters in Paris ('en métropole'). The capital is, or used to be, the cultural centre of the country; it is the place where the most important universities, opera houses and museums are. However, over the last ten or twenty years, things have been changing very gradually, with the rediscovery of old regional centres such as Toulouse, Lyons and Lille; slowly, the famous distinction between 'Paris et le désert' is losing its relevance.[29]

---

[28] See *Le Monde*, 23 February 2001. See also CC 9-5-1991, *Statut de la Corse, Rec.* 50, *Les grandes décisions* no. 46.

[29] It was once the title of a book: J. F. Gravier, *Paris et le désert français* (Paris, 1947).

The United Kingdom has a different tradition. Although there is a high degree of administrative centralization, it is less uniform in its application; and centralization does not affect non-governmental activities. The Scots have their own kirk and their own law, the Welsh their own language, Northern Ireland its own 'troubles'; the Anglican archbishops have their sees in Canterbury and York, not in London; Birmingham, Manchester and Edinburgh have always been cultural centres in their own right; and the oldest and most famous universities are in Oxford, Cambridge and St Andrews. The devolution laws of 1998 drew the appropriate conclusions from this situation by establishing dissimilar institutions for Scotland and Wales and by attributing dissimilar powers to them.

It is not completely obvious what the future will have in store. Some British authors think that devolution, hesitantly started in 1998, should be pushed much further. After the first experiences in Scotland and Wales, devolution should be extended to England itself, by the creation of regions in England; initially, that view seemed to have a certain appeal.[30] The Blair government was, however, unwilling to bring it on to the political agenda, and popular interest in further devolution plans seems to be petering out. Since 1998, the British have been living in a half-way house: the Scottish Parliament has its own powers, and the Welsh Assembly can exercise certain powers independently once they have been delegated to it by the Parliament in Westminister. However that may be, the situation of Scotland can in no way be assimilated, or even compared, to that of the *Länder* in Germany, like Bavaria or Saxony, or to that of American states such as Georgia or California. In the British case, ultimate power remains entirely in the hands of the national Parliament. And the national government retains important powers: the Home Secretary can, for example, 'direct' members of the Scottish executive not to take a certain action when he has 'reasonable grounds to believe' that this action would be incompatible with European Community law, or with any of the rights guaranteed by the European Convention on Human Rights.[31] In federal systems, such a task would quite naturally be assigned to the courts. It is also interesting to note that devolution in Britain had no effect on the organization of the judiciary:

---

[30] See Paul McQuail and Katy Donnelly, 'English regional government', in Robert Blackmun and Raymond Plant (eds.), *Constitutional Reform: The Labour Government's Constitutional Reform Agenda* (London and New York, 1999), ch. 13.

[31] See Art. 57 s. (2) and Art. 58 s. (1) Scotland Act 1998.

Wales continues to be under the jurisdiction of the English courts, Scotland continues to have its own system of courts with the House of Lords acting as final court of appeal.[32]

With respect to internationalization, British attitudes are traditionally ambivalent. Since Winston Churchill's day, British governments have always been slow to accept steps in the European integration process. The Conservative Party is vehemently opposed to any such step nowadays, and has been since the final Thatcher years; but it tends to accept blindly American guidance in military matters. Labour is strongly divided on both issues. In France, on the other hand, conservatives (*la droite*) are not generally hostile to European integration, but they reject American hegemony in military as well as economic and cultural affairs. In the media, American influence is often identified with pop music, bad movies and fast food ('la male bouffe'). Globalization is then the target of criticism.

From a legal point of view, the interesting thing about internationalization is that, unlike regionalization, it directly affects the organization of the judiciary and the jurisdiction of the courts. Since their first beginnings, the institutions of the European Communities have included the EC Court of Justice, which has constructed an important body of case law on the interpretation of the provisions of the European treaties, regulations and directives, as well as on the role of the Member State authorities in implementing these provisions.[33] In a comparable way, the national courts' interpretation of the rights guaranteed by the European Convention on Human Rights is influenced by the case law of the European Court of Human Rights. The World Trade Organization, established in 1994, has semi-judicial procedures for settling trade conflicts between States or groups of States, in the form of arbitration panels and an appeal panel. There seems to be a tendency to 'judicialize' matters concerning the implementation of treaty obligations, at least as far as economic issues and human rights protection are concerned.

Thus a new constitutional problem presents itself: is the transfer of these powers, including judicial powers, to a European or international organization compatible with the national constitution? And if not, is it up to the courts to assess this compatibility and to draw conclusions from their

---

[32] See for further materials Robert Reed, 'Devolution and the judiciary', in J. Beatson (ed.), *Constitutional Reform in the United Kingdom. Practice and Principles* (Oxford, 1998), ch. 3.
[33] See ch. 4.4.

findings? The problem does not arise in Great Britain, where the judiciary takes no notice of rules of international law unless specifically obliged to do so by statute. Nor does arise in the Netherlands, where the constitutional reform of 1953–6 opened the Dutch legal system to the direct application of rules of international law, even in case of incompatibility with national provisions.[34] The problem did, however, give rise to extensive legal debate in France and Germany. The constitutional courts of both countries had to pass judgment on it.

In France, the answer of the Constitutional Council was precise and legalistic, but it hardly helped to solve the problem. The preamble to the 1946 Constitution expressly states that France 'shall consent to those limitations of sovereignty necessary for the organization and defence of peace'. That means, said the court, that modifications to the EC treaty are compatible with the French Constitution so long as they only 'limit' the sovereignty of the Republic; however, any 'transfer' of sovereignty can only be accomplished after the necessary change of the Constitution.[35] This judgment led, of course, to an almost metaphysical debate on the exact boundary line between 'limitations' and 'transfers' of national sovereignty. As the debate continued, however, it was increasingly guided by pragmatic considerations rather than by statements of principle.

The German Bundesverfassungsgericht rendered an important judgment in 1984, but it defies any effort to trace intelligible boundary lines between permitted and forbidden steps in extending the powers of the European institutions. The case concerned constitutional complaints against the parliamentary approval of the Treaty of Maastricht.[36] That treaty established the European Union, of which the pre-existing European Communities were to be part; it also laid the foundation stones for a common European currency and for common policies in the field of defence and foreign relations. The court examined several questions of admissibility of the constitutional complaints, focusing on two substantive issues.

The first was whether the treaty empowered the European institutions to determine, within certain limits, their own powers. If that was the case, the powers of the European Union could be increased, and those of the

---

[34] See ch. 4.3.

[35] See Preamble Constitution 1946, s. 15; CC 30-12-1976, *Assemblée européenne*, Rec. 15, *Les grandes décisions* no. 25.

[36] *Maastricht-Urteil*, reported in English as *Brunner v. European Union Treaty* [1994] 1 CMLR 57.

German authorities correspondingly reduced, without any intervention by the Bundestag; that result would violate the constitutional rule that the citizens participate in the exercise of public authority by means of the representative system.[37] After some soul-searching, the Court came to the conclusion that the Maastricht Treaty did not give the European institutions the authority to extend their own powers. If those institutions nevertheless acted as if that authority had been granted to them, they would be acting *ultra vires*, said the Court. In a somewhat menacing tone, the Court added that in such an exceptional situation, it would itself have to draw the legal conclusions from the transgression of the limits of European powers.

The second issue represents a recurring theme in German case law: the public authorities of the Federal Republic cannot alienate the human rights of German citizens, and therefore the European institutions cannot have been empowered to disregard those rights. If in spite of that, a situation should occur in which rights guaranteed by the Basic Law were violated by European rules or decisions, these rules or decisions could not be considered as having been validly made. It is not entirely clear from the Court's reasoning whether, in such a case, the final judgment on validity of the European rules or decisions would be left to the European Court of Justice.

The *Maastricht* judgment raises a great many questions of European Community law. For our purposes, it is interesting because it illustrates the uncomfortable cohabitation of constitutional law with the growing internationalization of economics, politics and authority. Constitutional law represents stability; it incarnates inalienable rights and the unchangeable requirements of democratic government and the rule of law. In European and international matters, wholly different elements come into play, which may require rapid decisions, or be based on entirely novel considerations, or embody ideas commonly accepted in one State but not in another. The appropriate balance has yet to be found.

10.4. Judicialization

A debate on 'judicialization', or 'juridification', and its limits is now going on in most Western countries. The terms refer to the growing influence of the courts, in particular on matters which were once considered purely political. In previous sections of this book we have met different instances of this

---

[37] See Art. 20 s. (2), Basic Law.

trend. In a somewhat arbitrary sequence, I recall: the extension of judicial review of legislation to continental Europe; the highly disputed interference of the American courts in sensitive social issues such as abortion and affirmative action; the generalization of judicial review of administrative action; the critical attitude of judges with regard to political and administrative decisions; the growth of State liability; judicial involvement in European and international problems; and more.[38] Two or more of these developments are easily perceptible in each of the four constitutional systems we have examined.

From a strictly legal point of view, these developments can be divided into two groups. The first group is distinguished by extension of the jurisdiction of the courts. The growth of judicial review is the most obvious example. A second group does not concern the competence of the courts, but the way courts settle complaints about public authorities, in particular the decreasing deference to the assessments made by these authorities. To put it in simplified terms: courts are not only attracting new types of cases, they are also dealing with their cases in a more critical manner. To complicate things further, extension of jurisdiction is sometimes achieved by legislative reform of the system of remedies, sometimes by the mere action of the courts themselves. The introduction of judicial review of administrative action into English law, in 1977, was the fruit of a conscious effort to improve judicial protection, an effort supported by a parliamentary majority.[39] Especially on the European continent, courts have been inclined to increase their jurisdiction in tort actions by redefining conditions of admissibility (e.g. with regard to class actions) and by extending the concept of tort itself (e.g. with regard to air, water and soil pollution). It is therefore useless to look for one sole cause underlying judicialization.

Most of the time, judicialization debates are conducted in a national context. Participants discuss the role of their national courts, occasionally also of European courts, and the reactions to it of their national politicians and their national press. They seem to assume that the judicialization phenomenon is something unique, which has happened to their own country by some kind of accident. One of the rare exceptions I have been able to find is a discussion of judicialization in France by an English author in an English political review. The author first gives the elements of what he calls

[38] See, respectively, ch. 3.2; 3.4-3.5; 6.4-6.5; 5.3 and 7.4; 9.3; 10.3.
[39] See Order 53, Rules of the Supreme Court (1977); s. 31 Supreme Court Act 1981.

'the judicialization of public policy', and then sets out to explain the increasing recourse to the courts and to judicial processes.[40] Among the elements of judicialization, he lists the quantitative leap in litigation in all branches of law; the development of standards for public policy by the process of judicial review; the submission of nearly every important piece of legislation to the Constitutional Council; the use made by the courts of unwritten principles of law; the transfer to the courts of decision-making power in new policy areas, such as competition law, previously unregulated or scantily regulated by the government; the application of criminal law to activities of officials in the event of negligence (e.g. collapse of a bridge or a football stadium); and the growing autonomy of the judges with regard to the opinions of the politicians and their ministries in Paris. The explanations given by our author include the growing impact of European law on the application of French law; the dismantling of traditional State *dirigisme* in the French economy; the growing diversity of French society, which defies the homogenizing pressures of education and parliamentary legislation; technological change, raising urgent practical and ethical issues that regulators have neither the will nor the time to face; the growing collective demand from the judges for autonomy and independence; and the activity of individual judges in case of wrong-doing by well-known politicians. The separation between occurrences and explanations may look somewhat artificial, but it is clear enough that many of these factors have a structural character, in the sense that they are not just the result of temporary and typically French circumstances: parallels can be found in most Western democracies.

If even half of all this is true, we have come to a curious reversal of the situation as it presented itself when the first constitutions were adopted in the late eighteenth century, in the USA and in France. Shortly before that Montesquieu had already argued that judicial power should be organized in such a way that it does not express individual opinions of judges, but the words of the law; thus it would become more or less invisible: 'la puissance de juger [...] devient, pour ainsi dire, invisible et nulle'.[41] The current ideas were well expressed by Hamilton in the Federalist papers: the judiciary 'will always be the least dangerous to the political rights of the Constitution' when compared to the executive or the legislative powers. The former 'holds the

---

[40] Vincent Wright, 'The Fifth Republic: from the *droit de l'Etat* to the *état de droit*?', *West European Politics* 22/4 (1999), 92.

[41] *L'esprit des lois* book xi, ch. 6 (edn L'Intégrale, p. 587).

sword of the community', the latter 'commands the purse' and regulates the rights and duties of the citizens. 'The judiciary, on the contrary, has no influence over either the sword or the purse; no direction either of the strength or the wealth of the society'. It can truly be said, Hamilton thought, 'to have neither force nor will, but merely judgment'.[42] Two centuries later, an American observer wrote that this statement 'must have made a good bit of sense' in the years it was written, but that two hundred years of experience has taught us a different lesson, in particular as far as the US Supreme Court is concerned. 'The Court may be purseless and swordless', he said, 'but its ability importantly to influence the way the nation functions has proved great, and seems to be growing all the time.'[43]

With hindsight, the expression the 'least dangerous' branch seems singularly ill chosen. It may well have been the very lack of power over, and responsibility for, the 'sword' and the 'purse' which gave the American Supreme Court the courage to tackle complicated problems of society disregarded by the political institutions, perhaps because of their complexity. Racial inequality is the most obvious example: the Court's case law led first to severe disturbances of public order in the South, later to the re-districting of schools and the bussing of schoolchildren in the North. The power of the sword and that of the purse were both involved, but they had to be exercised by two departments of government that were not responsible for the basic decision. In a more general way, that may be one of the disadvantages of judicialization: the courts can, and do, sometimes take momentous decisions affecting the life of society without having to face up to the human or financial consequences. There are, of course, differences among the legal systems: the English courts are traditionally very cautious in taking new steps if they are not able to estimate the financial consequences of their ruling in comparable cases. Lord Wilberforce once used this argument when examining whether nervous shock could give rise to tort liability.[44] The work of courts engaged in civil litigation is perhaps not entirely comparable to that of courts which are, or act as, constitutional courts. Constitutional courts will necessarily take a larger view, not limited to the situation of the parties to the litigation. Nevertheless, the cautious approach of the law lords may have its merits.

The example of racial inequality in the USA also reveals, however, something about the dynamics of case law. Once racial segregation in schools

---

[42] *The Federalist* LXXVIII (Hamilton).   [43] Ely, *Democracy and Distrust*, p. 45.
[44] *McLoughlin* v. *O'Brian* [1983] 1 AC 410.

had been banned, the Court came quite naturally to its further decisions on desegregation in other public facilities and on the integration of the school system. New lines of case law were thus developed, not because the courts themselves loved to draw the consequences from the principles they have embraced but because litigating parties wanted to try out what they saw as a new beginning. Society adapts very quickly to new turns of legal evolution: it puts pressure on the courts to reveal the exact scope of their latest decisions. To that extent, case law has a kind of self-propelling effect. One decision can provoke a series of decisions on similar, or nearly similar, cases; and the consequences of the series of decisions may have an impact that can in no way be compared to that of the initial decision. At a certain point, however, the courts may put a stop to such a seemingly continuous expansion of their area of interference. There is a stage where they become aware that the political institutions may be better equipped to solve certain social problems, and that a way should be found to leave such problems to those very institutions.

An interesting illustration occurred in Germany in 1977. The Bundesverfassungsgericht was faced with an application from the son of a man of some fame, who had been abducted by left-wing terrorists ('urban guerillas') and subsequently killed by them, probably because he was the chairman of the German employers' association. The petitioner alleged that his father's death had been caused by the federal government's refusal to accept the kidnappers' demands (in particular, the release of other terrorists already imprisoned). This refusal had endangered the protection of human life guaranteed by the Basic Law. The state, the petitioner added, could not maintain that it was protecting a higher value, because no right could be of higher value than that to life itself.[45] The Court held, however, that it could not prescribe what decision the government should take under such conditions. It was true, the judgment states, that the state is obliged to protect human life; but the right of an individual cannot be the sole imperative in a case where the life and safety of a number of people are threatened. Only those measures would be justified that were adapted to 'the plurality of specific situations' ('die Vielfalt singulärer Lagen'). The government is in the best position, the Court seems to think, to assess all the elements of such situations. That view can seldom be detected in the constitutional court's

---

[45] BVerfGE 46 no. 12, *Schleyer*, 1977.

case law. However that may be, the judgment shows that the extension of the courts' scope of action is not ineluctable.

It is unlikely that the judicialization trend will continue unaltered in the years to come. The first reason for this assumption is the unavoidable overburdening of the judicial potential. In England, some judges have already warned that the combination of judicial review, the Human Rights Act and (possibly) devolution appeals is likely to create a situation where the workload of the courts will double and nobody has worked out how to find the judge-power to deal with it all.[46] Various expedients have already been invented in order to enable the courts to cope with the influx of cases: leave to appeal; selection of cases as under the American *certiorari* system; exclusion of appeals in cases of minor importance; reduced description of the grounds of the judgment, and others. These expedients are not always effective. Appointing more judges is not a suitable solution in the long run. Finally, it will encumber the judicial system, and facilitate the bureaucratization of judicial decision-making; it may thus be self-defeating.

The courts are in an unenviable position. They are being asked to examine more and more cases, whilst the pressure to shorten delays in proceedings is increasing. The European Court of Human Rights considers that Article 6 of the European Convention imposes an obligation on the courts to decide their cases within a reasonable time; and it is very strict in enforcing that rule. It does not accept the overburdening of the court system as a valid excuse for unreasonable delays. The citizen is entitled, under Article 6, to have his case examined and decided within a reasonable time, and should therefore not be the victim of an inappropriate organization of judicial remedies.[47] That, of course, is more easily said than done.

The second reason not to expect an unbroken development of further judicialization is psychological rather than legal or political. Part of the increased pressure on the courts appears to be due to persons or organizations that hope to find solutions to problems of society which the political institutions have not been able or willing to provide. They will probably be disappointed.[48] Occasionally, the judiciary can help to renew the legal system, as the American experience with racial equality illustrates. Without political backing, however, it will sooner or later have to stop: new case

[46] Lord Browne-Wilkinson, *The Times*, 19 October 1999.
[47] See ECHR 26-2-1993, *Salesi*, Series A no. 257-E.   [48] See also ch. 10. 2.

law cannot expand indefinitely in isolation. By way of example, we could point out that many important problems of modern society concern the beginning and end of human life: contraception, abortion, cloning, euthanasia, assisted suicide. The ethical issues raised by these problems used to be dominated by the teachings of the Church, or in Protestant countries of the churches, until some fifty years ago; but their voice is not regarded as decisive any more. Politics, however, tends to dodge these issues: they are not vote-getters as the reconquest of the Falklands once was, or as a firm appeal to law and order can still be; and they don't fit with the traditional divisions between political parties and political currents. The lack of an authoritative answer heightens the pressure on the courts. There are certainly things courts can do in this situation: they can help in emergency cases, or open up new lines of debate, or protect innocent third parties. But courts cannot achieve permanent solutions to these new moral problems. True solutions can be brought about only on the basis of a certain form of consensus in society; and only the political parties and the political institutions are in a position to provoke debates, to indicate roads to the future and to draw the consequences from popular convictions and feelings. The judiciary is in no such position.[49]

There may be a third reason why it is not very safe to rely on extrapolating the judicialization trend. Judges are inherently conservative, perhaps because of their very position in society. It is their role to maintain the established legal order; those who want to change that order should turn to politics. In other words, battles for renovation should be fought at the polls, not in the courtroom. This is, of course, a simplified picture of a complicated reality; some of the experience points in a different direction. In particular, courts have been instrumental in defining procedural standards to be observed in administrative decision-making; for example, they brought about important innovations in administrative law, and, in a certain sense, helped to create it. Moreover, courts may feel compelled to contribute to bridging the gap between constitutional principles and social realities, when this gap shows no signs of closing; case law on equal protection in the USA and in Germany illustrates the point. Sometimes, judges are led by the impetus of their own case law into areas of law reform. It happened with American criminal procedure, but the movement was brought

---

[49] See also P. S. Atiyah, *Law and Modern Society*, 2nd. edn (Oxford and New York, 1995), ch. 6; Robert Nisbet, *The Present Age* (New York, 1988), ch. III.

to an end when its instigators, such as Justice Brennan, left the Supreme Court. It is also true that in many countries courts have actively helped to impose substantive legal standards on areas of administration previously left to the total discretion of the government. Tax is the clearest illustration: by extending constitutional rules and principles, such as equal protection and protection of legal certainty, to tax matters the courts have helped to transform fiscal administration into tax law.[50] There is therefore evidence of the courts' active participation in law reform; nevertheless, the statement that judges cannot be considered as the prime agents for changing society remains fundamentally true. Like most fundamental truths, however, it is subject to variations and exceptions.

One additional observation should be made at this point. Supreme court judges are usually elderly gentlemen, occasionally ladies, who will not, as a rule, be very receptive to entirely new ideas. English judges will normally be appointed to the House of Lords when they are in their sixties, after a distinguished career at the bar, in the High Court and in the Court of Appeal; the Scottish law lords follow a somewhat shorter course. Sometimes the press, or the trade unions, or the Labour Party, reproach the law lords for their conservatism; it happened in particular during the 1970s.[51] It will be clear from the foregoing chapters that the situation is different in the USA, and that this difference may also be due to the way of appointing justices in the US Supreme Court: the political element that sometimes characterizes American appointments is absent in Britain. American justices, though often younger when appointed, can remain in the Court for a long time: as there is no age limit, some judges continue in the Court until well over eighty (sometimes, as in the case of the famous Justice Holmes, even over ninety).

It is not difficult, I feel, to find a word of consolation for politicians who complain about judicial interference in matters of public policy. On the one hand, further judicialization will probably not develop into a permanent feature of legal evolution in the liberal democracies of North America and Western Europe. There is nothing unavoidable, it appears, in the growth of judicial interference in matters which interest politicians. On the other hand, political institutions themselves can reduce the scope and importance

---

[50] For Britain, see Robert Stevens, *Law and Politics. The House of Lords as a Judicial Body* (London, 1979), pp. 410–14, 601–3. For France: CE 30-6-1995, *Polynésie Française, Rec.* 279. For Germany: BVerfGE 9 no. 31, *Feuerwehrbeitrag*, 1959.

[51] See David Pannick, *Judges* (Oxford, 1987), ch. 3 and 5.

of judicialization by tackling some of the problems of society they have neglected hitherto. When, however, governments solemnly announce their intention 'to put a stop to judicialization' without saying how,[52] they seem to be lashing the air, as a Dutch expression has it.

10.5. Law and politics

'Our tale is now done, and it only remains to us to collect the scattered threads of our little story, and to tie them into a seemly knot.' That is how Anthony Trollope introduced the final chapter of one of his novels.[53] I shall try to do likewise in this final section of my 'little story'.

I shall first devote some concluding remarks to the boundary line between law and politics; or, to be more precise, between the field of action of lawyers, particularly judges, and politicians, particularly members of governments and parliamentary institutions. One of the most conspicuous findings of our comparative study is that this boundary line does not follow the same pattern in all the constitutional systems under consideration. Capital punishment provides a good example. It is prohibited in the European countries by virtue of Protocol 6 to the European Convention on Human Rights; in the USA, the admissibility of the death penalty is nowadays a matter for the state legislatures to decide. In the American system, it is a political problem; in Europe, the political institutions are legally not empowered to reintroduce capital punishment. In the USA, the debate on reintroduction or abolition is a political debate; in Europe, constitutional law leaves no room for such a debate.

We found exactly the opposite situation as far as the lawfulness of abortion is concerned. Under the case law of the US Supreme Court, the due process clause of the American Constitution permits abortion during the first months of pregnancy; state legislatures are not allowed to limit the rights pregnant women derive from the Constitution. In the European countries, no such constitutional rights are recognised; abortion is lawful within the limits traced by statute, and these limits can be changed by the legislative bodies. Particularly in Britain and in France, the lawfulness of abortion is a problem to be faced by politics, not by the courts. Germany is perhaps in an intermediate position; but under German constitutional

---

[52] The Dutch government did so in 1998.
[53] Trollope, *The Warden*, ch. xxi (Oxford edn, 1989, p. 278).

law as currently interpreted, that lawfulness is at least primarily a problem for the legislative institutions.

These two examples also show that the European constitutional systems have a certain unity when compared to American constitutional law. It is interesting to notice that the European Convention on Human Rights has made a significant contribution to framing such a relative unity, although it was not established for that purpose (it is only intended to provide minimum standards).[54] On close analysis, European constitutional systems may have more in common than European opinion leaders are prepared to admit. It is, of course, an important fact that British constitutional law is not laid down in a document called 'Constitution' which has priority over statutory rules; or that the powers of the president of the Republic in France are completely dissimilar to those of his German counterpart. Nevertheless, it is also important that for subjects like the death penalty and the lawfulness of abortion, both subjects which touch the life of the citizens very directly, there is a common ground in Europe.

We found more examples of differences concerning the boundary line between law and politics. One further example is the distribution of legislative powers in federal systems. In the USA, Congress can only legislate on matters explicitly attributed to it by the Constitution; and the extent of these powers is determined by judicial interpretation. Powers not covered by the list of attributed subjects remain in the hands of the state authorities.[55] In Germany the situation is entirely different, because the Basic Law has a long list of 'concurrent' legislative powers. These powers can be exercised by the *Länder* as long as, and in so far as, the federal legislature has not established rules on the subject. Here, the definition of federal legislative powers is ultimately determined by decisions of the federal legislative institutions, in particular the Bundestag; the political debate decides.[56] This applies to some of the main subjects of legislation, for example for legislation on social and economic issues. There is, however, also a list of 'exclusive' federal legislative powers in the Basic Law.[57] Constitutional litigation can therefore arise, for example on the limits of the law relating to weapons and explosives, included among the subjects of concurrent legislation, with regard to matters of 'defence, including the protection of the civilian population',

---

[54] See Art. 53 European Convention on Human Rights.
[55] See Tenth Amendment, US Constitution.
[56] Art. 72 s. (1) and Art. 74 s. (1) Basic Law.   [57] Art. 73 Basic Law.

which are exclusive federal powers. Moreover, there is no doubt in German constitutional law that some subject matters can be dealt with exclusively by the *Länder*. I refer, in particular, to the cultural autonomy ('Kulturhoheit') of the *Länder*, which includes most matters of education. Things are rarely simple in German constitutional law. Nevertheless, the situation can in no way be assimilated to that under the US Constitution, where a mere change of case law, e.g. on the concept of 'interstate commerce', can profoundly modify the extent of federal legislative powers.

The second question is then whether the boundary line between the legal and the political debate is stable, or can shift, within a given constitutional system. There is no doubt about the answer: the American experience shows how the US Supreme Court has been able to shift the frontier, in particular in the post-*Brown* period, approximately between 1955 and 1975. First, the social practice of segregation, upheld by white activists and by the police in the Southern states, and accepted by the courts, was banned. Then the Supreme Court took control over the implementation of racial equality, in the schools and elsewhere. Finally, the task of surveillance brought the Court to a new and dynamic conception of the protection of civil liberties, with far-reaching consequences in the fields of public order, criminal procedure and the lawfulness of press publications. Issues previously considered as policy questions were subjected to constitutional requirements. The area of law increased, and the Supreme Court was often seen as the architect of legal renovation: it had been 'making and remaking the law of the land'.[58] Gradually, and in fits and starts, this period seems to have come to an end; and although our boundary line may still move occasionally, backwards as well as forwards, it is more stable than it has been over the last fifty years.[59] In recent years, it has been politics, in particular the action of Republican Congressmen and Christian movements, that has tried to bring abortion back into the field of political decision-making. Nothing is, of course, ever completely settled in American constitutional law. However, the judicial dynamism of the 1960s and 1970s seems to be on the wane.

That development, in its turn, raises a different question: was politics, in the sense of party politics, perceptible in the Supreme Court's decision-making processes? The answer cannot be a simple yes or no. The most

[58] Caption for review of two books on the Supreme Court in the *New York Times Book Review* in 1987 (20 September 1987).
[59] See also McCloskey, *The American Supreme Court*, Coda (pp. 236ff.).

important judgment, the first *Brown* decision, was rendered by a unanimous court; and although some judges were sometimes more cautious than others, the Court remained very much united over racial issues. On civil rights issues the Court was, however, often split. It was not so much a contrast between supporters and opponents of a wide conception of civil liberties, but rather between those like Justice Frankfurter, who saw more scope for congressional action, and those like Justice Douglas, who thought it was primarily the Court's role to uphold the freedoms the Bill of Rights is meant to guarantee. Slowly, the Court began to consist of two 'wings'. The liberals, symbolized by Justices Douglas and Brennan, were in favour of an extensive and individualistic interpretation of human rights; 'constructionists' such as Chief Justice Burger (1962–86) considered that the Court had to stick to the meaning traditionally ascribed to the rights protected by the Constitution. It should, the Chief Justice once said, avoid passing 'beyond the penumbras of specific guarantees into the uncircumscribed area of personal predilection'.[60] After the Reagan appointments in the 1980s, the somewhat loosely formed 'wings' developed steadily into a firm distinction between 'liberals' and 'conservatives' in the Court. That distinction also characterized American political debates and election campaigns at the time. Chief Justice Rehnquist, a Reagan appointee, was proud to be a true conservative. Thus the distinction tended more and more to be made on party lines.

Justices of the Supreme Court are, however, independently minded persons. The result has been that the press and public opinion in the USA has begun to describe the Court in terms of combats between liberals and conservatives, but it is often difficult to detect any such combat in the Court's case law. Conservatives in the country were not very happy, to say the least, when the Court refused to overturn the basic tenets of its abortion decisions; for part of the conservative majority of the court, the doctrine of *stare decisis* prevailed.[61]

There was, however, one occasion where the Court split exactly along political lines: the conservative judges appointed by Republican Presidents Reagan and Bush Sr constituted the majority in a case concerning the presidential election of 2000. From a legal point of view the case was not particularly exciting; but it touched a very sensitive political issue. The election did not produce a convincing result: the Democratic candidate attracted more

[60] In *Eisenstadt* v. *Baird*, 405 US 438 (1972). See also ch. 3.3.   [61] See ch. 3.4-3.5.

popular votes, but the Republican candidate gained more members of the electoral college (that is possible because in every state 'winner takes all'). In Florida the result had been very close, the Republican candidate, George W. Bush Jr, having got marginally more popular votes. His Democratic opponent complained that punch-card ballotting machines had been used in some Florida counties, and that a relatively high number of ballots had not been punched cleanly and completely. He therefore asked for a manual recount in two counties; the intent of the voters should be decisive, and it should not be frustrated by technical failures. The Florida Supreme Court accepted the argument: it ordered a manual recount and defined some standards to ensure how the intent of the voters should be determined. The US Supreme Court reversed the decision, on the ground that there was no assurance, in the Florida Court's ruling, 'that the rudimentary requirements of equal protection and fundamental fairness are satisfied'.[62] Without detailed guidelines, efforts to discover the intent of the voters might lead to arbitrary choices. The four dissenters thought that the interpretation of state legislation (the method used to select the presidential electors is reserved to the states) should be primarily left to the state courts. What caught attention at the time was, however, not the exchange of arguments by the Justices (there were five individual opinions, one concurring and four dissenting), but two political elements. First, the impression was given that the Supreme Court had decided that the conservative candidate was going to win the election, and secondly, the five conservatives in the Court had constituted the majority. The judgment was severely criticized.[63] Fortunately for the Court's reputation, later investigations revealed that Bush Jr would have been the winner even after a manual recount in the two counties.

It is safe to state that the US Supreme Court is much more politicized than supreme courts in Britain, France or Germany. In the 1960s, the German Bundesverfassungsgericht was said to have a 'red' and a 'black' chamber (it works in two chambers called 'senates'), but the labels gradually vanished from the German debates. In the French Constitutional Council, judges are often selected because of the political colour they are supposed to have; but it is difficult to find many traces of it in the case law of the court. Current French discussions on the boundaries between political and judicial

---

[62] *Bush* v. *Gore*, 531 US 70 (2000).
[63] Example: Ronald Dworkin, 'A badly flawed election', *The New York Review of Books* 48/1 1 (11 January 2001), p. 53. For further materials and comments see E. J. Dionne Jr and William Kristol (eds.), *Bush* v. *Gore. The Court Cases and the Commentary* (Washington, D.C., 2001).

action concern the interplay between political practice and criminal law (campaign financing, bribery, corruption); that is a somewhat different theme, however.

The English courts can be considered as the extreme opposite of the American Supreme Court from this point of view. Judgments of the House of Lords have a strictly legal kind of reasoning, and individual opinions ('speeches') almost never betray any kind of political allegiance on the part of the law lords. If choices are to be made, they are narrowly circumscribed, and discussed in terms of legal rules and traditional principles, rarely in terms of policy-making.[64] A closer look at English case law reveals, however, that some judges are occasionally inclined to base their decisions on personal opinions which they then disguise in terms of legal wisdom. Lord Denning, who was Master of the Rolls for a long time (1962–82), had a reputation for this kind of reasoning. He was a most original lawyer, who often had the courage to follow new avenues others only discovered much later, and he expressed his opinions in beautiful English; but he also believed very strongly in certain principles that could probably be described as convictions generally held by his social class, rather than as principles flowing from legal traditions. A famous example occurred in 1982, when the Labour majority of the Greater London Council had decided to reduce London Underground and bus fares by 25%; that would imply that extra money had to be provided by the (richer) outer boroughs. Lord Denning accepted that the GLC felt impelled to implement the Labour election manifesto; but, he said, such a manifesto should not be taken 'as a gospel'. He concluded that the GLC had not given 'genuine consideration' to the rights of other parties affected by the decision.[65] As these others were the well-to-do taxpayers in the more affluent areas of Greater London, the judgment gave the impression of being based on political bias rather than solid legal reasoning. A similar bias was often discovered in Lord Denning's decisions concerning the rights and obligations of trade unions.[66] These observations are not intended to diminish in any way the esteem in which Lord Denning was, and still is, held – he was rightly admired, even loved, by his fellow judges as well as by the general public – but they show something of the indirect way political opinions can play a role in judicial decision making by

[64] See Alan Paterson, *The Law Lords* (London, 1982, reprint 1984), ch. 8.
[65] *Bromley Borough Council* v. *GLC* [1982] 2 WLR 62. Upheld in appeal: [1983] 1 AC 768.
[66] See also, criticizing this generally held opinion, Edmund Heward, *Lord Denning, A Biography* (London, 1990), ch. 12.

the English courts. Legal reasoning may conceal policy choices, or criticism of policy choices made by others. In England this is done less often, and less openly, than in the USA; but it happens nevertheless.[67]

Is the American method 'better', or healthier for the body politic, than the English way of doing things? Or is it the other way round? These questions raise an important point I would not want to omit, although it seems to relativize the significance of much of the work that has gone into the composition of this book. Comparative studies help us to understand things, but they are a poor guide to determining what is 'good' or 'bad'. In the field of constitutional law, comparative study is a good method for disclosing constitutional basics, such as the main constitutional questions and how different constitutional systems handle them; lawyers normally take these things for granted within their own constitutional system. However, that does not always enable us to decide what kind of answer is the best answer, or the worst.

That is particularly true of the relationship between law and politics. The wisdom of constitutional choices depends on a great many background factors.[68] On the basis of our study, it is possible to isolate at least four variables influencing such choices in our field of inquiry.

The first is the type of judges: the law lords are selected on the basis of their professionalism, American Supreme Court Justices because they appeal to the President and to a majority of senators. The American method does not necessarily mean that professional considerations are absent; but other elements may prevail in the selection procedure. Justice Frankfurter, who had made a career as a law professor, was appointed by President Franklin D. Roosevelt in 1939 after having been an adviser to the President, and an intimate friend as well; Chief Justice Rehnquist was appointed in 1986 because he was a well-known conservative lawyer.[69] There are no parallels in Westminster.

The second variable is the scope of the courts' jurisdiction. The wide powers of the German Bundesverfassungsgericht promote judicial decisions that would hardly be conceivable in France. The French constitutional court has a limited jurisdiction, private litigants having no access to it, and it works on the basis of a constitutional text which is (relatively speaking) precise and

---

[67] See also *Ward* v. *James* [1966] 1 QB 273, and my comment ch. in 4.5.
[68] See also Tribe, *Constitutional Choices*, ch. 1.
[69] See Bernard Schwartz, *A History of the Supreme Court*, respectively p. 241 and p. 364.

clear. Access to the German court is possible by means of a great number of remedies, and the Basic Law employs many vague concepts that can only become operational through judicial interpretation: human dignity, *Rechtsstaat* and constitutional order are the most obvious examples.

The third element is historical experience. In Germany, confidence in the representative system suffered greatly from the experience of the Weimar Republic and the tragic month of January 1933.[70] Britain has never had a comparable experience. The consequence is that, in discussing the scope of action of the courts with regard to the political institutions, the German debate has undertones scarcely, it at all, perceptible in Britain.

The fourth element is the type of society to which the constitutional system applies. The French have a traditional belief in the merits of regulation; that has been so since the days of the Revolution and the codification of law in the early nineteenth century. The French say mockingly about themselves that they have 'le génie réglementaire'. The common law countries are in a different position: the common law tradition is a judicial tradition, which is suspicious of general rules and leaves room for individualized assessments of specific situations.

There must be more factors that can explain these politico-legal differences among the constitutional systems we have examined. However, the four circumstances I have just mentioned have the advantage of emerging directly from our comparative studies. They show something about the important differences among the four constitutional systems, and about the consequences these differences may provoke. They also, however, show us how difficult it is to draw axiological conclusions (conclusions in terms of good and bad) from studies of the kind we have undertaken. Constitutional law often aims at finding the balance between opposing tendencies, which are all, taken by themselves, 'good' for society: between democracy and the rule of law, stability and renovation, individual rights and the well-being of society, general principles and the requirements of the specific situation. Legal craftsmanship is not a great help when we try to find what is 'good' for society in general; but it is unbeatable when we are looking for the best possible solution in any given situation. Comparative studies help to understand that the balance to be found is not exactly the same in different constitutional systems, and that the differences in emphasis can only be understood against a background of non-legal circumstances.

---

[70] See also ch. 9.4.

The macrocosm of historical, sociological and cultural developments has contributed to shaping the micro-world of the law in its relationship to politics.

Politics, by contrast, aims higher. It may have lost its ambition to offer blueprints for changing society on the basis of a coherent set of opinions and beliefs; but it will nevertheless look for some general ideas that can guide the way society is to evolve in the near future; and it tries to assemble a maximum of citizens behind these ideas. As soon as politicians are content to merely run the shop, without being guided by any general idea at all, things might just as well be left to capable administrators, under the supervision of the courts. The judiciary can help to avoid such a situation, and thus sustain democratic government, by respecting the sphere of action that is the proper sphere of politics.

I am aware that I am coming dangerously close to stating the obvious. That is, however, also a comforting thought. It is good to know that some general truths will probably underlie the multitude of comparative materials collected in this book. We shouldn't generalize too much, though: there was no historical explanation, or sociological necessity, behind the American Supreme Court's interpretation of the due process clause of the Fourteenth Amendment to the US Constitution. Ultimately, life always defies general schemes, and so does the life of the law.

A French philosopher once observed that all general ideas are false; but he added that this is, of course, a general idea.[71] Both statements have the ring of truth. In the course of history, legal philosophers have often speculated about the existence, or non-existence, of certain maxims which are universally and eternally true. It would seem to me that it is not difficult to find such maxims, but their level of abstraction is so elevated that practising lawyers can't rely on them: in specific situations, general maxims will have to be reconciled with other principles or rules that may also apply. To that extent, the lawyer's view of such debates is not unlike Pascal's view of debates on theology. He said, speaking about sceptics, stoics and atheists, that all their principles are true; but their conclusions are false, because the opposite principles are true as well.[72] Comparative studies illustrate the truth of this statement in the field of constitutional law.

---

[71] Alain ('Toutes les idées générales sont fausses; ceci est d'ailleurs une idée générale').

[72] Pascal, *Pensées*, ed. Brunschvicq, no. 394; Krailsheimer translation, no. 619.

SELECT BIBLIOGRAPHY

I. General literature on comparative law and constitutional problems

Atiyah, P. S., *Law and Modern Society*, 2nd edn (Oxford and New York, 1995)

van Caenegem, R. C., *Judges, Legislators and Professors* (Cambridge, 1993)

  An Historical Introduction to Western Constitutional Law (Cambridge, 1995)

Cappelletti, Mauro, *The Judicial Process in Comparative Perspective* (Oxford, 1989)

de Cruz, Peter, *A Modern Approach to Comparative Law* (Deventer and Boston, 1993)

Dahl, Robert A., *On Democracy* (New Haven Conn., and London, 1998)

David, René, *Les grands systèmes de droit contemporains*, 3rd edn (Paris, 1969)

Eisenstadt, S. N., *Paradoxes of Democracy* (Washington, D.C., 1999)

Ellis, Evelyn (ed.), *The Principle of Proportionality in the Laws of Europe* (Oxford, 1999)

Finer, S. E., Vernon Bogdanor and Bernard Rudden, *Comparing Constitutions* (Oxford, 1995)

Friedmann, Wolfgang, *Law in a Changing Society*, 2nd edn (Harmondsworth, 1972)

Grewe, Constance, and Hélène Ruiz Fabri, *Droits constitutionnels européens* (Paris, 1995)

Guéhenno, Jean-Marie, *La fin de la démocratie* (Paris, 1993)

Henkin, Louis, *The Age of Rights* (New York, 1990)

Held, David, *Models of Democracy*, 2nd edn (Cambridge, 1998)

Lauvaux, Philippe, *Les grandes démocraties contemporaines* (Paris, 1990)

Lijphart, Arend, *Patterns of Democracy. Government Forms and Performances in Thirty-six Countries* (New Haven Conn., and London, 1999)

MacCormick, Neil, *Questioning Sovereignty: Law, State and Nation in the European Commonwealth* (Oxford, 1999)

Pound, Roscoe, *The Spirit of the Common Law* (Boston, Mass., 1921)

Schwarze, Jürgen, *European Administrative Law* (London and Luxembourg, 1992)

Stein, Peter, *Roman Law in European history* (Cambridge, 1999)

Sweet, Alec Stone, *Governing with Judges: Constitutional Politics in Europe* (Oxford, 2000)

Weiler, J. H. H., *The Constitution of Europe* (Cambridge, 1999)

Zweigert, K. and H. Kötz, *An introduction to Comparative Law*, 3rd edn, trans. Tony Weir (Oxford, 1998)

II. American developments

Bickel, Alexander M., *The Least Dangerous Branch. The Supreme Court at the bar of politics* (Indianapolis, Ind., 1963)

Bork, Robert H., *The Tempting of America. The Political Seduction of the Law* (New York and London, 1990)

Chemerinsky, Erwin, *Constitutional Law* (New York, 1997)

Cox, Archibald, *The Role of the Supreme Court in American Government* (Oxford, 1976)

Ely, John Hart, *Democracy and Distrust: A Theory of Judicial Review*, 11th edn (Cambridge, Mass., 1995)

Friedrich, Carl J., *The Impact of American Constitutionalism Abroad* (Boston, 1967)

Gillman, Howard, *The Constitution Besieged. The Rise and Demise of Lochner Era Police Powers Jurisprudence* (Durham, N.C., and London, 1995)

Grant, Alan, *The American Political Process*, 6th edn (Aldershot, 1997)

Jackson, Robert, *The Struggle for Judicial Supremacy* (New York, 1941)

Jones, Charles O., *The Presidency in a Separated System* (Washington, D.C., 1994)

Keefe, William J., *The American Legislative Process. Congress and the States* (Englewood Cliffs, N.J., 1993)

Kurland, Philip B., *Mr. Justice Frankfurter and the Constitution* (Chicago and London, 1971)

Lusky, Louis, *By What Right? A Commentary on the Supreme Court's Power to Revise the Constitution*, 2nd edn (Charlottesville, Va., 1978)

McCloskey, Robert G., *The American Supreme Court*, 3rd edn revised by Stanford Levinson (Chicago and London, 2000)

Morris, Charles R., *A Time of Passion. America 1960–1980* (Harmondsworth, 1986)

Nagel, Robert F., *Constitutional cultures. The Mentality and Consequences of Judicial Review* (Berkeley and Los Angeles, 1989)

Neustadt, Richard, *Presidential Power and the Modern Presidents* (New York, 1990)

Newman, Roger K., *Hugo Black, A Biography* (New York, 1994)

Scalia, Antonin, *A Matter of Interpretation – Federal courts and the Law* (Princeton, N.J., 1997)

Schwarz, Bernard, *Super Chief. Earl Warren and his Supreme Court – A Judicial Biography* (New York and London, 1983)

Schwarz, Bernard, *A History of the Supreme Court* (New York and Oxford, 1993)

Sunstein, Cass R., *Legal Reasoning and Political Conflict* (Oxford and New York, 1996)

Tribe, Laurence H., *Constitutional Choices* (Cambridge, Mass., 1985)

Westin, Alan W., *The Analysis of a Constitutional Law Case. The Steel Seizure Decision* (New York, 1968, reissue 1991)

Zemach, Y. S., *Political Questions in the Courts* (Detroit, Mich., 1976)

III. The British constitution; English law

Allen, T. R. S., *Law, Liberty and Justice. The Legal Foundations of British Constitutionalism* (Oxford, 1993)

Bagehot, Walter, *The English Constitution* (Fontana edn, introduced by R. H. S. Crossman, 11th edn, Glasgow, 1975)

Barber, James, *The Prime Minister since 1945* (Oxford, 1991)

Barendt, Eric, *An Introduction to Constitutional Law* (Oxford, 1998)

Bradley, A. W., and K. D. Ewing, *Constitutional and Administrative Law*, 12th edn (London and New York, 1997)

Brazier, Rodney, *Constitutional Reform. Reshaping the British Political System*, 2nd edn (Oxford, 1998)

Butler, David, Andrew Adonis and Tony Travers, *Failure in British Government. The Politics of the Poll Tax* (Oxford, 1994)

Cane, Peter, *An Introduction to Administrative Law*, 3rd edn (Oxford, 1996)

Dicey, A. V., *An Introduction to the Study of the Law of the Constitution*, 10th edn introduced by E. C. S. Wade (London, 1959)

Forsyth, Christopher (ed.), *Judicial Review and the Constitution* (Oxford and Portland, Or., 2000)

Goldsmith, Jeffrey, *The Sovereignty of Parliament: History and Philosophy* (Oxford, 1999)

Griffiths, J. A. G., *The Politics of the Judiciary*, 5th edn (London, 1997)

James, Simon, *British Cabinet Government*, 2nd edn (London and New York, 1999)

Jowell, Jeffrey, and Dawn Oliver (eds.), *The Changing Constitution*, 4th edn (Oxford, 2000)

McWhinney, Edward, *Judicial Review in the English-Speaking World*, 4th edn (Toronto, 1969)

Markesinis, B. S. (ed.), *The Gradual Convergence. Foreign Ideas, Foreign Influences and English Law on the Eve of the 21st Century* (Oxford, 1994)

Marshall, Geoffrey, *Constitutional Conventions* (Oxford, 1993)

Paterson, Alan, *The Law Lords* (London, 1982, reprint 1984)

Scarman, Sir Leslie, *English Law: The New Dimension*, 26th Hamlyn lecture (London, 1974) de Smith, Stanley, and Rodney Brazier, *Constitutional and Administrative Law*, 8th edn (Harmondsworth, 1998)

Stevens, Robert, *Law and Politics. The House of Lords as a Judicial Body, 1800–1976* (London, 1979)

Walkland, S. A., and Michael Ryle (eds.), *The Commons Today*, revised edn of *The Commons in the Seventies* (Glasgow, 1981)

Wade, H. W. R., *Constitutional Fundamentals, 32nd Hamlyn lecture*, (London, 1980)

Wade, H. W. R., and C. F. Forsyth, Administrative Law, 8th edn (Oxford, 2000)

IV. France and Germany

Avril, Pierre, *La Vme République. Histoire politique et constitutionnelle* (Paris, 1987)

Badura, Peter, *Staatsrecht* (Munich, 1986)

Bell, John, *French Constitutional Law* (Oxford, 1998)

Braibant, Guy, and Bernard Stirn, *Le droit administratif français*, 4th edn (Paris, 1997)

Brown, L. Neville, and John S. Bell, *French Administrative Law*, 5th edn (Oxford, 1998)

Cohen-Tanugy, Laurent, *La métamorphose de la démocratie* (Paris, 1998)

Crozier, Michel, *Le phénomène bureaucratique* (Paris, 1963)

Currie, David P., *The Constitution of the Federal Republic of Germany* (Chicago and London, 1994)

Debbasch, Charles, and Jean-Marie Pontier, *La société française*, 2nd edn (Paris, 1991)

Fisher, Howard A., *The German Legal System and Legal Language*, 2nd edn (London and Sidney, 1999)

Hamon, Léo, *Les juges de la loi. Naissance et rôle d'un contrepouvoir: le Conseil constitutionnel* (Paris, 1987)

Hamson, C. J., *Executive Discretion and Judicial Control*, 6th Hamlyn lecture (London, 1954)

Kommers, Donald P., *The Constitutional Jurisprudence of the Federal Republic of Germany*, 2nd edn (Durham, N.C., and London, 1997)

Laufs, A., *Rechtsentwicklungen in Deutschland*, 5th edn (Berlin and New York, 1996)

Lavroff, Dmitri, *Le système politique français*, 5th edn (Paris, 1991)

di Manno, Thierry, *Le juge constitutionnel et la technique des décisions interprétatives en France et en Italie* (Paris, 1997)

Markesinis, B. S., *The German Law of Torts, a Comparative Introduction*, revised 3rd edn (Oxford, 1997)

Maurer, Hartmut, *Allgemeines Verwaltungsrecht*, 12th edn (Munich, 1999)

Michalowski, Sabine, and Lorna Woods, *German Constitutional Law. The Protection of Civil Liberties* (Aldershot, 1999)

Rivero, Jean, *Le Conseil Constitutionnel et les Libertés*, 2nd edn (Paris, 1987)

Rousseau, Dominique, *Droit du contentieux constitutionnel*, 2nd edn (Paris, 1992)

Stirn, B., *Le Conseil d'Etat, son rôle, sa jurisprudence*, 2nd edn (Paris, 1994)

Stone, Alec, *The Birth of Judicial Politics in France: The Constitutional Council in Comparative Perspective* (New York and Oxford, 1992)

Viansson-Ponté, Pierre, *Histoire de la république gaullienne*, new edn, "Bouquins" (Paris, 1971)

INDEX